Issues in U.S. Foreign Policy

On the Front Burner:

Issues in U.S. Foreign Policy

Seyom Brown

Brandeis University

Little, Brown and Company

Boston Toronto

Library of Congress Cataloging in Publication Data

Brown, Seyom.
On the front burner.

1. United States—Foreign relations—1981– .
2. United States—Foreign relations administration.
I. Title.
E876.B76 1984 327.73 84-761
ISBN 0-316-11061-2

Library of Congress Catalog Card Number 84-761

ISBN 0-316-11061-2

9 8 7 6 5 4 3 2

MV

Published simultaneously in Canada
by Little, Brown & Company (Canada) Limited

Printed in the United States of America

Acknowledgments appear on page 210.

For Steven Darrow Brown
advocate of integrity

Preface

The front burner approach to foreign policy gives priority to those issues that are boiling already or about to come to a boil—issues that have already produced, or seem about to produce, a domestic or international crisis. Between crises the front burner approach gives priority to simmering problems of great potential significance that, if not constantly watched, could challenge or even destroy an administration's foreign policy. Officials typically occupy themselves more with threats than with opportunities, and spend more time on immediate or looming security requirements than on ideals of world order and justice or on defining and protecting what might be in the country's best interest over the long term.

The agenda of issues in this book reflects the front burner logic that prevails at top levels of the U.S. government. In my analysis of these issues, however, I emphasize the basic assumptions of policy and depart somewhat from a pure front burner approach. My approach is closer to the kind of analysis presidents and secretaries of state request from policy planners. It attempts to confront the typical conditioned-reflex, tunnel-vision, muddling-through perspective of harrassed and time-pressured foreign policy officials with some fundamental questions. It puts forward alternative assumptions and options of the kind that top-level decision makers solicit from their advisers at the outset of a new administration or when a crisis so dramatizes the deficiencies of prevailing policies that a review of basic assumptions cannot be avoided.

The opening chapters—"The National Interest" and "Who Decides?"—look at two fundamental problems rarely explored systematically by officials except when a newly elected administration takes office. The four chapters that follow deal with the usual agenda of the government's foreign policy planners in their order of priority: first, the problems of dealing with the presumed major security threat, the Soviet Union; next (because it is so closely connected to the Soviet-American relationship) U.S. policy toward China; then relations with the advanced industrial countries and with the developing countries. Chapter 7 is devoted to U.S. interests in the Middle East. (This chapter could well have been placed in order of priority immediately after the chapter on relations with the USSR. But because it cuts across East–West, North–South, and industrial-world problems, it was deferred until these problems had been treated.) Finally, the grand designs implicitly underlying or explicitly stated as goals for particular policies are spotlighted and analyzed.

My analysis of these issues is the product of more than two decades of consultation with policy-level officials and occasional direct participation in formulating foreign policy and national security policy as a social scientist with the RAND Corporation from 1963 to 1969; as a senior fellow with the Brookings Institution from 1969 to 1976; as director of the program of U.S.–Soviet relations of the Carnegie Endowment for International Peace from 1976 to 1978; and, since I joined the faculty of Brandeis University in 1978, as periodic consultant to the administration and the Congress.

Most of my dialogues with foreign policy and national security officials have been efforts to evaluate options from the presidential perspective—that is, to give prominence to the national interest considerations that are, or ought to be, controlling whenever foreign policy decisions are made at the presidential level. Almost invariably, the need for presidential deliberation and decision (as distinct from routine executive orders and bill signings) means that major issues boiling or coming to a boil on the front burner have not been resolved at lower levels of the government, and that their resolution can no longer be deferred. Presidential intervention usually reflects either a deadlock within the government involving different concepts of the national interest, or a contest between agencies that represent constituencies with different values, or basic disagreement between strategists and policy planners over the expected benefits, costs, and risks of alternative courses of action, or (more often than not) some combination of such unresolved issues. The president in rendering his decisions must be expected to weigh these competing considerations.

Accordingly, the most effective policy advocates in an administration are those who, in their own arguments, show an awareness of the very real dilemmas the president faces in choosing among alternative policies. Effective policy advocates therefore must be capable of understanding and evaluating dispassionately the *strongest* arguments of those who support policies opposed to their own. They must recognize that reasonable and intelligent people may sincerely disagree over what best serves the nation's interests.

The agnostic approach of this book, which may be exasperating to those who seek support for their policy preferences, derives from an awareness that the American republic is a great and diverse country, and that there will always be profound and legitimate disagreement among its peoples over how best to serve simultaneously special interests and the security and well-being of the country as a whole. To be sure, I have my own policy preferences. But they are subordinated here to the purpose of conveying the substance of the great foreign policy debates at the top levels of the government, and of providing conceptual frameworks for those who themselves might want to participate directly or indirectly in these debates.

Hundreds of policy makers and analysts have contributed (often without either they or I knowing it at the time) to this project during the years of its gestation. Their concerns for the nation's security and welfare and the logic of their policy prescriptions—sometimes conveyed only in oral discourse—is the raw material for my reconstruction here of the foreign policy debate in the policy community. I have cited written sources where I can, but some of the most cogent argument has never been committed to manuscript or cleared for publication.

Material that originally appeared in my article, "An End to Grand Strategy" *Foreign Policy,* No. 32 (Fall 1978), is included in Chapter 3. The debate over intervening in the Third World, analyzed at the end of Chapter 4, is the subject of my article, "The Trilemma of U.S. Foreign Policy," in the *AEI Foreign Policy and Defense Review,* Vol. 2, No. 5 (1980). I am grateful to these two journals for permission to adapt the articles for use here. I would also like to thank the Brandeis University National Women's Committee for allowing me to draw on material from my syllabus, *Issues in U.S. Foreign Policy,* prepared in 1983 for Women's Committee study groups.

Being a somewhat unorthodox venture, the book in no small part owes its existence to the imaginative and insightful encouragement of Little, Brown college editors Will Ethridge and Donald Palm. I am particularly indebted to Edith Musnick and Lisa Robinson of the Department of Politics at Brandeis for assistance in preparing the manuscript for publication. Matthew Morelock Brown helped with the index. Terri Gitler's sensitively responsive copy editing deserves special recognition.

I am uncomfortable with the traditional accolades to spouse that usually come at this point. It must be said, however, that Martha Morelock Brown, whose professional priorities are not entirely congruent with mine, has a right to expect this project to have an impact on its field. Only then will it have been worth the candle we both burned at both ends.

Contents

Chapter 1
Contending Concepts of the National Interest

Statesmen think and act in terms of interest defined as power.

—Hans J. Morgenthau (*Politics Among Nations*, 1954)

We have a simple but transcendent goal....It is, in President Kennedy's words, "a peaceful world community of free and independent states, free to choose their own future and their own system so long as it does not threaten the freedom of others...."

...America is at her best when she is true to the commitments we made to ourselves and to history in the Declaration of Independence. These are the ideas and ideals which give us allies, spoken or silent, among men and women in every corner of the earth.

—Secretary of State Dean Rusk (August 1962)

Our thinking about world affairs...has oscillated between an idealistic commitment to a world order yet to be shaped and a periodic swing toward fascination with Realpolitik.

—Zbigniew Brzezinski (*Power and Principle*, 1983)

A few elemental propositions about the purposes of United States foreign policy command widespread support in the policy community and from the populace: United States actions abroad and the country's national security and defense policies should be directed first and foremost to ensuring the physical survival and constitutional integrity of the nation. The American polity must not be dictated to or otherwise subverted by outside forces. United States foreign policy officials should also look after the material well-being of the country as a whole, insofar as the national well-being may be adversely affected or promoted by international events over which this country may have some influence. The essential purpose of foreign policy is, quoting from the Constitution, "to secure the blessings of liberty to ourselves and our posterity."

But underneath the apparent consensus there are intense debates of two kinds:

- What else—in addition to the survival of the country in a condition of political independence and material well-being—should be included in the category of essential national interests?
- By what means should the national interests be protected and advanced? (When alternative policies imply sacrifices in certain interests in order to serve other interests, the controversies tend to become quite bitter.)

All particular foreign policies are claimed by their champions to be in the national interest. By itself, the phrase is little more than rhetorical BOMFOG (Brotherhood of Man, Fatherhood of God). No policy maker would argue that the nation should act against its interests.

The controversies in policy making circles are often over claims that a particular interest is a "vital" national interest, which presumably must receive whatever support is necessary in human and material resources to sustain it. By implication, a vital national interest is one that the nation should be willing to incur great sacrifices—even to fight a war—to defend.

Accordingly, there is considerable disagreement, some of it philosophical, over the criteria for determining when an interest is vital. Indeed, the very notion of vital national interests is itself a matter of debate: geopolitically oriented policy makers and analysts claim that there are objectifiable criteria for determining essential national interests, while another school of thought asserts that, at base, all so-called national interests are no more than the subjective preferences of particular groups of Americans.

The National Interest Defined by Geopolitical Imperatives

The geopolitical perspective defines the national interest exclusively in terms of *power*, the power of the United States relative to that of other countries. The essence of power to the geopolitician is *control*—the ability to control the behavior of, or resist being controlled by, others. In the international system, the principal ingredients of power, so defined, are assumed to be military and economic strength. With sufficient military and economic strength, the country should be able to sustain at least its core value of independent survival in a condition of general material well-being. Insufficient military and economic strength will put the country at the mercy of others. On this much, all geopoliticans agree.

When geopoliticians disagree, it is over precisely what kinds of military capabilities and what economic resources will provide the country with sufficient strength in relation to other countries. For these assessments depend on an analysis not only of the capabilities of other countries but also of their intentions—that is, over where, when, how the interests of other countries are likely to conflict with the interests of the United States.

Despite the potential for disagreement, there has been a rather broad consensus among American geopoliticians since World War II on the most important threats facing the United States. The consensus has been built around the perception, which began to emerge during the war, that the Soviet Union could, and might if given the opportunity, put the core interests of the United States in jeopardy. It could pose a threat to United States interests simply by acting to serve its own geopolitical ones (which impelled it to expand its sphere of control), let alone by acting to implement Marxist-Leninist dreams of overthrowing the capitalist world order. (See the discussion in Chapter 3 on alternative assessments of Soviet intentions.)

Starting in the middle 1970s, a new primary geopolitical concern was added to the preoccupation with Soviet expansion—namely, that the United States and its allies in Western Europe and Japan might be denied access to crucial foreign sources of energy, particularly Persian Gulf oil. The new concern was the product of four related developments: (1) the nationalization by Middle Eastern and other Third World countries of the holdings of United States and European multinational oil corporations within their territories; (2) the formation of the Organization of Petroleum Exporting Countries (OPEC) cartel to control the marketing of oil; (3) the use of oil as a political weapon by the Arab members of OPEC during the 1973 Arab-Israeli war when they withheld exports to the United States and other countries deemed too sympathetic to Israel; and (4) the increasing dependence of the U.S. industrial system on imported oil. United States economists and military strategists now feared, for the first time, that the country's economy could be hobbled and its military power severely degraded by events in the Middle East and Persian Gulf area whether or not the Soviets were attempting to manipulate them.

The combination of a perceived threat of Soviet expansion plus fears that the Persian Gulf countries might deny the West and Japan access to the region's oil has provided the geopoliticians with what they regard as contemporary validation of the "heartland-rimland" thesis of traditional Anglo-American geopolitics. The traditional theory postulated a contest for control of the rimland of Eurasia between the great oceanic powers—Britain, the United States, and Japan—on the one hand and, on the other hand, the dominant heartland power which, in the contemporary period, would mean the USSR. The theory also postulated that if the dominant Eurasian heartland power ever came to dominate the rimland, then that power would control the world.[1]

This basic geopolitical world view has given rise to a number of national security and foreign policy imperatives:

- Ensure that the rival superpower, the USSR, does not gain a global preponderance of military power;
- Prevent the Soviet Union from enlarging the territorial extent of its sphere of control;

- Keep the other advanced, non-Communist industrial countries (the West European countries, Canada, and Japan) within the United States sphere of influence;
- Maintain access to foreign sources of critical raw materials (particularly the oil of the Persian Gulf area);
- Keep hostile forces out of the land, sea, and airspace adjacent to the United States; and
- (Derivative of all the above) Maintain United States naval superiority in the Atlantic and Pacific Oceans, the Mediterranean Sea, and the Indian Ocean.

The foreign affairs and national security agencies of the government attempt to justify many of their program requests with reference to these geopolitical imperatives.[2] Yet while opponents in the legislature or the bureaucracy rarely challenge the fundamental geopolitical assumptions, they often do challenge claims that this or that program or strategy is required by the agreed-upon geopolitical imperatives.

Thus there is disagreement over *how* to ensure that the Soviets do not gain military preponderance. Should reliance be placed primarily on arms control negotiations to limit Soviet military buildups or our own countervailing military buildups? Is it necessary to maintain essential equivalence with the Soviets in all components of the strategic arsenal and for every level of warfare, or can certain types of Soviet superiority be adequately countered by other types of United States superiority? Is it sufficient for the United States to be able to destroy Soviet society with strategic nuclear weapons to deter a Soviet first strike, or is a capability for fighting (and "prevailing") in a strategic nuclear war necessary for deterrence and defense? (These and related controversies over the military balance are detailed in Chapter 3, "Dealing with the USSR," and in the sections on common defense issues in Chapter 5, "Dealing with the Advanced Industrial World.")

Implementing the imperative of containing Soviet territorial expansion is no less controversial. The major contending approaches were elaborated just after World War II with George Kennan, the leading spokesman for containing the Soviets primarily by strengthening the socioeconomic and political fiber of societies in the non-Communist world,[3] and Paul Nitze and his coauthors of NSC-68, the advocates of containment through military strength.[4] Henry Kissinger's detente policies and the opposition they encountered in the Reagan wing of the Republican party expressed alternative approaches to containing Soviet expansion, as did the arguments between Zbigniew Brzezinski and Cyrus Vance in the Carter administration.[5] Another dimension of the debate over alternative means of containment concerns the economic problems and political turmoil in Third World countries and what posture the United States should take toward reformers and revolutionaries. These various controversies over containment are reflected not only in Chapter 3 but also in the discussion of "The Political Intervention Trilemma" in Chapter 6 and in Chapter 7 on "U.S. Interests in the Middle East."

Similarly, the geopolitical imperatives of maintaining access to critical raw materials and continuing to exercise control of the seas engender considerable debate when it comes to specific policies. Some geopolitically oriented policy makers support a wide range of commitments to countries in the Third World on grounds of their being suppliers of essential raw materials. Thus the United States Navy published a study in 1978 showing that the twenty-six raw materials most important for industrial and military purposes were imported in significant quantities from fifty-five countries.[6] But skeptical policy makers and resource economists challenge the *dependency* assumptions in the Navy study by pointing out that some of the producers of each of the commodities are located outside of the Third World and contending that U.S. industry, if pressed, could develop acceptable substitutes. The case for Third World involvements that might involve substantial costs and risks (especially the risk of U.S. military intervention), it is argued, has to rest primarily on other grounds.

Geopolitical concerns, by wide agreement, are a necessary consideration in the formulation and implementation of United States foreign policy. But specific policies cannot be derived directly from the geopolitical imperatives. Moreover, as indicated below, there is opposition to the priority given to geopolitical arguments in official foreign policy debates since World War II.

The National Interest as the Sum of Domestic Interests

Contending against the geopolitical concept of the national interest as the sum of the specific, core-security and economic interests of the nation as a whole is the notion of the national interest as neither more nor less than the variegated interests of the citizens of the United States. According to this view, it probably would be better to discard the term "the national interest" and to debate instead which of the many domestic interests at any particular time require and deserve the support of the United States government in the international arena.

This view also implies that interests are not purely objective in the sense that individuals or groups have their needs imputed to them by some analyst or expert who knows what is good for them, but rather that interests are in large measure subjective because they express what individuals and groups *want* for themselves and their community. Individuals or groups may, of course, seek the advice of strategic or international relations experts to determine how international events might impinge on their interests and what governmental foreign and defense policies they should therefore support in order to service their interests. But the determination of what the national purposes should be beyond the water's edge is no more the province of strategists and other experts than it is the province of economists to tell people what they should value.

If no individual's or group's wants have more inherent, intrinsic, objective merit than anyone else's, how is it possible to arbitrate among them when they are in conflict so as to be able to develop coherent foreign policies? Those who believe foreign policy to be an extension of domestic politics have a simple answer: The domestic political marketplace—elections and bargaining between different interests represented in the legislature and the executive branch—is the best arbiter among those urging different policies, foreign no less than domestic.

According to this view, the domestic political process provides legitimacy to foreign commitments and policies that might otherwise be rejected as unwarranted by vital national interest (meaning usually geopolitical) imperatives. An outstanding example is the continued support provided by the United States to the security of

Israel even in the face of serious geopolitical considerations that might argue for a decisive tilt toward the Arab side in the Arab-Israeli conflict. Support for Israel, after all, has given the Soviet Union the opportunity to intrude itself deeply into the Middle East as the benefactor of Arab governments and movements that might otherwise want to keep the Russian Marxist-Leninists at a distance. And it has put at risk United States access to the petroleum resources of the Persian Gulf. Were it not for the electoral clout of the Jewish community, and its members' influence in various interest groups in the life of the country, the chances that its moral appeals for continued U.S. support of Israeli security would be a decisive factor in U.S. Middle Eastern policy would be substantially reduced. Israel is not without strategic value to the United States, but if it is only basic strategic and economic value that determines which countries the United States favors, and if a choice has to be made between Israel and her opponents, continued support for Israel would be at least highly debatable. (See Chapter 7 for a more extensive discussion of this policy dilemma.)

Other religious and ethnic groups are also considered to have sufficient electoral clout to make public officials pay heed to their demands and sentiments on policies that can affect their brothers and sisters in foreign lands. This country is, after all, a nation of immigrants who can be expected to feel deeply about the well-being of other segments of their transnational communities. The decision not to bomb Rome during World War II reflected such a sociopolitical basis of defining the national interest, as did United States insistence at Yalta and Potsdam in 1945 that the Soviet Union allow free elections in the East European countries that would be under its postwar occupation, and as does the contemporary policy of imposing sanctions on the Soviets for their attempts to suppress Polish nationalism and liberalism. As American blacks have developed greater consciousness of their African roots and have translated this into an attentiveness to U.S. policies affecting Africa, it is no longer simply the geopolitical significance of particular countries in Africa that defines the national interest but also the anger on the part of politically influential American blacks about the apartheid regime in the Republic of South Africa and the reluctance of South Africa to grant full independence to Namibia. Moreover, if the United States is to provide economic assistance to Third World countries for purposes beyond U.S. national security itself, then the politicization and Africanization of the American black consciousness must be expected to affect the distribution of U.S. foreign aid resources. Similarly, the growing political influence of Americans of Hispanic origin in Florida and the American Southwest is increasingly acting as a constraint (and stimulus) on U.S. policies toward Latin America.

The influence of ethnic groups on United States foreign policy is not simply a function of their numbers in the population. Influence may also come from the intensity of their concerns and the effectiveness of their organizations at the grassroots level and in the Washington lobbying arena. It was because of such factors that the Greco-Americans successfully pressured Congress, despite objections from President Ford and Secretary of State Kissinger, to cut off military aid to Turkey in 1975–1976 in response to Turkey's invasion of Cyprus.

The ability of special-interest constituencies to shape United States foreign policy has long been evident in international commerce. Trade bills characteristically carry a long train of amendments sponsored by particular industry and labor groups to limit imports of competing products from foreign countries. Other special interests are resourceful in getting legislation to subsidize and otherwise promote their exports. One of the most effective special-interest lobbies has been that of American grain farmers, which in the 1980 election was successful in getting the Republican National Platform to promise removal of the grain embargo the Carter administration had imposed on shipments to the Soviet Union as a sanction against the Russian invasion of Afghanistan—a promise that President Reagan honored shortly after taking office.

Geopolitical purists ask, "Is this any way to run a foreign policy?" If it is subversive of rational policy making in the domestic sphere to allow special-interest constituencies to dictate the shape of government programs that can affect everyone's welfare, is it not even more illegitimate to entrust the national security, common defense, and strategies for maintaining an acceptable global balance of power to narrow self-interest and parochial groups?

Defenders of the pluralistic concept answer that the whole can never be greater than the sum of its parts; and if the geopoliticians feel the national interest as *they* define it is implicated in certain developments, then it should be their business to show and convince the rest of us that the interests that are most meaningful to us will also be served by the particular foreign policies the geopoliticians favor.

The National Interest as a Part of the World Interest

A third concept defines the national interest more broadly as integral to a system of world order and justice within which the security of the country as a whole and the particular values of its constituent groups can be realized. It starts from the premise that—like it or not—the world has become a society of highly interdependent nations and that, therefore, a foreign policy designed principally to secure the independence of the country has become an anachronism. Indeed, to many who hold this view, the traditional international norms of nation-state sovereignty and independence have become part of the problem for they get in the way of the kinds of global cooperation and accountability between national societies that are required to ensure the survival of the human species. The world-interest logic intersects the pluralist logic at the point where the latter accords legitimacy to efforts by transnational ethnic and economic groups to shape United States foreign policy around interests that transcend the borders of the country. But the world-interest logic departs from the justification for special-interest parochialism inherent in the pluralist logic by making the common fate of humankind its dominant frame of reference. The interests of the national community as well as particular transnational communities are viewed as unsustainable over the long run without a concept of a world community operating to restrain and channel the otherwise selfish, and ultimately self-destructive, policies of the narrower groups.

Those who view the national interest as part and parcel of the world interest believe that United States foreign policy must give high priority to countering threats to international peace—threats that, through political chain reactions, might bring on World War III. Tangible U.S. interests need not be in clear and present danger for the United States to want to devote substantial resources to help resolve international conflicts. The United States should not only provide its own good offices, as President Carter did in his Camp David approach to facilitate a peace treaty between Egypt and Israel, but should also support the buildup of international processes and institutions of conflict control and resolution. (It is not clear, however, to all supporters of this approach that the United Nations system is any more the best structure within which to conduct international conflict resolution in light of its increasing exploitation in recent years by those who use their voting majorities in the UN to condemn and isolate their opponents.) No grand design for world order flows directly from these premises, and some of the alternatives will be explicated in the final chapter of this book, but the logic does dictate an active role by U.S. statesmen in international dialogues and negotiations directed toward subordinating the behavior of the separate nation-states to universal rules and perhaps even the universal institutions, such as the rules and institutions in the United Nations Law of the Sea Treaty (which the Reagan administration was unwilling to sign).

The world-interest logic also dictates restraint by the United States and other militarily well-endowed countries on the sale to other countries of advanced weapons and technologies—conventional, nuclear, chemical, biological, or what have you. These weapons are now being sold or otherwise transferred for often petty motives of earning foreign exchange or immediate political influence and without regard for their effects on regional and global balances of power.

Another world interest that, according to the logic of this approach, encompasses the national interest and should constrain national decisions, is that of preserving the earth's essential ecological balances and the overarching life supporting balances of the biosphere. National societies and private interests in pursuing their perceived economic self-interests tend to pass off the ecology-destabilizing effects of their industrial and agricultural processes as externalities that they should not have to pay to correct. As pointed out in a report on such practices prepared for President Carter by the Council on Environmental Quality and the Department of State, current irresponsibility may have disastrous effects on the earth's climate and life-support systems in the twenty-first century.[7]

The case for a world-order orientation to United States foreign policy often parades under the concept of Enlightened Self-Interest. By this it is meant that to be for world order is not in the least unpatriotic; rather, it is to be concerned with the security and well-being of the people of the United States over the long term, recalling the words in the U.S. Constitution, not only for "ourselves" but for "our posterity."

There is a version of the world-interest approach, however, that emphasizes global "justice" as well as order. In this version there is a strong strain of pure altruism: The people of the United States should be interested in the well-being of the people of other countries, not because this will promote the security, well-being, or influence of the United States but simply because we are all part of the community of mankind and are, accordingly, obligated to attempt to help at least the most destitute and suffering members of the community. As stated by President John F. Kennedy in his inaugural address:

> To those peoples in the huts and villages of half the globe struggling to break the bonds of mass misery, we pledge our best efforts to help them help themselves, for whatever period is required—not because the communists may be doing it, not because we seek their votes, but because it is right.[8]

The obligation extends to efforts to remedy the political conditions as well as the economic ones that are the cause of the misery of peoples. Thus there was generally wide support in the country at the outset of the Carter administration for his promise to make human rights the centerpiece of U.S. foreign policy—and it was clear that by "human rights" Carter initially meant political and civil liberties.

The political support for policies whose principal rationale is to bring justice to the people of the world is soft and flimsy, however, when the policies carry costs and risks and are not presented as part of a package for attaining more tangible national self-interests. Thus President Kennedy found he could get no monies for foreign development assistance from Congress unless his programs were rationalized as necessary means of countering Soviet power drives in the Third World. And President Carter felt compelled to soft-pedal his insistence that governments the world over are obligated to respect the human rights of their citizens in order not to alienate friendly but repressive regimes such as Iran's under the Shah and the governments of Saudi Arabia, South Korea, and China.

In the United States political marketplace, altruistic definitions of U.S. national and world interests, so far, have not sold well. And the moral issues are given slight attention in the councils of decision.

The alternative concepts of the national interest whose rationale and basic implications are outlined in this chapter face their sternest tests of validity when there is an attempt to apply them to more specific policy issues—the subjects of Chapters 2 through 7. And since they are too broadly formulated to provide operational guidance in particular situations, their meaning and action implications can only be defined by the country's responsible policy makers on a case-by-case basis. As will be elaborated in Chapter 2, *who* decides will therefore often be as important as the substantive content of any national consensus on the national interest.

Notes

1. The sources for the traditional geopolitical view are Alfred T. Mahan, *The Problem of Asia and its Effects upon International Relations* (Boston: Little, Brown, 1900); Halford J. MacKinder, "The Geographical Pivot of History," *Geographical Journal,* Vol. 23 (1904), pp. 421–441; and Nicholas Spykman, *The Geography of the Peace* (New York: Harcourt Brace, 1944). The similarities between Mahan, MacKinder, et al. and recent geopolitical views are developed in Stephen B. Jones, "Global Strategic Views," *Geographical Review,* Vol. 45 (1955), pp. 492–508.
2. See the Annual Reports to the Congress by the Secretary of Defense on the proposed military budget.
3. George F. Kennan (writing under the pseudonym "X"), "The Sources of Soviet Conduct," *Foreign Affairs,* XXV (July 1947), pp. 566–582.

4. NSC-68, U.S. Department of State, *Foreign Relations of the United States* (Washington, D.C.: U.S. Government Printing Office, 1950), Vol. I, pp. 237–239.
5. See Seyom Brown, *The Faces of Power: Constancy and Change in United States Foreign Policy from Truman to Reagan* (New York: Columbia University Press, 1983), pp. 335–359.
6. Office of the Chief of Naval Operations, *U.S. Lifelines: Imports of Essential Materials—1967, 1971, 1975—and the Impact of Waterborne Commerce on the Nation* (Washington: U.S. Government Printing Office, 1978).
7. *The Global 2000 Report to the President* (Washington: U.S. Government Printing Office, 1979).
8. Inaugural Address of President John F. Kennedy, January 20, 1961.

Chapter 2
Who Decides?

We are confident in the good sense of the American people, and so we let them share in the process of making foreign policy decisions. We can thus speak with the voices of 215 million, and not just an isolated handful.

—Jimmy Carter (May 22, 1977)

The fact that the [Cuban missile] crisis did not become public in its first week obviously made it easier for President Kennedy to consider his options with a maximum of care and a minimum of outside pressure. Not every future crisis will be so quiet in its first phase, but *Americans should always respect the need for a period of confidential and careful deliberation in dealing with a major international crisis.*

—Dean Rusk, Robert McNamara, George Ball, Roswell Gilpatrick, Theodore Sorensen, McGeorge Bundy (September 27, 1982, essay in *Time*)

The way the government is organized to make and conduct policy is itself frequently a matter of controversy because *who* decides often determines *what* will be decided.

Two principal criteria are invoked in debates over who decides:

- The criterion of *efficiency*—ensuring the most expeditious and least costly accomplishment of the international objectives of the country.
- The criterion of *accountability*—ensuring that those who commit the country to international undertakings are answerable to the

whole body politic, that their actions are consistent with, if not always explicitly mandated by, the democratic will of the nation as expressed through the Congress and the election of the president.

These two criteria sometimes operate at cross-purposes: The fewer government agencies foreign policy decision makers have to satisfy, the more quickly they can respond to developing international crises. As legislative mandates governing U.S. diplomatic moves become more explicit and detailed, United States diplomats have less flexibility for effective bargaining.

But efficiency and accountability are sometimes mutually reinforcing considerations. A foreign policy that requires commitments of resources over the long term needs to be thoroughly aired before the nation and to be based on popular support if it is to be sustained. A congressionally mandated policy, like human rights, requires skilled and resourceful execution by the foreign policy bureaucracy if it is to be more than just a popular rhetorical stance lacking practical significance.

Elitist versus Democratic Approaches

More often than not the efficiency versus accountability debate is only the analytical, neutral sounding, expression of the underlying highly charged and emotional controversy between the proponents of *elitist* and *democratic* approaches to United States foreign policy.

The elitist approach views foreign policy making as a fine art performed effectively only by persons with special training and wide experience in foreign affairs. Popular approval is considered desirable but not necessary. The principal aim of this approach is efficiency.

The democratic approach views foreign policy making as an extension of domestic politics. Popular approval is an essential criterion for the legitimacy of policy. Choices are to be formulated in terms accessible to lay persons and should be responsive to public opinion. The principal aim of the democratic approach is accountability.

Elitism

The elitist attitudes often are closely associated with geopolitical definitions of the national interest that come to the fore in wartime or in periods, of which the cold war is the prototype, dominated by confrontational and highly militarized diplomacy. Sometimes, however, they are associated with periods of quiescence and popular indifference, even boredom with foreign affairs, such as the late 1920s. Their common denominator is a view of foreign policy making as a type of boardroom activity for those with ultimate power and knowledge that need not, often should not, be shared with the general public. The Kennedy administration was highly elitist in its approach to foreign affairs, as was the Nixon administration; and each had a number of "successes" as well as failures" that could be attributed in part to their elitism.*

The Kennedy administration's "best and brightest approach[1] was particularly appropriate for managing the Cuban missile crisis of October 1962 and appeared to have been vindicated by the outcome in which the Soviet Union, in one of the most dramatic reversals in the annals of international politics, contritely dismantled the missiles that it was erecting on Cuban soil. The definition of Soviet deployment of the intermediate-range ballistic missiles in Cuba as a direct and intolerable threat to the security of the United States was the product of deliberation by the president and about ten other persons, as were all the key moves during the thirteen days it took to get Nikita Khrushchev to remove his missiles. Those moves included the naval blockade around Cuba; decisions to follow up the blockade if necessary with military action against Cuba and to present an ultimatum to this effect to the Soviets; the offer of a public pledge by the United States not to invade Cuba and a secret promise to dismantle U.S. missiles in Turkey in return for the removal of the Cuban missiles; and the fateful threat, publicly stated by Kennedy, that any nuclear missile fired from Cuba that landed in this hemisphere would be met by a full

*Quotation marks are put around success and failure to indicate that these are simply conventional and popular judgments. The international relations analyst is reluctant to make such one-dimensional evaluations of historical events, the full implications of which are most difficult to discern and may emerge over the course of decades.

strategic retaliation against the Soviet Union.[2] Each of these moves was more than tactical. Every one of them involved a commitment of the whole nation to a course of action with wide and long-term ramifications for the security and well-being of the country; and every one of them, if submitted to Congress or the wider public for discussion and guidance, would have occasioned intense and long debate (which, of course, was one of the principal reasons the administration's deliberations were kept super-secret and confined to the very few officials who had full trust in one another and "a need to know"). Clearly, a surfacing of the range of options and the staging of a public debate on them would have diluted the strong and unequivocal stances that the administration believed were necessary to convince Khrushchev that he had made a terrible mistake and must immediately reverse himself.

The elitism of the Kennedy administration did not serve the country so well, however, in the policy making that led to United States involvement in the Vietnam war. As documented in Secretary of Defense MacNamara's 1968 study of the increasing U.S. involvement—a study that probably would not have been revealed to the public had it not been given to the press, unauthorized, by one of its authors, Daniel Ellsberg—actions involving the United States deeper and deeper in the Vietnamese civil war were authorized by the Kennedy administration. And with conscious calculation, not only the details but also the basic policy premises underlying these actions were shielded from public view.[3] Yet these actions, taken by a small group of public officials, made it virtually inevitable that the United States would become a cobelligerent in a war in Southeast Asia in which the lives of tens of thousands of Americans would be lost and the resources of this country would be drained for a decade.

Some of the secret decisions that eventually led to direct United States military participation in the Vietnam war went back to the Roosevelt, Truman, and Eisenhower administrations, and the first actual large-scale U.S. military involvement was ordered by President Lyndon Johnson. But it was during the Kennedy administration that previously indirect and marginal assistance to the regime in Saigon was transformed into direct paramilitary participation and a degree of military and economic assistance that made South

Vietnam a virtual protectorate of the United States. To most of the officials who collaborated in this effort, this transformation meant that the United States was now unalterably committed to preventing the communists from taking over South Vietnam, even if its commitment required the use of American troops.

The costs to America of the Vietnam involvement were exactly the kinds of large social and economic consequences of any decision to go to war that led the founding fathers of the United States constitutional system to lodge the basic war making powers in the so-called popular legislative branch and to provide congressional checks and balances of the executive's crucial diplomatic and military powers that could lead to the country's involvement in war.

But the founding fathers also understood the need for swift and decisive actions at times—especially to prevent or fight wars—and therefore gave the president complete authority to act in the national interest as commander in chief. The Constitution itself does not resolve this contradiction but wisely leaves it to the political leadership of the time to determine within the prescribed constitutional boundaries what degree and kind of cooperation between the branches is necessary. It is not constitutionally illegal for the executive to take actions, without a firm popular mandate, that will involve the country in a large-scale war, but such action usually will be imprudent because popular support will be necessary to provision and otherwise sustain a war. It may also be constitutionally imprudent, since (as will be discussed further below) an unpopular war that has been entered into and fought without adequate congressional consultation can very well result in subsequent congressional restrictions on executive flexibility that may hobble effective foreign relations.

As it turned out, it was the inability to President Johnson to sustain the Vietnam war against growing popular discontent that turned him, at the end of his term, toward negotiating a withdrawal of United States forces from Indochina.

Elitism was elevated to a high art in the execution of the Nixon administration's proudest accomplishment in foreign affairs—the rapprochement with the People's Republic of China. In July 1971, National Security Adviser Henry Kissinger flew secretly to Pakistan and from there went on to Peking in Pakistani President Yahya Kahn's personal airplane on a super-secret trip to lay the diplomatic groundwork for this historic demarche, which was to be climaxed by President Nixon's spectacular visit with Mao and Chou En-lai in February 1972. "Yahya was enthralled by the cops-and-robbers atmosphere of the enterprise," recalls Kissinger.[4] And because of this "great service for our country," Pakistan was rewarded by Nixon's favoritism in the India-Pakistan war over Bangladesh. All the other world leaders, who had been kept in the dark about what was transpiring, were not at all pleased at being excluded when they heard President Nixon's surprise radio-TV address on July 19, 1971, announcing the completion of Kissinger's clandestine mission and its result—the invitation extended the president to visit China and his acceptance of this "journey for peace."

Looking back on the event, Kissinger defends the secrecy attending his mission and the lack of prior consultation, domestic and international, about the major shift in United States policy that was coming: If the cat had been let out of the bag prior to his visit,

> Foreign countries would ask for briefing and reassurances about a meeting whose agenda consisted of nothing other than permitting each side to raise the issues important to it. All this would become public and be recited back to the capital with which we were able to communicate only via third parties. Some countries might have attempted to preempt our visit; others to thwart it. The tender shoot so painstakingly nurtured for more than two years might well have been killed....I have no doubt now that the secrecy of the first trip turned into a guarantee of a solid and well-managed improvement of relations.[5]

Even after the public announcement of the planned presidential trip to China, however, Nixon and Kissinger held the China card close to their vests and only allowed the world to get a glance at its face in the formal Shanghai Communiqué issued at the close of Nixon's February 1972 visit.

This secretive elitist style did not work so well for Nixon and Kissinger in conducting the detente relationship with the Soviet Union. By failing to consult adequately with Congress, especially on the economic arrangements that were central to the strategy of giving the Soviets a "stake in the equilibrium" (Kissinger's phrase), the administration left itself vulnerable to after-the-fact insistence by the legislative branch on certain conditions to be attached to these arrangements that, in effect, negated much of what had been agreed to by Nixon and Brezhnev in Moscow in May 1972. The centerpiece of the economic side of detente was supposed to have been the extension to the Soviets of normal trading privileges in the United States market (the so-called Most Favored Nation arrangements) and substantial financial credits guaranteed by the U.S. Export-Import Bank. These new opportunities for Soviet-American commerce were crippled by congressional amendments requiring a liberalization of Soviet restrictions against Jewish emigration from the USSR as a condition of implementing the Moscow commercial accords.[6]

By failing to consult adequately with Congress prior to making economic arrangements with the Kremlin, Nixon and Kissinger lost an opportunity to gain the legislative branch's support of their grand strategy, which required a buildup of Soviet economic dependence on and appetite for United States commerce prior to the exertion of economic leverage on them. Nixon and Kissinger also failed to avail themselves of opportunities to show a genuine responsiveness to the growing popular human rights concerns and to devise in cooperation with Congress more productive ways of bringing pressure on the Soviet Union in the matter of Jewish emigration.

Democratic imperatives

The American polity is supposed to be a consent-of-the-governed system. The president and cabinet-level foreign policy officials, aware that sooner or later they must answer to the public at large for their actions, normally attempt to discern the prevailing popular mandate (or to create one) before committing the United States to major international actions—especially those carrying a high risk of war or involving large expenditures of material resources.

The popular mandate may be broad: Do all that is necessary to ensure continued access to oil resources in the Persian Gulf. Or it may be highly restrictive: Do not do or say anything that could again get the United States involved in a war on the Asian mainland. Such permissive or restrictive mandates may be informal, expressed through newspaper editorials, public opinion polls, and political speeches that add up to a rather solid popular consensus; or, they may be formally expressed through congressional resolutions or legislation. Sometimes the popular mandate is given quasi-formal reinforcement by statements of the president, secretary of state, and other high officials indicating their interpretation of the national will; this was the aim of the "Carter Doctrine" that asserted U.S. vital interests in the Persian Gulf and a determination to protect them with military force if necessary and the denials by Ronald Reagan early in his presidency that he had any intention of intervening in El Salvador with U.S. troops.

Periods when foreign policy making tends to be relatively democratic—when the executive feels highly constrained by popular attitudes or mandates often reflected in detailed congressional stipulations on United States international programs and actions—tend to give expression to either isolationism or ideologically determined interventionism.

In isolationist periods, influential segments of the electorate are extremely eager to prevent United States actions abroad that might require a diversion of resources from domestic pursuits of high interest to themselves. Also at such times, there is usually a broad-based consensus against foreign adventures that might result in higher taxes, military conscription, or other disruptions of domestic normalcy. Characteristically, such swings toward popular isolationism follow wars or periods of activist intervention; and the strong popular impulse to pay attention to things back home is reflected in journalistic scrutiny and legislative restrictions to ensure that U.S. foreign commitments are kept to the minimum necessary to fend off direct threats to the core national interests.

The longest of the isolationist periods in the twentieth century lasted from the end of World War I until the Japanese attack on Pearl Harbor in 1941. A similar isolationist response to World War II was turned around in 1947 by the Truman administration's ability to alarm the public about the Soviet threat. Popular reactions against costly foreign involvements—"no more Vietnams"—became a weighty constraint on U.S. foreign policy in the late 1960s and appear to have peaked about 1972. The post-Vietnam isolationist mood has been gradually eroding since the early 1970s but is still quite pervasive. Thus opinion surveys show nearly 50 percent of the electorate in the 1971-1973 period believed that the country was spending too much on defense whereas by 1978 less than 20 percent believed defense expenditures were too high. Similarly, whereas in the early 1970s, less than 30 percent of the public approved committing U.S. troops to combat in the event the Soviets invaded Western Europe, by the early 1980s, approval was back up to almost 60 percent.

Popular pressures do not always operate as a restraint on the country's foreign involvements. At times, aroused by patriotic sentiments or a crusading spirit to do battle globally against the forces of "evil," the populace, or at least its most politically active sectors, might send strong signals to the elected leaders that it expects them to act abroad in the service of the nation's honor and what the United States stands for in the world over and above what more tangible geopolitical interests would require. Such a crusading spirit in the populace drew a reluctant executive into the Spanish-American War in the late nineteenth century and sustained an interventionist mode of dealing with political turbulence in Latin America until World War I. Public pressures on behalf of an activist-interventionist foreign policy were generated by the Truman administration in 1947, particularly by the president's "Truman Doctrine" speech, to bring pressure on Congress to approve economic and military aid to Greece and Turkey. Furthermore, the crusading anticommunist ethos created by the administration's good guys versus bad guys definition of the global struggle subsequently operated as a goal to U.S. foreign policy makers to oppose any extension of communist influence even in places where this was not warranted on geopolitical or strategic grounds.

Indeed, it was policy planner George Kennan's fear of a hyper-stimulated public impelling the government to make universal commitments that would exceed the nation's capabilities that led him to oppose, unsuccessfully, the ideologically crusading formulations that were the hallmark of the Truman Doctrine. Kennan would later point to the United States involvement in the Vietnam War as confirmation of his fears.

Attempts to ensure a democratic foreign policy frequently come in the form of congressional assertions of control over executive actions (see below). In their more radical manifestations, the democratic or populist challenges to elitism are expressed in mass demonstrations or even organized civil disobedience to laws held to be wrong. All matters—from the general issue of how much the government should spend on national security programs as opposed to domestic social programs, to more specialized issues such as which countries because of their human rights records are worthy of receiving United States economic and military aid, to highly esoteric issues such as what kind of basing scheme should be approved for ICBMs—can become causes for which the people take to the streets to compel public officials to heed the popular will.

A result of a major flareup of populist reaction to elitism can be temporary paralysis on the issues that have been thrust into the public arena. This seriously inhibits diplomacy that requires detailed and patient negotiations, such as arms control, even though these may be the kinds of issues on which the public wants action. The Reagan administration, for example, was pressured by popular agitation to begin negotiations with the Soviets in late 1981 on limiting nuclear missiles in Europe; but the proposals it presented at the outset were designed more to diffuse the popular agitation than as a serious negotiating stance.

Presidential Prerogatives versus Congressional Control

The conduct of foreign policy is essentially an executive responsibility. Few would contest that proposition for the other countries with which this country interacts, negotiates, makes agreements, and has confrontations must be able to know that some*one* (or his executive secretaries) has authority to credibly commit the country to particular international obligations and courses of action. And to effectively perform these responsibilities, especially when bargaining with or attempting to coerce other countries, the executive often requires considerable leeway to decide and act quickly and with complete authority, to make promises and threats that his foreign counterparts will believe he can deliver.

The controversy, rather, centers on the fundamental issue of the accountability of the executive to the country for whom he presumably speaks. To whom should the executive be answerable, to what mandates, when committing the country to certain courses of action abroad? Who determines the extent of the executive's negotiating leeway? Who, in short, formulates the basic policy and sets the guidelines for implementing the policy in fields that require interaction with other nations? A failure to clarify the accountability issue and a lack of consultation with and advance guidance from those to whom the executive is expected to be accountable can produce foreign policy crises and disasters—such as the agreements to extend credits and trading privileges to another country (like President Nixon made with President Brezhnev in 1972) that Congress fails to honor, or, worse yet, military deployments that get the country into a war for which there is insufficient popular support (such as the Vietnam involvement of the 1960s).

The question is not only to whom the foreign policy executive should be accountable but also in how much detail, how intensively. In other words, should the foreign policy executive be on a short leash or a long leash? There tends to be a fluctuation, historically, between long-leash and short-leash approaches to constrain the executive's foreign policy and authority. Thus, the period of relatively large leeway, the cold war era of interventionist foreign policies capped by the Vietnam war, produced the 1970s backlash against the rather freewheeling "imperial" executive—a reaction manifested primarily in legislation requiring increased congressional oversight and authorization of United States actions abroad, especially in the field of intelligence gathering and covert operations, in the transfers of military equipment to other countries, and, of course, in the deployment of U.S. military forces. By the 1980s, there was growing recognition among analysts and congressmen (apparently also supported by their constituents) that the short leash was cutting too much against the minimum flexibility the executive needs to exercise U.S. power effectively in the international arena, and during the first two years of the Reagan administration a start was made on gradually dismantling the extraordinary legislative restrictions of the 1970s. But as it became evident, by the third year of the Reagan presidency, that the executive was inclined to revive the cold war pattern of covert and military interventions without substantial prior congressional consultation, the trend toward removal of the previous decade's constraints was abruptly halted, and Congress began once again to reassert its prerogatives.

The struggle between the president and the Congress for control over foreign policy was built into the American political system from the start. The United States constitutional provisions make the president commander in chief of the armed forces, but give the Congress the power to "provide for the common defense," raise and provision the army and navy, and declare war; they give the president the power to make treaties and appoint ambassadors but subject both of these diplomatic functions to "the advice and consent of the Senate;" and, they accord Congress the responsibility for regulating foreign trade.

This struggle in many respects overlaps the elitism versus democracy issue, but they are actually two different dimensions of the larger "who decides" issue. The assertion of presidential power over foreign policy may be made in the name of the general welfare of and responsiveness to the whole electorate (which is the president's constituency) against the legislative branch's alleged representation of special interests. Thus, in the area of foreign economic policy—especially trade legislation on tariffs and other barriers to foreign imports—the president characteristically champions the general consumer interest in having a wider choice of product and price, while members of Congress characteristically act as brokers for their districts' special industry and labor groups that fear displacement from foreign competition. Similarly, the president is not always the culprit behind wastefully large military programs that violate popular mandates to keep defense expenditures to the minimum consistent with national security; in many cases, excessive expenditures are the result of "pork barrelling" exchanges of votes in the Congress between representatives attempting to keep lucrative defense contracts for firms in their districts.

Unitary versus Pluralistic Approaches

The presidential versus congressional dimension of the "who decides" issue is more accurately viewed as the axis of tension between unitary and pluralistic approaches to foreign policy than as between democratic and antidemocratic impulses.

The champions of the unitary approach usually argue that the presidency is and the Congress is not capable of detailed policy formation and guidance, rapid and decisive command and action, and sustained secrecy of deliberations—all of which are deemed necessary for effective international bargaining and the exercise of power. As put by Secretary of State Kissinger in response to the growing congressional assertiveness of the mid-1970s:

> We do not ask for a blank check. . . . We welcome the indispensable contribution of Congress to the general direction of national policy. At the same time, it is important to recognize that the legislative process—deliberation, debate, and statutory law—is much less well-suited to the detailed supervision of the day-to-day conduct of diplomacy. Legal prescriptions, by their very nature, lose sight of the sense of nuance and the feeling for the interrelationship of issues on which foreign policy success or failure so often depends. . . . The growing tendency of the Congress to legislate in detail the day-to-day or week-to-week conduct of our foreign affairs raises grave issues. American policy—given the wide range of our interests and responsibilities—must be a coherent and purposeful whole.[8]

The pluralistic approach emphasizes the essential role of Congress in ensuring that foreign policies are sustainable, in ensuring that they are rooted in the real interest and domestic power configurations prevailing in the country, which presumably are better represented in the Congress than anywhere else in the government. Without substantial congressional participation in the foreign policy process, the conduct of foreign relations by the president and his subordinates will lack constancy and credibility for they will have to be pursued without adequate ensurance of funding and political support.

A moderate middle position between assertions of presidential prerogatives and assertions of heavy congressional participation holds that explicit congressional mandates are important for setting the country's basic course in foreign affairs and setting broad boundaries to executive actions. Within these basic mandates and broad boundaries, however, the president should be allowed maximum flexibility (including secret deliberation with his aides) for implementing policy—namely, designing strategies and tactics, funding and staffing specific programs within generally authorized categories, and negotiating with other countries.

Rhetorically, most executives and legislators accept the validity of this moderate middle position. In fact, however, there is an ongoing struggle as each side attempts to protect and add to its power.

The current phase of this struggle features attempts by the executive to recapture some of the flexibility denied to the president by the restrictive congressional resolutions and legislation passed as part of the popular backlash against the "imperial presidency" of the High Cold War and Vietnam years.

During the cold war and Vietnam periods, according to Senator J. William Fulbright, former chairman of the Senate Foreign Relations Committee, Congress abdicated its powers to initiate war and to authorize significant foreign commitments. "So completely have these powers been taken over by the president," said Fulbright, that the United States became, in effect, "a presidential dictatorship."[9] Fulbright himself, to his subsequent regret, had been a part of this congressional abdication when he was floor manager for the famous Gulf of Tonkin Resolution in 1964, by which President Johnson got the Congress to approve in advance "all necessary steps including the use of armed force" that the president might determine were necessary to assist countries covered by the Southeast Asia Collective Defense Treaty (which included South Vietnam as a protocol state). It was under authority of the Gulf of Tonkin Resolution that over 500,000 U.S. troops were sent to Vietnam, of which more than 50,000 lost their lives without the Congress ever having a full debate on a declaration of war.*

Fulbright and other legislators who felt they had been taken for a ride were determined to get even, and starting in the late 1960s they began to take every opportunity to impose detailed constraints on presidential foreign policy options. By the time Jimmy Carter assumed the presidency in 1977, there were some seventy specially restrictive congressional amendments and resolutions on the books,

*The Gulf of Tonkin Resolution was not atypical of the congressional abdication of its war making powers during the cold war. Similar resolutions gave the president advance authority to use force to achieve specific objectives in the Formosa Straits (1955), the Middle East (1957), Cuba (1962), and Berlin (1962). See Cecil V. Crabb, Jr. and Pat M. Holt, *Invitation to Struggle: Congress, the President and Foreign Policy* (Washington: Congressional Quarterly Press, 1980), p. 125.

including various "war powers" resolutions giving the Congress shared responsibility in some of the traditional functions of the commander in chief, the 1974 Congressional Budget and Impoundment Act, the 1975 Clark Amendment stopping covert aid to pro-U.S. elements in Angola, and various amendments to military assistance and sales legislation that, in effect, gave Congress a veto on the transfer of military equipment to other countries. Some of the legislation injected human rights criteria for determining which countries qualified for U.S. help, others put restrictions on aid to "socialist governments." Liberals and conservatives in the Congress joined with one another against the common opponent: the "imperial presidency."[10]

The War Powers Resolution

The most important congressional-imposed restriction on the president's authority to conduct foreign policy—practically and symbolically—is the War Powers Resolution of November 1972, which was passed over President Nixon's veto. Its rationale is stated clearly:

> It is the purpose of this joint resolution to fulfill the intent of the framers of the Constitution of the United States and insure that the collective judgment of both the Congress and the President will apply to the introduction of United States Armed Forces in hostilities, or in situations where imminent involvement in hostilities is clearly indicated by the circumstances, and to the continued use of such forces in hostilities or in such situations.[11]

In its specific restrictive clauses, the War Powers Resolution requires the president to report in writing to the Congress within forty-eight hours of any introduction or nonroutine enlargement of United States armed forces abroad and requires the termination of any such deployment within sixty days after the president's report if the Congress within that period has not explicitly authorized the continuation of the deployment (Sections 4, 5, and 7). The Congress, by this resolution, also has the authority to terminate such a deployment by a concurrent resolution before the expiration of the sixty-day deadline for positive action (Section 5).

President Ford, like President Nixon, contended that the resolution was an unconstitutional interference in the president's powers as commander in chief but complied with its reporting requirements when he dispatched special units to Vietnam in 1975 to effect the final evacuation of Danang, Pnom Penh, and Saigon and in the marine rescue of the crew of the Mayaguez from Cambodia.[12] President Reagan also reluctantly complied with the reporting requirements in a number of instances, including the U.S. marine invasion of Grenada in 1983. Each of these actions ended quickly before Congress moved to implement the withdrawal provisions of the legislation. The Reagan administration at first refused to consider the War Powers Resolution binding on the dispatch of U.S. marines to Lebanon, but as casualties mounted and Congress made known its intention to act, the administration conceded and in return obtained a positive grant from Congress to continue the marine deployment in Lebanon for eighteen months without congressional reauthorization.

The legislation remains on the books and portends a great debate and even a constitutional crisis on the unresolved boundary between presidential prerogatives and congressional control.

The Special Issue of the CIA and Other Intelligence Agencies

In a political system that is supposed to be governed by officials responsible to the general public, the important foreign relations function of obtaining information about the intentions and capabilities of other countries encounters special difficulties and engenders intense controversy. This is because—inevitably—some of this intelligence gathering must be done secretly and against the wishes of foreign governments and through methods and agents that cannot be disclosed to the public. The twin brother of such espionage, covert action to affect the political situation in other countries, is even more controversial.

The case for *some* clandestine intelligence gathering would seem to be indisputable (although voices and petitions are raised from time to time to prohibit all such activities). Most of the governments hostile to the United States are closed societies, and it is characteristic of the game of power politics between sovereign states that even relatively open societies often will mask their true intentions and capabilities and systematically deceive their adversaries. A surprise attack or a surprise unveiling of military capabilities that would suddenly tip the balance of power against the United States could fatally endanger the country; and, therefore, it is the government's responsibility to do what it reasonably can to anticipate such occurrences even if stealth is required to do so. Similarly, the balance of international power affecting the well-being of the people of the United States can shift dramatically from changes of government in geopolitically significant foreign countries; and since our adversaries may be engaged in clandestine operations to generate coups or other sudden changes in their favor, the United States wants to have the ability to uncover such plots while there may yet be time to counter them.

Once the rationale of gaining intelligence information secretly is granted, it becomes impossible to avoid the implication that not only most of the public but also most of the public officials will not be able to share in these secrets. A highly restricted set of "need to know" criteria should set the boundaries on who has access to the personnel and methods that gather the intelligence and also on the content of much of the information gathered.

Granting the requirement, however, does not dispose of the issue of *who* should have access to different categories of intelligence information and *who* should determine the access rules.

At one extreme are those—many of whom are intelligence professionals—who feel that even the question of access criteria should be as far removed from public scrutiny as possible. Once the public and the ordinary member of Congress starts asking such questions, secrecy of operations are bound to be compromised. For most of the post World War II period, the national leadership in and out of Congress tended to defer to this philosophy, and the Congress was not even allowed to know the operating budget of key intelligence agencies for fear this might reveal where and by whom certain activities were being conducted. The public by and large went along with this policy that granted to the intelligence agencies special immunity from even rudimentary legislative oversight. And within the executive itself, only a handful of officials were exposed to even the gross magnitudes of funding for the various types of intelligence operations.

Public and congressional forbearance changed rather dramatically, however, in the late 1960s and early 1970s as a part of the general populist mood affecting attitudes toward all executive prerogatives and elitist justifications for unexposed decision processes. A series of disclosures and events evidently produced the critical mass of concern that makes for a change in the life of a society. One of these was the publication of *The Pentagon Papers* with its chapter-and-verse accounts of how clandestine intelligence operations to gather information and to influence political events in Southeast Asia were important factors in the deepening involvement in Vietnam which now—with the wisdom of hindsight—was widely regarded as one of the worst mistakes in the history of the country. Another spur to public and congressional demands for more information about what the intelligence agencies were doing was the journalistic revelation in 1972 of efforts by the International Telephone and Telegraph Company (ITT) to get the CIA to help prevent the Marxist socialist Salvador Allende from being elected president of Chile. It was one thing for a handful of public officials, presumably responsible to the president of the United States, to be privy to CIA operations. It was quite another matter for the executives of a multinational corporation to have access to the CIA and, perhaps, even to be determining what the agency would be doing in foreign countries. If the journalistic reports were true, then this would be an outrageous example of the tail wagging the dog and the grossest violation by the CIA of the privileged trust heretofore accorded it. The Senate Foreign Relations Committee, responding to these suspicions, authorized its Subcommittee on Multinational Corporations to investigate the alleged ITT-CIA connection in Chile. The Subcommittee hearings, while unable to document any foul play by the CIA, did stimulate even greater public and congressional skepticism about the agency's rectitude; and when in September 1973, the then-President Allende was overthrown and murdered in a coup in Santiago, the lid was blown off the traditional congressional restraint in keeping hands off the intelligence field. Various committees held hearings of their own, and rather rapidly the press and public were given a picture of an activist covert arm of U.S. foreign policy that was not only doing secret work for the top political levels of the United States government, but also, apparently, often calling its own plays and running with the ball in ways that could commit the entire nation to courses of policy that had not even been debated in the executive branch, let alone the Congress.

Parallel with the hubbub over CIA activities in Chile, the Watergate affair was evolving toward its climax with President Nixon's resignation in August 1974 and a confused picture of to what extent intelligence and counterintelligence operatives and agencies had anything to do with the scandal.

The upshot of all of this confusion and agitation was that the CIA was now clearly on the defensive. The rules of the national discourse had changed almost overnight: The burden of proof was now on the intelligence agencies to demonstrate their fidelity to the national interest and foreign policies—both of which were being increasingly defined by the Congress. Consistent with this changed national sentiment, the Senate and the House of Representatives empowered special committees to investigate the CIA and related intelligence agencies. The most influential of these, the Senate Select Committee on Intelligence, was made a permanent committee in 1976 after the publication of voluminous reports detailing the wide range of information gathering and covert political activities engaged in by the intelligence agencies.

President Carter was philosophically in favor of reducing secrecy and the role of covert action in U.S. foreign policy and instructed the members of his administration to keep the appropriate committees of Congress maximally informed about the government's intelligence activities. President Reagan, however, has authorized major covert operations in Central America and generally has been attempting to give back to the intelligence agencies their traditional prestige and freedom of action, explaining:

> I think covert actions have been a part of government and a part of government's responsibilities for as long as there's been a government...and [when the government does practice covert activity] you can't let your people know without letting the wrong people know—those that are in opposition to what you're doing.[13]

Despite Reagan's efforts, the premise of rather detailed congressional oversight and substantial budgetary control has been established. Secrecy is still granted but with much greater access now afforded selected members of the popular branch of the government. The fundamental dilemmas remain: Too much accountability to the political agencies of the government can compromise the independent judgment about events in other countries that is required for an effective foreign policy. Too much openness can make it impossible to engage in the covert operations that are periodically essential to national security. But the debate over the degree of accountability to be imposed on the CIA and its sister agencies is now a real one; and the guardians of accountability to the public have made it clear that it is *they* who will be setting the ground rules.

The Issue of Foreign Policy Control within the Executive Branch

The contest for control of foreign policy within the executive branch involves few basic constitutional or philosophical issues of accountability. The issues mainly involve questions of efficiency and efficacy in policy formulation and implementation. What degree of centralization of foreign policy making and execution in the Department of State or, alternatively, in the White House and National Security Council (NSC) will assure that the most informed and pertinent decisions are made, that priorities are not distorted by bureaucratic politics and procedures, and that decisions are loyally, conscientiously, and effectively carried out in the national interest? What other agencies should be given decision making weight in particular foreign policy categories to ensure that all the relevant factors are considered and that those who will be expected to carry out policy understand fully the rationale for what they are expected to do?

Maintenance of control: Through the Department of State

The arguments for centralizing the formulation and implementation of foreign policy in the Department of State imply that only an agency like the Department of State, with its special mission of maintaining U.S. interests abroad, can ensure the steadiness of course, effectiveness in international bargaining and negotiations, properly informed decision making, and thorough professionalism in execution that are necessary to good foreign policy. Other agencies, it is argued, have responsibilities that are either too narrow or too broad to perform this role adequately.

The Department of Defense is too focused on the military balance of power and on the use of force in international relations to generate the wide range of options and policy instruments needed for a prudent foreign policy. The Pentagon may be the source of the sticks and the strategies for their employment, but the carrots of diplomacy are not its responsibility, nor is its forte the diplomatic art of dangling carrots and sticks in international encounters so that conflicts of interest can be adjusted short of war.

Treasury, which in some countries has been accorded a prime foreign policy role, is too concerned with the balance sheets of international payments and trade and the national budget to give adequate weight to the nonmaterial values embodied in the national interest. Both on the costs and benefits sides, its assessments of the wisdom of policy are likely to be blind to the intangible factors behind many of this country's commitments at home and abroad. Treasury can tell us what we can afford to do but not whether we should want to do it. And if it were given the central role in policy coordination, the financial terms of reference would dominate the interagency deliberations.

The White House, operating through the NSC system, is alleged to be too responsive to immediate domestic political considerations, which can prematurely restrict the range of options during foreign policy formulation and distort efficient implementation. But, as will be reflected in the discussion below, whether or not these problems are overbalanced by the advantages to a president of having more direct control of the foreign policy decision making process is a matter of persistent debate.

Secretaries of State normally will attempt to keep the overall coordination of foreign policy in their department, but they do not always succeed in this effort.

George Marshall and Dean Acheson did quite well in this regard, even with the new NSC (created by act of Congress in 1947) under legislative mandate to advise the president on national security and help him to coordinate policy. President Truman's respect not only for the wisdom of secretaries Marshall and Acheson but also for the traditional departments of the government had the effect of keeping the NSC in largely a custodial role prior to 1950. But as the Korean War dramatically expanded the portion of national resources and effort devoted to national security, NSC staff and functions began to grow accordingly.

President Eisenhower enlarged upon this natural growth of NSC staff and functions but more on the side of coordinating policy implementation than formulation because the prerogatives of chief foreign policy maker were jealously guarded and cultivated by Secretary of State John Foster Dulles.

Secretary of State Rusk waged a losing contest for control over the foreign policy agencies against the powerful White House staffs of presidents Kennedy and Johnson, though he was able to retain State Department chairmanships for a new set of Interdepartmental Groups set up by Johnson to do program budgeting across agencies in the foreign affairs field.

Under President Nixon, Secretary of State William Rogers presided over a State Department virtually emasculated by National Security Adviser Henry Kissinger's determined accumulation of power over foreign policy formulation and implementation (including NSC chairmanships of all the key interdepartmental committees), until Kissinger himself was appointed secretary of state in 1973. Between 1973 and 1975 there was no possibility of major conflict between the NSC and the State Department, for Secretary of State Kissinger retained his role as head of the NSC staff. President Ford's appointment of Kissinger's trusted NSC deputy, Brent Scowcroft, as the new NSC chief in 1975, was hardly the resurrection of an independent center of power.

President-elect Jimmy Carter and his foreign policy entourage pledged to restore the Department of State to its rightful role as top foreign policy agency; Carter would have only one spokesman beside himself in foreign affairs—Secretary of State Cyrus Vance—and the NSC under Zbigniew Brzezinski would serve mostly as an administrative staff to the president. Brzezinski was not to be a formulator and advocate of policy, only a facilitator of interagency deliberations and of information flows to the president to allow him to make the most informed decisions as well as a coordinator of policy implementation for the president and the departments. But by the end of Carter's presidency, Brzezinski and the NSC staff were clearly the center of foreign policy making as well as implementation in the government; Secretary of State Vance had resigned, only to be replaced by former Senator Muskie in what turned out to be little more than a caretaker role at State.

In 1981, just before the inauguration of Ronald Reagan, Secretary of State-designate Alexander Haig attempted to restore the department he would head to unchallenged preeminence in the foreign policy field. He presented the following arguments to the president-elect (according to the Haig "talking paper" that was released to the press in 1982 after Haig resigned):

- Reagan's "concept of 'Cabinet Government'...requires that the Secretary of State be your Vicar for the Community of Departments having an interest in the several dimensions of foreign policy."
- The issues that cross departmental lines and impinge upon United States strategic interests, and, as a consequence, must be coordinated by the secretary of state include:
  —Foreign Economic policy
  —Energy policy, "not only with respect to petroleum reserves, but nuclear power and our policy toward the sale of civil reactors as it relates to nonproliferation."
  —Trade Policy. "How do we exercise the powerful level of trade to influence Soviet behavior?"
  —Food policy.
  —Technology transfer.
  —Crisis contingency planning.
- "To manage the development of policy alternatives in all of these areas you must have a single manager who can integrate the views of all of your Cabinet Officers and prepare for you the range of policy choices."
- "To assure that, I propose to establish a number of interdepartmental groups which will include representatives from all of the Departments who have a role to play. All of these NSC subcommittees will be chaired by State except where there is a clear prevailing interest as, for example, at Treasury or Defense."
- "All contacts with foreign officials must be conducted at the

State Department—Otherwise, allies and adversaries will exploit the opportunity to drive a wedge between us on matters of policy."

- "In the same vein, there must be no independent press contact with the office of your National Security Adviser. I must be your only spokesman on foreign affairs."[14]

However rational this design for organizing the government for foreign policy might be, President Reagan, on the basis of strong advice from his White House staff and the new National Security Adviser, Richard Allen, firmly rejected Haig's bid to be the president's "Vicar" and to make the State Department *the* external affairs agency. Reagan's aides at the White House and NSC were his long-time associates from his California days and the presidential election campaign, and they were not now about to let the ambitious ex-general and Kissinger protégé become "Reagan's Kissinger." In this they were supported by the new Secretary of Defense, Caspar Weinberger, also a Reagan crony from California days. The battle over "turf" continued throughout Haig's secretaryship until his resignation in June 1982. Although it was usually expressed in the form of disagreements over policy substance, the policy disputes themselves were in large part a function of the conflicting bureaucratic interests of the principals and their jockeying for position of closest access to the president.

Haig's letter of resignation from the post of secretary of state referred only to his disappointment in the departures from substance of the grand design that he and the president presumably had worked out in January 1981:

> We agreed that consistency, clarity and steadiness of purpose were essential to success. It was in this spirit that I undertook to serve you as secretary of state. In recent months, it has become clear to me that the foreign policy on which we embarked together was shifting from that careful course which we laid out.[15]

However, Haig's phrases were transparent euphemisms for considerations that were somewhat less lofty. James Reston of the *New York Times* summed up what was common knowledge among the Washington press corps:

> Mr. Haig's mistake—he made it repeatedly from the beginning—was to take these incidents [rejections of his policy preferences,

> bureaucratic rivalries] as an affront to him personally and the authority of his office. It is a very old tragedy in Washington: people here fail in politics and the press when they begin to think they *are* what they, for a short while, merely *represent*.[16]

Maintenance of presidential control: Through the National Security Council

The principal argument for centering control of foreign policy in the National Security Council under immediate White House direction is that the State Department itself is also too narrow in its functions and perspectives to structure and manage choices for the president. The president is the only officer in the executive branch of government with the constitutional responsibility enforced by the requirements of standing for election before the *whole* country, of balancing domestic against international considerations and the needs of one sector of the society against another. And the National Security Council comes closest to being the kind of agency that can assist him in making these choices.[17]

By legislative mandate, the National Security Council is composed of the president, the vice-president, and the secretaries of state and defense, plus three "advisers": the chairman of the Joint Chiefs of Staff, the director of the Central Intelligence Agency, and the director of the Arms Control and Disarmament Agency. The president also has the authority to designate other high officers of the government to participate in the deliberations of the NSC. In recent administrations, these other officers typically have been the secretary of the Treasury, the attorney general, the chairman of the Council of Economic Advisers, the director of the Office of Management and Budget, the United States ambassador to the United Nations, and the assistant to the president for National Security Affairs. The last-named official is the head of the *staff* of the Council and is directly responsible to the president. Most often, the Council does its work at the level of subcabinet officials or below—interagency committees—chaired by the assistant to the president, also called the NSC adviser (Kissinger for Nixon; Brzezinski for Carter; and Allen, succeeded in turn by William Clark and Robert McFarlane, for Reagan).

How the president actually uses the NSC system is left up to him and has varied with each occupant of the Oval Office. The tendency, however, is for much of the day-to-day work of coordination and the formulation of options for formal NSC deliberation to be delegated to the assistant to the president for National Security Affairs. And therefore, in fact, this official becomes, next to the president, the most powerful foreign policy official in the United States government unless the president makes a special effort to defer more to the secretary of state. And, indeed, during especially hectic periods of foreign policy making or crises, when the president must make quick responses to rapidly unfolding events, it is not at all unusual for foreign policy to be conducted by the president and his national security adviser alone, acting in the name of the National Security Council.

One school of thought regards the tendency of foreign policy making power to gravitate toward the national security adviser as, in the nature of things, inevitable and functional. And if that is the way a particular president chooses to conduct foreign policy no one should object, since it restores to the president the authority and control necessary for him to perform his chief executive role.

Opponents of a powerful national security adviser, which does appear to be the inevitable consequence of lodging the authoritative coordinating role in the National Security Council rather than State, argue that this particular official is too insulated from public accountability to be accorded so much power. His appointment does not need to be confirmed by the Senate, as do the appointments of all other heads of cabinet departments, their deputy secretaries, and assistant secretaries. And a president can protect him from congressional interrogation by claiming "executive privilege." These problems could, of course, be remedied by congressional legislation if the legislative branch in its wisdom chose to make the national security adviser more publicly accountable.

Maintenance of presidential control: Through a system of task forces

The virtually inevitable gravitation of influence to the national security adviser and his staff points up the fact that the NSC system—the elaborate formal structure of interagency committees—is both a cumbersome and inefficient means for maintaining presidential control of foreign policy and for assuring timely and effective decision making. Presidents soon find that in order to make the administration work for them, they have to operate it largely on an ad hoc basis. Each foreign policy decision has a unique set of requirements for expertise, advice, and other resources. There is only one authority in the executive branch who can draw on these resources with the snap of his fingers, and that is the president himself. The principal foreign policy coordinating tasks, therefore, fall naturally to the White House staff, particularly those on it whose special responsibilities are for foreign affairs, and coordination at this high level becomes tantamount to policy making. Instead of waging a futile battle against the crucial coordinating role played by the White House staff, it is argued, institutionalize it through explicit presidential guidelines and directives—even, perhaps, legislation—mandating the principal staff officers to the president to formulate and reformulate interagency task forces, as each situation requires, to present the president with options for decision and to effectively carry out his decisions. A special planning staff might be created in the White House with the mission of ensuring that all important linkages between domestic and foreign considerations and across policy sectors are taken into account, both in the policy-formulation and decision-implementation phases of the process.[18]

The consequences of the president's failure to take firm control of the reins of foreign policy, it is claimed, are disastrous. "Turf" conflicts between ambitious cabinet officers and between the cabinet officers and White House staffers trying to protect the president and to enhance their own roles tend to substitute for foreign policy deliberations. A president who starts out with a weak immediate staff for foreign policy, as was the case with President Reagan, finds he has to remedy the situation if the country is to have any foreign policy worth the name. Accordingly, Reagan soon replaced his first national security adviser with a close associate from his California days and gave him a mandate to knock heads together within the administration to achieve meaningful substantive deliberations and coordination.

In short, the issue of who is the principal foreign policy decision making authority *within* the executive is a false one. It has to be the president. The issue is who are to be his principal subordinates—for advising him and for carrying out his decisions. The historical record shows this to have varied from presidency to presidency and to have been, often, a bitterly fought contest within each administration. The case for keeping it this way, for allowing each president to organize the executive largely according to his predilections and personality, invokes the record to demonstrate that any more rigid general prescriptions will crack anyway under the pressures for rapid and flexible decision making to maintain United States interests in a fast-moving world.

Notes

1. From the title of David Halberstam's critical book, *The Best and the Brightest* (New York: Random House, 1972).
2. Robert F. Kennedy, *The Thirteen Days: A Memoir of the Cuban Missile Crisis* (New York: W.W. Norton, 1969); see also Dean Rusk, Robert McNamara, George Ball, Roswell Gilpatrick, Theodore Sorensen, McGeorge Bundy, "The Lessons of the Cuban Missile Crisis," *Time*, September 27, 1982, pp. 85–86.
3. *The Pentagon Papers: The Department of Defense History of United States Decisionmaking on Vietnam*, Senator Michael Gravel, ed. (Boston: Beacon Press, 1971).
4. Henry A Kissinger, *The White House Years* (Boston: Little, Brown, 1979), p. 739.
5. Kissinger, *ibid.*, p. 725.
6. See Seyom Brown, *The Crises of Power* (New York: Columbia University Press, 1979), pp. 145–146; and Paula Stern, *Water's Edge: Domestic Politics and the Making of American Foreign Policy* (Westport: Greenwood Press, 1979).
7. John E. Rielly, *Public Opinion and U.S. Foreign Policy 1983* (Chicago: Chicago Council on Foreign Relations, 1983).
8. Henry A. Kissinger, Address before the Los Angeles World Affairs Council, January 24, 1975, *Department of State Bulletin*, Vol. LXXII, No. 1960 (February 17, 1975), pp. 197–204.
9. J. William Fulbright, *The Crippled Giant* (New York: Vintage Books, 1972), p. 193.
10. See Arthur M. Schlesinger, Jr., *The Imperial Presidency* (Boston: Houghton Mifflin, 1972), for a warning by someone who, although sympathetic to the congressional counterattack, believed that it was probably going too far.
11. Public Law 93-148, 93rd Congress, H.J. Res. 542, November 7, 1973.

12. Cecil Crabb and Pat Holt, *Invitation to Struggle: Congress, the President and Foreign Policy* (Washington, D.C.: Congressional Quarterly Press, 1980), p. 128.
13. President Reagan's News Conference of October 19, 1983; text in *New York Times,* October 20, 1983.
14. Talking Paper for Meeting Between President-Elect Reagan and Secretary-Designate Haig, July 6, 1981, published in the *Washington Post,* July 13, 1982.
15. Transcript of Resignation Letter from Secretary of State Haig to President Reagan, *Boston Globe,* June 26, 1982.
16. James Reston, "Who's Now in Charge," *New York Times,* June 30, 1982.
17. A compelling argument for lodging the Central coordinating functions in the NSC and the National Security Adviser is provided by Robert Hunter, *Presidential Control of Foreign Policy: Management or Mishap* (New York: Praeger, 1981).
18. See Lincoln Bloomfield, *The Foreign Policy Process: A Modern Primer* (Englewood Cliffs: Prentice Hall, 1982), especially pp. 28–31, for suggestions along these lines.

Chapter 3
Dealing with the Soviet Union

The United States of America and the Union of Soviet Socialist Republics,

HAVE AGREED as follows:

First. They will proceed from the common determination that in the nuclear age there is no alternative to conducting their relations on the basis of peaceful coexistence. Differences in ideology and in the social systems of the U.S.A. and the U.S.S.R. are not obstacles to the bilateral development of normal relations based on the principles of sovereignty, equality, noninterference in internal affairs and mutual advantage.

Second. The U.S.A. and the U.S.S.R. attach major importance to preventing the development of situations capable of causing a dangerous exacerbation of their relations. Therefore, they will do their utmost to avoid military confrontations and to prevent the outbreak of nuclear war. They will always exercise restraint in their mutual relations. . . . Discussions and negotiations on outstanding issues will be conducted in a spirit of reciprocity, mutual accommodation and mutual benefit. . . .

—Richard M. Nixon and Leonid I. Brezhnev
(Moscow, May 29, 1972)

In its global activities the Soviet Union pursues a "grand strategy" involving the use of a great variety of means to attain the ultimate end: the reduction of any potential opponent's ability to resist. These means include economic, diplomatic, political, and ideological strategies against a background of military strength, to be used separately or together as instrumentalities of power.

—Committee on the Present Danger (April 1977)

The central preoccupation of U.S. foreign policy since World War II—how to deal with Soviet efforts to expand their sphere of control beyond the borders of the USSR—is also the subject of the most intense controversies. The controversies are less over the objective of containing Soviet power and expansion (see Chapter 1) than over the most appropriate means for doing so. Is "force . . . the only thing the Russians understand," as President Harry Truman came to believe,[1] or can the Soviet power drive also be contained and moderated by giving the Kremlin a stake in the legitimate international order, as Henry Kissinger argued in defending the Nixon-Brezhnev detente negotiations of the early 1970s?[2]

The question of how to deal with the Soviet Union periodically extends to the issue of whether containment of Soviet expansion is a *sufficient* objective. Should the "liberation" of countries that the Soviet Union has made its satellites be a goal of U.S. policy once again, as it was at the beginning of the Eisenhower administration? Should U.S. policy extend even farther, as during the first year of the Carter administration, to efforts to enlarge the "human rights" of citizens of the USSR? Should the policy extend even farther, as under Reagan, to basic regime changes in the Soviet domestic polity?

All of these grand strategic questions—What mix of carrots and sticks should be used to contain Soviet expansion? How much should the United States attempt to affect the conditions of people now under Soviet control?—beg the so-called intelligence questions: What are the *intentions* of the Soviet leaders? And what *capabilities* do they possess for implementing their intentions and resisting the efforts of others to change their behavior?

Soviet Intentions: What Are They Really Up To?

Behind many of the policy debates over how to deal with the USSR lie different assessments of the reasons for the Soviet regime's domestic and international behavior. These assessments can be stated in the form of a set of alternative, but not necessarily mutually exclusive, propositions:

PROPOSITION 1. *The Soviet leaders are essentially insecure and defensive.* They are attempting to secure a domestic and international environment that continues the socialist experiment in the USSR and that perpetuates their own rule (or more generously, the Communist party's rule), which they consider indispensible to the survival of Soviet socialism. What looks like aggressive expansion—such as the Soviet military invasion of Afghanistan in 1979—is for the most part the regime's reaction to its feelings of being threatened and encircled by a still-hostile capitalist world and by traditional enemies around the borders of the USSR. Such "protective" expansionary moves by the Soviets can be viewed as attempts to provide greater defense in depth of the USSR and to establish bases from which aggressive moves against the Soviet regime can be interdicted.

PROPOSITION 2. *The Soviets are contemporary carriers of imperialist Russian traditions.* They have inherited the aims of the geopolitically oriented czars (most notably Peter the Great and Catherine the Great) to obtain warm water ports, to become an international commercial power, and to develop friendly client states around the world that will allow them to assure the Soviet Union's access to all continents, as would befit any great power. The Soviet leaders are aware that this outward thrust to establish themselves as one of the world's great powers must inevitably clash with the historic counterthrust of the oceanic powers. Those nations want to keep the Russian empire from expanding from its traditionally confined existence in the Eurasian heartland into the geopolitically significant rimland stretching from the Mediterranean to the Sea of Japan; the Kremlin's strategists know that their Western counterparts are schooled in the Anglo-American geopolitical lore postulating that if the power that controlled the heartland were also to control the rimland, it would be in a position to control the world. (See discussion of U.S. geopolitical imperatives, Chapter 1, pp. 3–6.) Accordingly, Soviet grand strategy is premised on a protracted conflict with the oceanic powers (led by the United States) for dominance of the rimland—a conflict of such high stakes for each superpower that it could result in war. Soviet military planning and deployments, therefore, must be expected to exhibit capabilities for engaging the United States and its allies in battle even beyond the shores of the rimland: in the Pacific, the Indian Ocean, and the Atlantic. From this perspective, Soviet Russia exhibits no particularly new (or novel, for an imperialist power) expansionary intentions as compared with czarist Russia. What are new are her expansionary capabilities.

PROPOSITION 3. *The Soviet leaders are dedicated Marxist-Leninists strongly motivated to communize the world.* They consider themselves to be the advance guard of a historically ripe worldwide revolution that will replace the capitalist system with socialist states that, through the eradication of economic classes, will institute communism and the elimination of states. This mission demands of the Soviet leaders an aggressive effort to seek and exploit opportunities all around the world that will give the revolutionary forces a push against the forces holding on to the old order. A softer verison of this proposition sees the Soviets helping foreign revolutionaries on the condition that there is a "full maturation of the contradictions" of the old order in any particular country, meaning, in effect, that revolutionary movements deserve Soviet help only when they require very little of it.

PROPOSITION 4. *The Soviets are pursuing a grand strategy motivated by and including a combination of ideological, geopolitical, and domestic-control interests.* The various interests are systematically ordered, and the greatest urgency is given to the protection of the leadership's immediate bases of power. Thus first priority is given to securing the power of the Communist party (or its current ruling clique) within the USSR. Their second priority is the protection of the USSR from outside attack and domination and from this is derived the requirement for a belt of loyal satellite states in Eastern Europe. The third priority is to carry out a successful and dynamic Marxist-Leninist program of socialist transformation of human society in the Soviet Union. Fourth is the Soviet Union's realization of Russia's traditional great-power geopolitical ambitions. And fifth is the Kremlin's maintenance of its leadership of the Marxist world-revolutionary cause. All five of these objectives are important to the Soviet leaders, but they will not sacrifice those higher on the scale to obtain those lower in priority.

PROPOSITION 5. *Soviet foreign policy, no less than Soviet domestic policy, is an expression of contending impulses and attitudes within the leadership toward the Marxist-Leninist experiment in the USSR and toward the world outside.* The Soviet Union, despite Russian imperial traditions and the bolshevik ideology, perpetually is trying to find where its head and heart are. The character of Soviet foreign policy at any time, therefore, is likely to be a tentative reaction to complex domestic and international pressures.

Each of these propositions about Soviet intentions has implications for United States' policies toward the USSR.

1. If the Soviet Union's expansionist tendencies are essentially a defensive reaction to perceived threats to the USSR, then the containment and moderation of these expansionist tendencies might best be accomplished by policies designed to reassure the Soviet leaders that the United States has no hostile designs toward them—certainly that it has no objective of fomenting anti-Soviet counterrevolutions in the USSR or in its East European sphere of control. Detente and arms control negotiations would be necessary facets of the containment policy. The United States would refrain from undertaking military deployments that might be interpreted by the Kremlin as preparations for inflicting harm on the Soviet Union or for intimidating it. The United States would exercise restraint in its association with China, particularly when it came to U.S. transfers to China of sophisticated military technologies and weapons. On the positive side, the West would attempt to draw the USSR into cooperative economic ventures for mutual benefit. It could, for example, provide financial credits and technologies for the development of Soviet energy resources, and those resources could be sent to the West in repayment for its help. Since the West would not be helping the Soviets if it expected to do them harm or to go to war against them, such cooperative projects would be highly reassuring of the West's pacific intent. Such policies of reassurance are based on the assumption that the traditional Russian paranoid fears of a hostile West are not so deeply ingrained that even sincere efforts of help and cooperation will be viewed as

strategems to weaken the USSR. The proponents of such policies feel that if such paranoia does dominate Soviet attitudes toward the world, little will have been lost by at least attempting to reassure the USSR of our benign intent.

2. If contemporary Russians are indeed inheritors of the expansionary traditions of the imperialist czars, then policies of reassurance will miss the mark completely. The Russians will place a high value on expanding their sphere of control into the Eurasian rimland and on developing forward positions to protect this enlarged domain from efforts by the oceanic powers to dislodge them. The realistic prospect is for continuing Soviet-American rivalry, at least for dominance of the rimland, which cannot be relieved by professions of peaceful coexistence for this rivalry is geopolitically determined on both sides. According to this perspective on the rivalry, the United States would be naïvely deluding itself were it to believe and act upon the assumption that the United States and the Soviet Union have common interests, short of the avoidance of thermonuclear war, that override their interests in winning the power competition. Were the United States to refrain from entering this power contest and let the Soviets realize their geopolitical ambitions so as to become a satisfied state, it would be tantamount to allowing the USSR to become the dominant world power.

3. Alternatively, if Soviet expansion is deemed an expression, for the most part, of the Marxist-Leninist ideology of the leadership in Moscow, and if that ideology is perceived as imbuing it with the mission of communizing the world, then the United States cannot be secure until the USSR changes its regime or at least modifies its ideology. A sufficiently impressive and successful containment of Soviet expansion over a considerable period of time, however, might eventually relegate the Marxist-Leninist mission to a myth—it might change the operative Soviet goal to a more modest one of securing the "socialist world." Thus the assumption of ideologically motivated Soviet expansion is not necessarily incompatible with a spheres-of-influence approach to U.S.-Soviet relations or to detente and peaceful coexistence between the Soviet and Western spheres, provided that any *modus vivendi* is backed up by a

balance of power capable of keeping the latent Soviet expansionism from reasserting itself.

4. The view of the Kremlin as guided by a systematic grand strategy, with its components ordered from the topmost objective of securing the regime's power within the USSR down to the fifth-order, but nonetheless important, objective of effecting a worldwide Marxist-Leninist revolution, has the virtue of providing U.S. policy makers with the basis for a countervailing grand strategy. The United States could take tough, unequivocal, militarily backed stances against Soviet actions remote from the Soviet homeland which, while expressions of the Kremlin's world revolutionary pretensions, are not required by the Soviets for their own security. Confrontations in opposition to Soviet geopolitically motivated expansion, especially into the rimland areas, could also be tough, and they could be credibly backed by threats of military counteraction to Soviet military moves beyond their existing sphere of control; but such confrontations would need to be managed prudentially and with a capacity to back off of particular forward-containment positions where the Soviets during a confrontation demonstrate a comparatively higher commitment and capacity to sustain *their* forward positions. The greatest forebearance, especially when it comes to the threat of U.S. military action, would have to be exercised in attempting to challenge the Soviets within their existing sphere of control, and there would need to be virtually a total inhibition on U.S. actions that the Soviets could reasonably interpret as threats to the territorial integrity of the USSR and to the political rule of the Communist party within the Soviet Union.

5. Finally, the view of the Soviet leadership as a far from unified group, but rather one beset with massive uncertainties about the domestic and international effects of its decisions calls for a United States policy toward the USSR that asserts our own interests and unambiguously defines for the Kremlin those that are geopolitically vital. But the premise that the Soviets themselves are highly ambivalent about what they should attempt to accomplish internationally also points to the adoption of United States policies that are designed to probe for areas of common interest and cooperation

and to the avoidance of policies that will enlarge the influence within the USSR of those who are paranoid and belligerent toward the outside world. In other words, the view of the Kremlin as unsettled on a grand strategy ought to produce great caution as well as flexibility in U.S. policy for it portends serious potential danger as well as constructive opportunities. It suggests the motto: Prepare for the worst but try for the better.

Soviet Capabilities: What Can They Really Do?

Given such uncertainties about the Soviet leaders' real intentions, intelligence analysts and foreign policy decision makers are compelled to give great weight to Soviet capabilities for actions that would have important implications for United States interests. Even in situations where Kremlin intentions are clearest, such as in Eastern Europe where it is determined to prevent an erosion of Soviet control over the other Warsaw Pact countries, exactly what it will do and what options exist for U.S. counteraction will be profoundly affected by Soviet military, economic, and political capabilities for influencing events. As the Soviets themselves phrase it, "the correlation of forces" is the primary determinant of Soviet foreign policy. The comparable American expression is "the balance of power." Both formulations recognize that any meaningful capability assessment must be *relative*—that is, the power of either side's military forces or other tools of influence can only be evaluated in relation to those of its adversaries. Accordingly, much of the debate in policy circles over which side has the edge in the global balance of power or in regional and local balances reflects the difficulty of making these relational comparisons. The question is if Soviet capabilities were confronted with those of the U.S. and other countries in a dynamic interaction, who would prevail?

The range of plausible answers and the content of the policy debate, of course, vary with the scope of the situation being assessed—whether it is global, regional, or local, and what types of capability (military, economic, political organization) are assumed to have a bearing on the situation.

Varying assessments of the East-West military balance

There is a wide consensus (governmental and nongovernmental, Democratic and Republican) within the United States policy community that at the level of all-out thermonuclear war the superpowers have essentially equivalent capabilities for inflicting vast damage on each other, damage so vast that an all-out thermonuclear war is almost universally characterized as "mutual suicide." Military strategists have labeled this aspect of the Soviet-American military balance Mutual Assured Destruction (MAD). There has been disagreement in the policy community, however, over the capabilities of each side for fighting nuclear wars at various levels of intensity short of an all-out strategic exchange.

The Department of Defense has been warning since the mid-1970s that, without compensatory United States weapons programs, the Soviet Union before the end of the 1980s would be able to destroy over 90 percent of U.S. land-based intercontinental ballistic missiles (ICBMs) in a first strike and in the process would have to use up only a fraction of its own ICBMs. Such an imbalance would present the United States with a dangerously unstable situation, argue Defense Department strategists, for then the Soviets in some future intense crisis might be tempted to launch a strike at the U.S. ICBM force while withholding the bulk of their own strategic forces to deter the United States from retaliating at Soviet cities.[3] Some strategists and arms controllers argue that the Soviet strategic threat has been exaggerated. They doubt that any Soviet leadership would ever launch such a first strike at the vulnerable U.S. ICBMs under the assumption that the United States would refrain from retaliating with its remaining ICBMs, submarine-launched ballistic missiles, and bombers, which still would carry enough megatonnage to incinerate most of the major Soviet cities and industry. The Soviets, it is argued, would still lack a disarming first-strike capability and would not gamble on the theoretical possibility that the U.S. president could be deterred from launching a retaliatory second strike by the existence of a Soviet third-strike capability. The consequence of the Soviets taking such a risk and being wrong would be the loss of everything (and more) than they might have hoped to gain by launching a nuclear attack in the first place.[4]

There have also been different assessments of the military and political significance of Soviet deployments of medium-range ballistic missiles and bombers in the western USSR targeted on the European members of NATO. The standard evaluation in the United States government of these Soviet "Euro-strategic" capabilities is that they pose a blackmail threat to the West Europeans for being allies of the U.S. and for being potential enemies of the Soviet Union on their own behalf. An alternative evaluation, one compatible with how the Soviets define the situation, is that a rough balance exists between the medium-range nuclear forces the Soviets have aimed at NATO Europe and the forces of NATO countries (including France) deployed on the continent, in England, and in the seas around Europe that are capable of striking the Soviet Union.

Most military analysts in the West, governmental and nongovernmental, credit the Warsaw Pact with capabilities superior to NATO's for fighting a war in Europe that did not escalate to a general war between the United States and the Soviet Union. NATO's major assets—technological sophistication, firepower, and more versatile tactical nuclear weapons—have been substantially negated by Soviet qualitative improvements in the 1970s. Additionally, Soviet quantitative superiority in manpower and especially tanks deployed in Central Europe is a potentially decisive Warsaw Pact advantage.[5]

Those who discount the military and political significance of the asymmetries in the force balance of the European Theater argue that a major war in Europe would surely escalate into a general war between the United States and the Soviet Union. NATO, after all, was designed precisely to disabuse the Soviets of any expectation that they could attack Western Europe without starting World War III, and the over 300,000 American troops stationed in Germany are tangible reassurance that the United States would be a cobelligerent at the outset. The NATO disadvantages are not so great that the Soviets and their Warsaw Pact allies could simply roll out their own red carpet to the Channel; the East would have to contemplate launching a blitzkrieg so massive in its proportions that it could not possibly be interpreted as anything else but the opening of World War III, and in any such general war, the overall global force balance (in which the Soviets far from hold a decisive advantage) would dominate the Theater balance.

Some analysts throw additional doubt onto the assessment of Soviet-Warsaw Pact superiority in the European Theater by pointing to the prospect of major sabatoge of essential Soviet lines of supply and communication from the western USSR to the Central European front as these lines cross Eastern European nations with pent-up hostilities toward the Russians.

There is a wide consensus in the United States policy community that the ability of the Soviet Union to project its military power beyond the Warsaw Pact region and Central Europe has obviously been growing. There is much conjecture and debate, however, over the degree to which the Soviet power projection capabilities are beginning to equal those of the United States. The USSR maintains massive deployments along the Sino-Soviet border and has used nearly 100,000 troops in its invasion and occupation of Afghanistan. Yet among U.S. strategists there is considerable uncertainty over whether the Soviets have a capacity to sustain a major two-front war. Their new Backfire bomber and their improvements over the past decade in naval mobility and firepower appear to give them an ability to project military power into the Persian Gulf area but with what effectiveness in relation to U.S. capabilities to use military force in the region is highly debatable. As yet the Soviets have not intervened overseas with their own military forces, although they have transported thousands of Cuban troops into Angola and the Horn of Africa. What these Cuban ferrying operations indicate about Soviet capabilities to sustain a remote intervention remains unsettled among U.S. analysts.

Varying assessments of Soviet nonmilitary capabilities

Most of the competition between the Soviet Union and the United States for influence in the world is in the nonmilitary arenas of economics, sociopolitical organization, and ideology. The employment by either superpower of its military forces outside of its own immediate sphere of control in order to influence the politics of other countries or regions, as the United States did in Indochina and as the Soviets are doing in Afghanistan, is rare. Countries are more likely to fall under the sway of one side or the other or to remain nonaligned because of dependencies they develop with each or both of the superpowers and with other countries; it is, therefore, the respective capacities of the superpowers to respond to the needs of others that determines the global scope of their influence.

The strength of the Soviet economy and its ability to support a large role for the Soviet Union in the international economy is a matter of considerable dispute among Western sovietologists and economists. The Soviet Union in recent years has been a trade-deficit and debtor country, unable to earn sufficient foreign exchange with its exports of petroleum, hard minerals (including gold), and armaments to pay for its principal imports of food grains and advanced technologies. Some analysts contend that this is a systematic and long-term weakness that will persist or get worse for it over the coming decades. Others see the trade deficits and international debt (by 1982 the USSR owed some $20 billion to Western creditors) as a temporary condition exacerbated by a few years of poor wheat harvests because of bad weather and deliberately incurred as a part of its grand strategy of internal development. That strategy required expensive imports of Western and Japanese technology and industrial-expansion equipment to help the USSR develop its vast energy resources for future export and for modern industries that can produce goods for the world market.[6]

For the time being, the USSR is essentially self-sufficient in providing petroleum and other energy resources and earns needed foreign exchange by importing cheaper grades of petroleum while exporting more expensive ones. The persistence of this condition is debated among energy analysts. The CIA has itself fluctuated in its forecasts of if and when the Soviet Union might have to become a net importer of energy (perhaps in the latter 1980s) and when it might become a net exporter (perhaps near the end of the century). In part these estimates depend on assumptions about the Soviets being able to obtain sufficient international credits and high technology imports to rapidly develop their Siberian resources.[7]

There is not necessarily a significant correlation between the current international debtor status of the USSR and its international influence. Among Western and Japanese credits and suppliers of technologies there are many who are willing to gamble on the long-term potential of the USSR for agro-industrial and energy-resource development; and once they extend present help in the anticipation of future payoffs, these investor countries and corporations develop a stake in the health of the Soviet economy and in the maintenance of sufficiently amicable political relations with the Soviets to allow for at least a continuation, if not expansion, of East-West commerce. Meanwhile, the Soviets, in order to relieve their current foreign exchange and debt servicing problems have become vigorous entrepreneurs in the international market, one of the expressions of this being their burgeoning arms sales to Third World countries. They are also earning foreign exchange by providing commercial ocean shipping services all around the world at rates just under those charged by their competitors.

The larger political significance of this new Soviet commercial aggressiveness is at issue in the American foreign policy community. Does it indicate a basic transformation in the Soviet Union from a revolutionary power to one with a stake in international order? Are they creating two-way dependency relationships that constrain them as much as their customers and creditors from power plays that might result in alienation? Does this development give the United States special levers on Soviet behavior?

Another cluster of questions revolves around the appeal of the Soviet Union as the source of leadership for Marxist regimes and movements and other leftists around the world: Has their record of brutally suppressing dissidents within their own camp—as in Hungary (1956), Czechoslovakia (1968), and now Poland—severely eroded their "moral" authority as leader of the world's "progressive" forces? How badly fragmented and inhibited from disciplined action is the world communist movement as a result of the Sino-Soviet split and the rise of the "Eurocommunist" challenge to the doctrinal leadership of the Communist party of the Soviet Union? Was Egypt's severance of its military client relationship with the USSR after the 1973 Arab-Israeli war a symptom of festering resentment in the Third World at Russian arrogance and insensitivity toward other peoples? How deeply did the Soviets alienate themselves from Muslim leftists by their invasion of Afghanistan? Has the sluggishness of the Soviet economy and the Soviets' need to rely on the industrial West and Japan for modernization assistance, more than sixty-five years after the bolshevik revolution, tarnished the image of the USSR as a model for socio-economic development?

The answers to these questions circulating in the American policy community reveal a wide spectrum of assessments about the sources and strength of Soviet influence in the contemporary period. At one end of the spectrum are those who believe that the Soviet Union has virtually no influence over other countries and movements except that which they can impose by force of arms. At the other end are those who see the continuing enlargement of Soviet commercial, organizational, and ideological presence around the globe as a product not only of their enlarged reach but also of the respect, even awe, the Russian communists inspire for having converted their country in less than three generations into one of the world's two superpowers. In between these characterizations of the Soviets as crude, blundering, unpopular, and internationally ineffective on the one hand and ten-feet-tall, deft Machiavellian imperialists on the other are a bewildering array of mixed and highly uncertain assessments.

U.S. Policy Dilemmas and Choices

Given the varying assessments and uncertainties about Soviet intentions and capabilities, almost every aspect of United States policy toward the USSR is highly debatable; and no matter how confident a face and how coherent a rhetorical wrapping an administration puts on its Soviet policy, underneath there is great ambivalence and fear from the realization that the policy rests on assumptions that might be wrong. At the level of grand strategy, there is ambivalence between the alternatives of containment as opposed to peaceful engagement. With respect to managing the military competition there is ambivalence about maintaining an advantageous (or at least not disadvantageous) balance of power through the arms race or through negotiated arms control. When it comes to commercial relations, there is ambivalence on whether to attempt to weaken Soviet power through policies of economic denial or whether to attempt to gain leverage on Soviet behavior through economic and technological intercourse. There are risky choices to be made in responding to maturing nationalist and pluralist tendencies in the Soviet sphere of control in Eastern Europe: What kinds and how much American help to these decentralizing forces will weaken or strengthen the Kremlin's intentions and capabilities to suppress them? Intense debate also surrounds the issue of how much the United States should collaborate with China to build her up as a counterweight to the USSR. This issue is given special attention in Chapter 4.

Confrontation versus cooperation

United States policies have fluctuated widely from the emphasis on Soviet-American cooperation in the Grand Alliance against Hitler in World War II, to the confrontationist containment policies of the High Cold War period during the Truman through the Johnson years, to the Détente and China card period of "carrot and sticks" diplomacy initiated by Nixon and Kissinger and carried on through most of the Carter administration, and to the return to a predominantly confrontationist approach under Ronald Reagan. Each emphasis has its own rationale.

The rationale for confrontation. The rationale for containing the Soviets by essentially coercive threats and policies designed to deny them economic and political gains is that the Soviet leadership has an unrequitable appetite for expanding its imperium over the entire globe, that it views (and consequently so must we) the Soviet-American rivalry as a "zero-sum" game: a gain for one side is *ipso facto* a loss for the other. Any Soviet bids for peaceful coexistence and cooperation (in arms control or commercial relations) must, therefore, be regarded as a strategem designed either to give the Russians an opportunity to build up their strength for the next round of conflict, or to lull the United States and its allies into letting down their guard, or both. The Soviets presumably will regard any Western willingness to enter into cooperative East-West arrangements as indicative of naïvete or weakness on the part of the West. Moreover, it is argued, the Soviets are correct in their assumption that East-West cooperation will lull the West into letting down its guard because democracies are essentially inward looking in their politics and find it difficult to respond to abstract and hypothetical future threats. The rationale for keeping up a confrontationist stance is most articulately presented in the works published during the late 1970s by the Committee on the Present Danger—the group from which Ronald Reagan drew his foreign policy brain trust.[8]

The rationale for cooperation. The rationale for cooperating with the Soviets in reducing tension between East and West, in arms control and arms limitation schemes, in trade and technology exchange, and in running international institutions is twofold: First, there is no rational alternative to working to avoid confrontations between the United States and the Soviet Union in the thermonuclear age, and the leaders of the Kremlin know this; therefore, they must be serious about detente. (Witness the observation by Krushchev that in a thermonuclear war the workers will be incinerated along with the capitalists.) Second, partly because another world war is intolerable and partly because Soviet leadership has discovered that making the Marxist experiment work in its own country is an all-consuming task, the present generation of Soviet leaders is sincere in their professed desire for peaceful coexistence with the West. In short, the Kremlin's highest motivations are to preserve the security and independence of the USSR and to make the Soviet Union a model of a successful socialist society; all else, including what may appear to be the Soviets' international expansionary moves and aggressive arms buildup, is, for the most part, derivative of these objectives. The United States, therefore, should help the Soviets to pursue their basic domestic goals and thereby relieve their fear of attack from the capitalist powers and their consequent need to establish geopolitical and military positions of strength as matters of highest immediate priority.[9]

The mixed approach: Carrots and sticks. Those who argue for conducting U.S.-Soviets relations on a mixed cooperative-adversarial basis depending on the situation base such a grand strategy on either of three assumptions or some combination of them: (1) The Soviets themselves are pursuing a rational mixed grand strategy (Proposition 4, above) and are giving highest priority to securing their domestic political and economic goals within the USSR while opportunistically probing for weak spots in the rest of the world that will allow them to pursue their expansionary goals; (2) The Soviets themselves are confused and ambivalent as to what their international goals should be (Proposition 5, above); or (3) We know too little about both Soviet intentions and capabilities to pursue other than a highly flexible and experimental strategy on a situation-by-situation basis. Coercion may well be required to periodically remind the Kremlin that adventuristic expansion might result in high risks to Soviet security goals. But cooperation can be used to reward moderate Soviet international behavior and to enlarge the stake various political and economic sectors in the USSR have in true long-term peaceful coexistence.[10]

Arms race versus arms control

In addition to the argument that arms control negotiations can lull the Western democracies into a false sense of security, the case for a largely unconstrained competition in armaments rests on the assumption that the Russians are now reaching their upper limits insofar as weapons innovation and resource diversions to armaments are concerned. The catch-up game they have been playing with the United States over the past three decades has strained their scientific, technological, and economic resources, while the United States is now ready to come off the plateau it has been on for over a decade. It is understandable that the Soviets would want to freeze the military balance of power at essentially where it is, for this would allow them to retain the most lethal fruits of their recent and incompletely exhausted buildup, while inhibiting the United States from establishing momentum in its new rearmament program. The Reagan administration, which took office in 1981, planned to devote an additional 7 percent of financial resources each year to the improvement of the U.S. military arsenal and argued that the Russians were in no position to make comparable additions to their weapons programs. The president knew that his actions might make the Russians angry. "They're screaming like they're sitting on a sharp nail," said the president, "simply because we are now showing the will that we're not going to let them get to the point of dominance where they can someday issue to the free world an ultimatum of surrender or die. And they don't like that."[11]

Arms control agreements should be pursued seriously only after it has become evident to the Soviets that the momentum in the arms race has again shifted to the side of the United States. Then we might be able to negotiate from strength. A variant of this argument is that the United States should use its advanced weapon systems such as the MX ICBM and the Pershing II intermediate-range missile as bargaining chips for Soviet-American arms control negotiations.

By contrast, those who favor a strong and continuing commitment to Soviet-American arms control are doubtful that the Soviets, having struggled this long to reach the military level of the United States, especially in the strategic weapons field, would allow the United States to regain the edge in the arms race. Instead the Soviets will squeeze the civilian sectors of their economy even harder; and to justify the further delay in bringing the better life to citizens of the USSR, the leaders of the Communist party will need to paint the intentions and capabilities of the United States in the most terrifying terms. The arms controllers fear an action-reaction cycle of spiraling military expenditures on both sides, which will only result in less security all around, a revival of cold war paranoia, and increased chances of hot war.

The debate between the rearmers and the arms controllers is reflected in the debates over particular strategies and weapons systems. A central issue pervading both the general and specific debates is whether the United States strategic arsenal should be designed only for deterring a nuclear war or also for fighting one. The deterrence-only school believes that capabilities for ensuring that unacceptable levels of destruction will be inflicted on the Soviet Union (should it initiate a strategic war) are sufficient; a corollary usually is attached to this argument: It is that this assured destruction capability should not contain elements that threaten comparable Soviet capabilities to deter the United States, for then, in an intense crisis, the Soviets might be panicked into shooting their vulnerable weapons first. This is the basic rationale for attempting to limit the U.S.-Soviet balance, through SALT or other agreements, to one of *Mutual* Assured Destruction or MAD.

The war-fighting school, on the other hand, argues that only a capacity to respond to a Soviet strategic attack in ways that do not lend automatically to the total destruction of both sides, yet promise to inflict costs on the Soviets greater than any gains they might hope to achieve by their attack, constitutes an adequate deterrent and, beyond that, an adequate defense for the country in case deterrence fails. If the U.S. does not have the capability to fight a "limited" strategic nuclear war—so the argument goes—the Soviets might, in some intense crisis, be tempted to demolish some of our vulnerable forces with a surprise first strike, while withholding most of their society destroying forces as a deterrent against our retaliation.[12]

Critics charge that this limited strategic nuclear war strategy undermines deterrence because it conveys in advance to the Soviets that we would be afraid to retaliate massively to their first strike; moreover, the prospect of actually fighting a nuclear-strategic duel gives both sides high incentives to obtain superiority and, therefore, negates any prospect for meaningful arms limitation agreements. This approach, say the critics, transforms MAD into NUTS, an acronym coined out of the words Nuclear Utilization Target Selection.[13]

The argument between the war-deterrers and the war-fighters translates into the more esoteric debates on particular weapons systems and specific technical problems, such as how to close the so-called "Window of Vulnerability" that will be opening on the United States land-based ICBM force as the Soviets improve their counterforce accuracy. The war-deterrers urge that U.S. correctives be restricted to efforts to reduce the vulnerability of the ICBMs—possibly through "hardening" their protection or making them mobile—or, if this is impractical, to compensate by giving the principal retaliatory strike missions to less vulnerable forces in the U.S. arsenal such as submarine-launched ballistic missiles. The war-fighters advocate rectifying the potential U.S.-Soviet strategic imbalance by programs that give the United States an equally impressive counterforce capability against Soviet ICBMs. This is the principal rationale for the MX ICBM. But arms controllers oppose such counterforce deployments on grounds that they would give both sides an incentive to launch "preemptive" blows against the other side's vulnerable but also highly threatening forces.

The provocative vulnerability of the MX missile was a concern of President Reagan's special committee organized in order to assess alternatives to basing this highly accurate 10-warhead ICBM. The Commission on Strategic Forces, headed by General Brent Scowcroft (President Ford's National Security Adviser) and comprising former secretaries of defense and other former high national security officials, concluded that it would be safer to substitute a new generation of small single-warhead (Midgetman) ICBMs for the existing and planned multiple-warhead missiles. If both sides could be induced to field ICBM forces composed primarily of accurate single-warhead missiles, argue the adovcates of this strategic posture, neither would find it advantageous to attempt a disarming first strike, but both would retain second-strike options in addition to possessing the capability to attack cities.[14]

War-fighting as opposed to purer war-deterring philosophies also pervade the debate over alternative NATO strategies and deployments in Western Europe. These and other common defense problems will be discussed in Chapter 5.

Deterring and defending against specific Soviet expansionary moves[15]

Although a wide range of policies and instruments are available to the United States to counter Soviet expansion, each carries costs and risks. Accordingly, in any specific situation, each will be likely to generate support as well as opposition within councils of decision. The logic and rationale of the most important options as well as the standard objections to them are summarized below:

On-the-spot confrontation. By making it clear to the Soviets that they cannot persist in a particular power play without coming into direct conflict with the United States itself, the United States can attempt to persuade Soviet decision makers that they have significantly underestimated their risks. The Soviets, wishing to avoid a costly local humiliation, will presumably back down. The essence of this type of counteraction (for which the Cuban missile crisis is a model) is a physical presence conveying determination to prevent or repulse an objectionable Soviet action.

On-the-spot confrontation, therefore, requires a convincing capacity to alter the immediately available coercive balance so that the Soviets will have to anticipate incurring more costs if they persist in their provocation. But it also requires an ability and a willingness on the part of the United States to engage the Soviets at a higher level of conflict in case they do not choose to back down. Unless these basic requirements are satisfied, it is the United States that risks being drastically humiliated in a direct confrontation. Accordingly, those who favor enhancing U.S. capabilities for on-the-spot confrontation tend to be supporters of the Rapid Deployment Force notion of quickly deployable tactical assault units. They want to be able to lower the threshold under which the Soviets might hope to intervene in local conflicts without having to face U.S. counterintervention. Otherwise, given mutual strategic deterrence and the new Soviet, all-oceans, tactical mobility, the Russians will find an increasing number of tempting targets for future military power plays.

Reliance on proxies. This approach contemplates letting others engage in on-the-spot confrontations. Proxy support activities can range from transferring military equipment to indigenous forces all the way from using United States ships and planes to ferry another country's combat troops to the scene of conflict. The standard reasons for relying on this option are several. Local anti-Soviet elements, particularly in the Third World, will often find it less embarrassing to accept direct assistance from neighbors or even former European patrons than from Uncle Sam. This is especially true in areas where the Soviets have been relying primarily on their own proxies to establish an initial foothold. Proxy war averts, or at least postpones, a dangerous test of wills between the United States and the Soviet Union with the whole world watching—a situation in which the superpower that backs down risks suffering an enormous loss of international prestige. This fact in particular makes it easier for both superpowers to accept, or even to sponsor, compromise outcomes in local conflicts involving only their proxies and not yet Soviet or American forces.

Critics of the proxy approach contend that it makes it easy—too easy—for American officials to defer the tougher evaluation of whether a threat to United States interests really warrants a major commitment of resources and prestige. The danger is that initially neither side will have to face the starkest implications of widening the conflict, yet both, inevitably, will be likely to find themselves increasingly involved, especially if their proxies engage in irresponsible escalations.

Linkage. This strategy centers on providing the Soviets with extraneous inducements, negative and positive, to modify their behavior in a particular situation. Linkage tends to become a preferred strategy where on-the-spot confrontation or the reliance on proxies is deemed infeasible, undesirable, or insufficient. Its most compelling rationale is that it allows American decision makers to choose areas in which to take a strong stand, rather than allowing the Soviets to trap the United States in local conflicts where the indigenous factors are unfavorable. United States cooperation in East-West commerce and science and technology exchanges can be linked to Soviet restraint in a local situation. Leverage over the Soviets can also be sought by playing the China card—that is, by enlarging the fields of cooperation between the United States and the Russians' principal Asian opponent. This strategy includes increased weapons transfers to China.

But effectively linking commercial and science and technology deals to local U.S.-Soviet conflicts is inherently difficult. Most such transactions are handled by private American firms or buyers and sellers who do not wish to see their profitable arrangements with the Soviets used as political playthings. The Kremlin knows it can rely on American farmers to lobby against linkages in the agricultural field and that many industrial corporations also will lobby against trade and credit restrictions on their exchanges with the Soviets. Moreover, to have any tangible impact, such restrictions must be imposed on items that the Russians cannot obtain elsewhere in the world market, which often leads the United States into disputes with other supplier countries, many of whom are likely to be U.S. allies, who do not feel that the particular situation warrants their making the sacrifices required to have the linkage strategy work.

Efforts to link central arms control negotiations to Soviet behavior in other arenas has the inherent pitfall of indicating to the Soviets that U.S. negotiating positions on particular items of the strategic or tactical military balances are not determined by essential United States security requirements. To the extent that the Soviets believe a U.S. arms control negotiating stance is based on such "soft" considerations, they will be encouraged to harden their own arms control negotiating stances.

Similarly, playing the China card as a linkage strategem can make U.S.-China relations dependent upon the upturns and downturns in U.S.-Soviet relations, which a Machiavellian Soviet leadership could manipulate to its advantage. The U.S.-China relationship is important and complicated enough in its own right (see Chapter 4) not to be made the mere instrument of U.S.-Soviet policies.

Anticipatory involvement. The United States might choose to establish ties and acquire influence with national governments, multilateral associations, and unofficial organizations in areas likely to be on the Soviet opportunity list. In some cases this might mean permissive military sales policies. In others it might mean the slackening of insistence on human rights conditions while extending military and economic assistance. Where the basic conditions in a country portend chronic political instability or civil conflict that the Soviets could exploit to their advantage, the United States could sponsor economic and institutional development programs aimed at strengthening the structure of the economy and society and at the same time avoid identification with particular factions. These alternative interventionary approaches are explored in Chapter 6. The difficulty with all of them is that they presume that U.S. experts and policy makers sufficiently understand the intricacies of foreign societies so that they can design effective "nation building" programs for them. The fiasco of the U.S. involvement in Vietnam is the main case in point for those who challenge the wisdom of such involvements.

Transcending the Soviet threat. This approach ties to subordinate containment of Soviet expansion, to make it a by-product, as it were, of American attention to world-order goals. The notion is that the United States should make such goals the first-order consideration in its relations with specific countries and in its activities in international institutions. United States material and political support would be given to regimes that act in accord with U.S. preferences on human rights, economic development, and international order. Such an emphasis on basic U.S. interests, in contrast to a defensive, reactive foreign policy determined by Soviet decisions, would presumably allow for a cool, unruffled response to particular Soviet actions. It would also convey a belief in the larger compatibility of American ideals with the aspirations of the world's peoples. It would reduce the likelihood of the United States being drawn into local fights in order to prove its political machismo and would contrast favorably with cruder Soviet interventionist strategies.

Opponents of such an aloof approach to Soviet power plays argue that it can concede too much immediate and short-term gains to the Soviets, which cumulatively could amount to important shifts in the global balance of power. They remind American decision makers that Hitler and other aggressors throughout history have exploited such aloof detachment on the part of status quo powers that trusted too much to the long-term job of building a viable world order. And they doubt that in the present era the Soviet threat can be so readily transcended.

Notes

1. Harry S. Truman, *Memoirs: Year of Decisions* (New York: Doubleday, 1955), I, 551–552.
2. Henry A. Kissinger, Testimony to the Senate Foreign Relations Committee September 19, 1974, *Department of State Bulletin,* Vol. LXXVII, No. 1842, (October 14, 1974), pp. 505–519.
3. A typical scenario depicting the Soviets' withholding capabilities for a strategic "third strike" appears in *Department of Defense, Annual Report: Fiscal Year 1979,* pp. 62–65.
4. Spurgeon M. Keeny, Jr., and Wolfgang K.H. Panofsky, "MAD Versus NUTS: Can Doctrine or Weaponry Remedy the Mutual Hostage Relationship of the Superpowers?" *Foreign Affairs,* LXX (Winter 1981/82), pp. 287–304.

5. International Institute of Strategic Studies, *The Military Balance 1982–83* (London: IISS, 1982).
6. On the strengths and weaknesses of the Soviet economy and how these are reflected in the international economic policies of the USSR, see U.S. Congress, Joint Economic Committee, *Soviet Economy in the 1980s: Problems and Prospects, Selected Papers,* 97th Congress, 2d Session, 1982.
7. *Ibid.*
8. See the following publications of the Committee on the Present Danger: *Countering the Soviet Threat* (May 9, 1980); and *What We Have Said 1976–1980* (November 11, 1980).
9. Exemplary expressions of the rationale for Soviet-American cooperation are found in Fred Warner Neal, ed., *Detente or Debacle: Common Sense in U.S.-Soviet Relations* (New York: Norton, 1979).
10. Henry A. Kissinger, Statement to the Senate Foreign Relations Committee, September 19, 1974, reproduced in Kissinger, *American Foreign Policy* (New York: Norton, 1977); and Kissinger's address before the Commonwealth Club, San Francisco, February 3, 1976, in *ibid.*
11. Ronald Reagan, News Conference, August 13, 1981, *Weekly Compilation of Presidential Documents,* Vol. 17, No. 33, pp. 868–877.
12. The logic of the war-fighting school has become the official U.S. military doctrine since 1979 when President Carter, in Presidential Directive #59, approved a "flexible response" philosophy for the design and use of the U.S. strategic arsenal. See Secretary of Defense Harold Brown, *Department of Defense, Annual Report: Fiscal Year 1981.*
13. See Keeny and Panofsky, "MAD Versus NUTS," *Foreign Affairs, ibid.*
14. See essay by Henry Kissinger, "A New Approach to Arms Control," *Time,* March 21, 1983, pp. 21–23; and Presidential Commission on Strategic Forces, Report of April 11, 1983 (Washington, D.C.: Publication of the Commission, 1983).
15. This section is adapted from my article, "An End to Grand Strategy," *Foreign Policy,* No. 32 (Fall 1978), pp. 22–46.

Chapter 4
Managing the Relationship with China

We were convinced that a genuinely cooperative relationship between Washington and Beijing would . . . be to U.S. advantage in the global competition with the Soviet Union. . . .

However, the Soviet dimension was one of those considerations of which it is sometimes said, "Think of it at all times but speak of it never." I, for one, thought of it a great deal, even though I knew that publicly one had to make pious noises to the effect that U.S.-Chinese normalization had nothing to do with U.S.-Soviet rivalry.

—Zbigniew Brzezinski (*Power and Principle*, 1983)

There is broad agreement in policy circles today on the overriding imperatives of United States policy toward the People's Republic of China (PRC)—namely, China must continue to be a counterweight to Soviet power; China must not become alienated from the United States (as it had been from 1949 to 1969); and the Sino-American cooperative relationship established by the Nixon administration in 1972 should be sustained.

There is intense controversy, however, over the costs and risks to be borne in the pursuit of this basic China policy. Some policy analysts and decision makers are worried about negative effects on on Soviet-American relations. Others are opposed to a further downgrading of United States relations with Taiwan. Still others question the extent to which current support for China, especially if it involves assisting her in a major military buildup, could eventually backfire in the event that China mends her rift with the USSR or becomes a major threat to countries and interests supported by the United States.

Playing the China Card

There is debate over precisely how to use the U.S.-China connection as a diplomatic and military counter to the Soviet Union.

A principal concern is that if the Soviet-American relationship is allowed to be the primary determinant of the U.S. relationship with the PRC, then both Moscow and Peking may be accorded more influence over United States policy than would be prudent. While the prospect of China's playing a major role in the U.S.-led coalition might give the Kremlin an incentive to be more cooperative toward the United States (Kissinger's principal rationale for the Sino-American rapprochement engineered in 1972), it could put the Soviets in a position to reduce the degree of cordiality between the United States and China. Credible indications from the Soviets that they were moving toward U.S. positions on important arms control measures and were prepared to accede to U.S. conditions (such as withdrawal of Soviet troops from Afghanistan) might induce the United States to play down its developing geopolitical relationship with the PRC. But this would make the Chinese resentful, and elements in the PRC leadership who have alleged that the United States has all along been setting up China as a sacrificial pawn would claim confirmation of their suspicions.

To prevent a reduction in the American interest in a strong China, Peking has high incentives to spoil efforts by the United States and the Soviet Union to recreate their detente relationship of the early 1970s. The Chinese have become propagandists against Soviet-American arms control and for a U.S. military buildup in NATO, and they are adamant against any thinning out of forces in Europe that would give the Soviets more freedom to deploy forces in East Asia.

It is argued that to use the Sino-American relationship as a "card"—to be played or held back—in what is essentially a Soviet-American game can only provoke the Soviet and Chinese leaders to play analogous games to neutralize the China card strategem. The Chinese can dangle in front of the Russians the prospect of the PRC once again opposing U.S. bases and deployments in Asia or, alternatively, consolidating a full-blown alliance with the United States, depending upon Moscow's responsiveness to Peking's demands concerning their border dispute and the role of Vietnam in Indochina. Or both the Russians and the Chinese, each for their own purposes, can exploit the worst-case fear in Washington of a reconstituted Sino-Soviet alliance—openly playing their Red (ideological) cards, so to speak—to put the United States in a weak bargaining position against each of them.

A sounder approach, it can be argued, would be for the United States, as part of a considered long-term policy of preventing one-power dominance in Asia, to help China and Japan build up capabilities to agreed levels for balancing Soviet power in Asia. This basic balance-of-power strategy would not be altered by any particular Soviet moves, such as a withdrawal of Russian troops from Afghanistan, a letup of Soviet-sponsored repression in Poland, or even a general revival of detente. However, substantial reduction of Soviet military deployments in Asia, either as part of a U.S.-Soviet arms control accord or as a unilateral Soviet move, could reduce the levels of military capability the United States would help the Chinese and Japanese maintain under the persisting objective of balancing Soviet power.

The Taiwan Issue

The issue of what to do about Chinese objections to the continuation of United States relations with Taiwan, particularly in the area of arms sales, remains the most controversial one in the China policy field. The PRC insists that the persisting U.S. special relationship with Taiwan is the principal obstacle to Chinese-American cooperation. The U.S. policy community is divided between those who contend that the standing commitments to Taiwan are a geopolitical liability and should be sloughed off as rapidly as possible and those who insist that the United States continues to have important moral, ideological, and national security reasons for sustaining the ability of Taiwan's regime to defend itself against attack from the mainland.

In order to effect full diplomatic relations with the PRC, the United States, since 1971, has moved substantially toward full acceptance of the Chinese position that there is only "one China" and that, therefore, the regime in Taiwan (which is a part of China) is illegal. Ronald Reagan, however, campaigned on a platform that pledged to upgrade the status of Taiwan and to preserve its independence and capacity for self-defense. The Reagan administration, accordingly, slowed the momentum that had been established by its predecessors—but it did so not without intense controversy.

From 1972 to 1980, United States policy toward Taiwan operated within the ambiguous outlines of the Sino-American agreement to disagree negotiated by Nixon and Kissinger with Mao Tse-tung and Chou En-lai and expressed in the Shanghai Communiqué of February 1972.

> The Chinese side reaffirmed its position:...The Government of the People's Republic of China is the sole legal government of China; Taiwan is a province of China which has long been returned to the motherland; the liberation of Taiwan is China's internal affair in which no other country has a right to interfere; and all U.S. forces and military installations must be withdrawn from Taiwan. The Chinese Government firmly opposes any activities which aim at the creation of "one China, one Taiwan," "one China, two governments," "two Chinas," and "independent Taiwan" or advocate that "the status of Taiwan remains to be determined...."
>
> ...The U.S. side declared: The United States acknowledges that all Chinese on either side of the Taiwan Strait maintain there is but one China and that Taiwan is a part of China. The United States Government does not challenge that position. It reaffirms its interest in a peaceful settlement of the Taiwan question by the Chinese themselves. With this prospect in mind, it affirms that ultimate objective of the withdrawal of all U.S. forces and military installations from Taiwan. In the meantime, it will progressively reduce its forces and military installations on Taiwan as the tension in the area diminishes.[1]

The full normalization of relations between the United States and the PRC, effected by the Carter administration on December 15, 1978, perpetuated this agreement to disagree over Taiwan. There were some concessions on each side, however, from the stances taken at the time of the 1972 rapprochement. The United States agreed to complete the withdrawal of its military personnel from Taiwan and to terminate the Taiwan-U.S. defense treaty, but Peking gave in to the American request that the treaty be given a year to expire. In return for U.S. reiterations of the standard line that Taiwan was a part of China, Peking agreed not to contradict accompanying U.S. statements indicating that we expected a *peaceful* resolution of the Taiwan issue. The formal joint statement between China and the United States did not refer specifically to U.S. relations with Taiwan, but in the delicate negotiations during the fall of 1978 that led up to the December agreement, Brzezinski and other U.S. representatives made it clear that the United States would continue to trade with Taiwan and even to sell the Taiwanese selected defensive arms after the expiration of the Taiwan-U.S. defense treaty. The Chinese would have to understand, explained Brzezinski, "that normalization would run into major political difficulties in the United States if we were not clear on this subject."[2]

The Carter administration, even if it should have desired to slough off the legacy of U.S. commitments to Taiwan, was restrained by the Taiwan Relations Act, passed by the Congress in April 1979, which recommended that the United States "provide Taiwan with arms of a defensive character" in order to help Taiwan "maintain a sufficient self defense capability."[3]

Consistent with the terms of the Taiwan Relations Act, the Carter administration approved $280 million in sales of "selective defensive equipment" to Taiwan in January 1980. But the administration did not approve Taiwan's request for fighter aircraft that could be used in offensive operations against the Chinese mainland.

Peking's objections to the 1980 arms sales to Taiwan were deflected by indications from Washington that, in the wake of the Soviet invasion of Afghanistan, the United States might be prepared to sponsor a major military buildup of China. The prospect of a military relationship between the United States and China was given reality by Secretary of Defense Harold Brown's visit to China. The simple act of an American secretary of defense visiting China was itself unprecedented and one of enormous geopolitical symbolism, but apparently the decision to have Brown undertake this mission occasioned no significant debate within the administration.[4]

Despite Ronald Reagan's election pledges to treat United States relations with Taiwan as official and actively to implement the provisions of the Taiwan Relations Act authorizing sales of defensive arms to Taipei, the value of a friendly China prevented Reagan as president from adhering fully to his inclination to undo the "injustice" inflicted on Taiwan by the Nixon, Ford, and Carter administrations. The geostratic considerations advanced by Secretary of State Alexander Haig tended to prevail over the insistence of the pro-Taiwan lobby in the Congress and over Reagan's purely ideological preferences. China was a crucial weight against the Soviet Union in the global balance of power; so at least for the time being, anti-Sovietism would take precedence over anticommunism.

But the Reaganites' desire to restore at least a measure of legitimacy to the regime on Taiwan would not be so easily deflected. The geopolitical logic of the Soviet-American-Chinese relationship could be invoked on behalf of this ideological preference. The PRC's need of the United States to redress China's weakness vis-à-vis the USSR was so strong, it was argued, that Peking might holler and scream but really had no place to go.[5]

The assumption that "the Chinese need us more than we need them" allowed the Reagan administration to resist Peking's anger at the United States for continuing to interfere in what the Chinese claimed was their domestic conflict. Still, threats by PRC leaders that they might feel compelled to reassess the value of the Sino-American relationship if the United States persisted in selling military equipment to Taiwan could not be totally discounted.

The Chinese maintained that the progress being made toward peaceful unification of Taiwan with the mainland would be advanced if the United States made it clear to Taipei that the time was at hand to make peace with Peking and that receiving further arms from the United States was no longer appropriate.

The dominant view in Washington remained opposed to summary termination of United States military support for Taiwan's armed forces. As put by Richard Solomon, an Asian specialist formerly on Henry Kissinger's National Security Council staff,

> Such an abrupt cutoff . . . could degrade the political stability of the island's leaders, undermine their confidence to enter into talks [for unification], or impel them to seek arms elsewhere. Pressure for termination of arms sales to Taiwan also risks erroding American support for the PRC, as there is strong bipartisan backing in Congress for prudent sales of defensive weaponry to the island. And countries such as Japan . . . would be disrupted by U.S. abandonment of its residual security link to the island.[6]

United States and Chinese diplomats labored over a ten-month period from November 1981 to August 1982 in an effort to find some formula that would satisfy the seemingly incompatible positions of the PRC and the Reagan administration on the U.S.-Taiwan arms transfer issue. The result was the joint communiqué of August 17, 1982 in which the Chinese reiterated that "the question of Taiwan as China's internal affair" but also again pledged "to strive for a peaceful solution to the Taiwan question." In response the United States government said that it "does not seek to carry out a long-term policy of arms sales to Taiwan . . . and intends to reduce gradually its sales of arms to Taiwan."[7] This ambiguous formula provided the context for the summit-level exchange of visits in 1984 between Reagan and top Chinese officials, where the talk emphasized Sino-American commercial opportunities.[8]

How Close a Sino-American Alignment?

The strategies of keeping the Kremlin worried that the United States and China could well collaborate against the USSR, and of reassuring the Chinese leadership that, despite the lingering American support for Taiwan's "self defense," the United States is fundamentally committed to a friendly and cooperative relationship with the PRC have implied a more unequivocal endorsement of

Peking policies than might otherwise be in the U.S. interest. Lying just below the surface of public reaffirmation of common interests between the two countries, this problem has the potential to give rise to considerable controversy in the future.

If the United States had not been so anxious to court Mao Tse-tung and Chou En-lai in the early 1970s, it is doubtful that Kissinger would have been as determined as he was to tilt toward Pakistan in the Indian-Pakistan war over Bangladesh independence. (India, after all, has much more significant weight than Pakistan in the global balance of power.) "The issue burst upon us while Pakistan was our only channel to China," recalls Kissinger. "A major American initiative of fundamental importance to the global balance of power could not have survived if we colluded with the Soviet Union in the public humiliation of China's friend—and our ally."[9]

The anomaly of the Carter administration in effect exempting the largest and one of the most totalitarian autocracies in the world from its human rights campaign could only be explained by the high level anxiety in Washington not to say or do anything that might alienate the presumably sensitive PRC leaders and reverse the progress toward full normalization of Sino-American relations.

Geopolitics first. But how durable is the special exemption of China on human rights? Will it outlast the first major crisis in the new Sino-American relationship? One of the country's leading specialists on Asian relations, Thomas Robinson, posed such questions in a summer 1980 seminar sponsored by the Department of Defense and attended by prominent policy analysts closely associated with the Carter administration and with candidate Ronald Reagan: "The United States wants a world of states similar to itself politically and philosophically," observed Robinson. He went on to say:

> Certainly China does not meet this test. Leninist-type communism, of which the Chinese Communist Party is an example, is inimical to closely held American political and social values. This fact cannot be obscured by *realpolitik*-based political rapprochement.

There was general assent at this seminar (which the author of the present volume chaired) to Robinson's proposition that "this poles-apart and ultimately irreconcilable ideological situation severely limits the ultimate character of Sino-American relations." To allow cooperation to reach the point of substantial interdependence between the two societies would require that Americans avert their eyes from "Chinese domestic politics at variance with American values." This would require a double-standard in U.S. policy—one that submitted "America's [other] Asian allies to a higher test of moral and political goodness and China to a more relaxed standard" —that would severely undercut other important U.S. relationships in the region, particularly ones with Indonesia, the Philippines, and South Korea.[10]

Devotees of Henry Kissinger's earlier brand of *realpolitik* (no longer vocal in the United States policy community of the early 1980s) would argue that the principal implication of such a potential clash between American liberal capitalism and Chinese authoritarian communism would not be to reduce U.S. ties with the PRC but rather to purge from U.S. foreign policy ideological predilections that inhibit cooperation. However, a harbinger of possible change in the other direction was a remark in November 1980 by President-elect Reagan that the PRC subscribed to "an ideology based in a belief in destroying governments like ours."[11]

During the Carter administration, the PRC took advantage of our tentative approach to the Sino-American relationship still prevailing in Washington by orchestrating its 1979 threats and invasion of Vietnam to coincide with the finalization of its normalization accords with the United States government. Premier Deng Xiaoping used the occasion of his January 29–February 5, 1979 visit to the United States to seal the normalization with President Carter as a time at which to issue belligerent threats against Hanoi for Vietnam's bullying of Cambodia. Not particularly pleased with the implication that the United States endorsed the Chinese threats (the U.S. government was then in the process of trying to resume the temporarily stalled SALT II talks with the USSR, Vietnam's principal ally), the Carter administration nevertheless did not dissociate itself from Deng's remarks. And China's invasion of Vietnam started less than two weeks after Deng departed from the United States.

Because the Carter administration was itself at odds with Vietnam for its expansionary moves in Indochina since the 1973 Peace Accords ending United States involvement there, it was not too displeased to have China now teach this arrogant Soviet ally a lesson. There was worry in the White House and the State Department, however, that the Chinese invasion could provoke the Soviets to reopen hostilities on the Sino-Soviet border, which would present the PRC with a two-front war and compel China to seek even greater assistance from the United States than we were prepared to offer. Wasington's counsels of restraint were followed by Chinese troop withdrawals from Vietnamese territory—the Chinese explained that their invasion was a limited reprisal to punish Vietnam for its imperialistic actions and was not designed to be a military occupation.

Whether China's limitations on its military moves against Vietnam were mostly self-imposed or were in response to U.S. admonitions is not known, but the flareup of this quadrangular conflict among the communist states (China, the USSR, Vietnam, and Cambodia) did point up the incongruence between the alignments and antagonisms of the United States on the one hand and of the PRC on the other.

If the Reagan administration and its successors contemplate closer military ties with the PRC, even if purportedly only for the purpose of balancing Soviet power in Asia, they will need to face some complicating facts:

- The interests of the United States and the PRC do not coincide on the degree and kind of hostility each has for the Soviet Union and on how best to play upon the Sino-American connection in dealings with the Russians.
- The interests of the United States and the PRC are even less congruent when it comes to dealing with other countries in Asia, particularly India, Japan, Indonesia, Korea, Thailand, Malaysia, and, of course, Taiwan—none of which want to supplement Russian hegemony with a Chinese variety.
- China still refuses to sign the nuclear nonproliferation treaty.

The implication, which no administration would be able to escape, is that, despite the shared geostrategic objective of containing Soviet expansion in Asia, United States policy toward China needs to be elaborated carefully and managed with a sophisticated awareness of the intersecting American and Chinese interests, some of which are complementary but quite a number of which are potentially antagonistic. Case-by-case, the conduct of Sino-American relations will occasion increasing controversy as the bloom on the rose of normalization fades and romantic illusions are supplanted by realistic dilemmas.

Notes

1. Text of Joint Communiqué, Issued at Shanghai, February 27, 1972, *Department of State Bulletin,* Vol. 82, No. 1708 (March 20, 1972), pp. 435–438.
2. Zbigniew Brzezinski, *Power and Principle: Memoirs of the National Security Adviser 1977–1981* (New York: Farrar, Strauss, Giroux, 1983), pp. 196–233; quotation from p. 232.
3. Taiwan Relations Act, April 10, 1979.
4. See Banning Garrett, "China Policy and the Constraints of Triangular Logic" in Kenneth A. Oye, Roger J. Lieber, and Donald Rothchild, eds., *Eagle Defiance: United States Foreign Policy in the 1980s* (Boston: Little, Brown, 1983), pp. 237–271.
5. *Washington Post,* June 22, 1980.
6. Richard H. Solomon, "East Asia and the Great Power Coalitions," *America and the World* (*Foreign Affairs,* Vol. 60, No. 3, 1982), p. 699.
7. U.S.-China Joint Communiqué, August 17, 1982, *Department of State Bulletin,* Vol. 82, No. 2067 (October 1982), p. 20.
8. See reports in the *New York Times,* January 11 and 12, 1984, covering the visit of Prime Minister Zhao Ziyang to the United States.
9. Henry A. Kissinger, *The White House Years* (Boston: Little, Brown, 1979), p. 913.
10. Thomas W. Robinson, "Choice and Consequence in Sino-American Relations," a paper presented at the Seventh National Security Affairs Conference, National Defense University, Washington, D.C., July 21–23, 1980 and published in *Proceedings: Rethinking U.S. Security Policy in the 1980s* (Washington: National Defense University Press, 1980), pp. 37–54.
11. Ronald Reagan, quoted in *New York Times,* November 29, 1980.

Chapter 5
Dealing with the Advanced Industrial World

The industrial countries are still groping to reconcile the imperatives of their domestic policies with the realities of interdependence.

—Henry A. Kissinger (*Years of Upheaval,* 1982)

The most extensive and intensive diplomatic intercourse of the government of the United States is with the industrialized countries outside of the Soviet orbit—in particular, Canada, the members of the European Community, and Japan. In this area of foreign policy, there are two clusters of issues, which sometimes overlap: (1) those having to do with relations between the countries in the "advanced industrial world;" and (2) those having to do with relations between members of this grouping and countries outside of it. Additionally, an overarching question, often not openly expressed, permeates the debates over these "internal" and "external" relationships: How much of its own independence should the United States sacrifice in the service of peace and harmony among the members of the advanced industrial world and for the common security and well-being of this community against external enemies?

The independence of the United States always has been one of its highest values, but it also always has been an elementary fact of international life that the country has to depend to some degree on the cooperation of other countries in order that Americans may lead the good life. Indeed, some rather important sacrifices of independence have proven necessary even to secure a minimum condition of independence.

One of the most significant historical examples of this paradox (that dependence is necessary to secure independence) was the Monroe Doctrine of 1823, through which the United States announced a policy of independence from the politics of Europe and insisted that the European countries not intervene in this hemisphere. In order to enforce the prohibition on foreign intervention in the hemisphere, the United States had to accept the protection of the British navy.

The most dramatic departures from the ideal of political independence have come since World War II in the form of the North Atlantic Treaty Organization (NATO) and the U.S.-Japanese Mutual Security Treaty. The U.S. entered into these entangling alliances because they were essential for a balance of power against Soviet expansion, which if not contained would threaten the independence of the United States.

In the economic field, the unprecedented restrictions on United States independence of action in monetary and trade matters instituted after the Second World War in the Bretton Woods system and the General Agreements on Tariffs and Trade (GATT) were supported on the grounds that they were necessary for inducing limitations on the unilateral economic policies of the other industrial countries. Without a multilateral system of restraints on unilateral currency revaluations and protectionist barriers to international trade, it was argued, the ability of the United States to secure the well-being of its people could be overwhelmed by another collapse of the global economy such as occurred between the two world wars.

Given the rather solid postwar consensus in the United States on the need for mutual security arrangements in the military field and mutual accountability arrangements in the economic sphere among the industrial powers, the controversies in recent years have turned on the *degree* of inhibition on United States unilateral action and the *distribution of sacrifices* among the partners in these multilateral undertakings.

The Case for Community Building

One variant of the case for a strong commitment by the United States to multilateral undertakings in its relations with the other advanced industrial countries is, without apologies, visionary. It looks forward to the eventual political integration of the noncommunist industrial world, perhaps in a federal system analogous to the United States of America. The premise is that a society's political system should be congruent with its economic system—or put another way, its pattern of political and legal accountability should match its pattern of material interdependence.

This vision was popular in the United States foreign policy establishment during the 1950s and 1960s when it was fashionable to talk of the North Atlantic Community. The American Atlanticists drew much of their inspiration from the European federation builder, Jean Monet, who dreamt of an enlarged organically intertwined community of Western nations growing out of the European Common Market.

President Kennedy found an idealistic rationale in the Atlanticist vision, which journalists labeled the Kennedy Grand Design, for pressuring the Europeans for greater cooperation with the United States on military and economic matters. Whatever contributed to a broadening and deepening of transatlantic interdependence, such as Britain's entry into the Common Market or more integrated NATO defense plans, was good; whatever retarded or reversed the building of the North Atlantic Community, such as President deGaulle's military and economic nationalism, was bad—not simply on the grounds that it weakened the anti-Soviet coalition but because it was subversive of the goal of building the North Atlantic Community.

The construction of a more integrated Atlantic Community, as envisioned by President Kennedy, was to proceed at two levels: The first, already well underway, was for "our European friends to go forward in forming the more perfect union which will someday make this [Atlantic] partnership possible." But it was not too early to look ahead. As the Europeans achieved success in their own community building experiment, the United States will be ready for a Declaration of Interdependence.

> ...We will be prepared to discuss with a United Europe the ways and means of forming a concrete Atlantic partnership between the union now emerging in Europe and the old American Union.[1]

It was time for the Americans to "learn to think intercontinentally," said Kennedy, just as the founders of the American Constitution had to learn to think continentally.

> Acting on our own, by ourselves, we cannot establish justice throughout the world; we cannot insure its domestic tranquility, or provide for its common defense, or secure the blessings of liberty to ourselves and our posterity. But joined with other free nations we can do this and more....For the Atlantic partnership of which I speak would not look inward only....It must look outward to cooperate with all nations in meeting common concerns. It would serve as a nucleus for the eventual union of all free men.[2]

A similar formulation of a staged process of community building among the advanced industrial countries underlay the work of the Trilateral Commission during the years when Zbigniew Brzezinski was its executive director. Founded by David Rockefeller in the early 1970s, the Trilateral Commission was a nongovernmental organizaton made up of prominent corporation executives, bankers, publishers, public officials, former public officials, and a few academics—almost all of whom came from North America, Western Europe, and Japan. Among its American members were luminous exiles from past administrations (Cyrus Vance, George Ball, Paul Warnke, Harold Brown, Paul Nitze) and media executives, Arthur Taylor (of CBS) and Hedley Donovan (of *Time*).

The commission did not purport to speak for or negotiate among the governments of the individuals participating in its deliberations. It met in nongovernmental settings to work out common approaches to the problems of advanced industrial society, to strive for cooperative means of dealing with their increased interdependence, and to strive for unified responses by the advanced industrial countries toward countries in the Soviet camp, OPEC, and the Third World.

The informal transnational associations developed in meetings of the Trilateral Commission were supposed to be the contemporary analogue of the transnational bonds between the aristocrats of nineteenth century Europe who, in the period following the Napoleonic wars, were able to effect an unprecedented degree of cooperation among the great powers.

The *weltanschauung* animating the Trilateral Commission's work was elaborated by Brzezinski in his 1970 book *Between Two Ages: America's Role in the Technetronic Era*. Brzezinski envisioned stages of community building, made possible by technology-generated interdependence:

> The first of these would involve the forging of community links among the United States, Western Europe, and Japan, as well as with other more advanced countries (for example, Canada, Australia, Israel, Mexico). The second would include the extension of these links to the more advanced communist countries [in Eastern Europe].[3]

The third phase would feature the association of the Soviet Union with the advanced community:

> The Soviet Union may come to participate in such a larger framework of cooperation because of the inherent attraction of the West for the Eastern Europeans—whom the Soviet Union would have to follow lest it lose them altogether—and because of the Soviet Union's own felt need for increased collaboration in the technological and scientific revolution.[4]

Brzezinski's Trilateralist-*plus* vision found expression in Jimmy Carter's election campaign rhetoric pledging to supplant "balance-of-power" international politics with "world-order" politics, and in early statements of the Carter administration indicating that the new foreign policy would discard preoccupation with the Soviet threat.[5]

By the middle of Carter's term in the White House, concerns over the Soviet military buildup and Soviet and Cuban power plays in the Horn of Africa had revived the cold war preoccupations; and the need for mutual security cooperation in NATO and with Japan against an increasingly aggressive Soviet Union became, once again, the predominant rationale for community-mindedness among the advanced industrial countries. United States efforts to further consolidate the "free world coalition" against the Soviet threat were sharply spurred by the Soviet invasion of Afghanistan in late 1979, which revived fears in Washington of Soviet designs on the oil-rich Persian Gulf.

However, the frustrations of the Carter administration in unsuccessfully attempting to reforge a tightly coordinated anti-Soviet coalition in response to the Afghanistan invasion, and similar frustrations experienced in 1981–1982 by the Reagan administration in attempting to organize an alliance-wide set of economic sanctions against the USSR for its repression of Polish liberalism, indicate the extent to which the previous decades' assumptions of increased integration of the advanced industrial societies were being challenged by centrifugal forces. The 1980s and 1990s could well feature a return to a more traditional unilateral diplomacy by members of the erstwhile free world coalition.

The Case for Unilateralism

The classic case for American unilateralism was stated by George Washington in 1796 in his Farewell Address:

> Europe has a set of primary interests which to us have none or a very remote relation. Hence she must be engaged in frequent controversies, the causes of which are essentially foreign to our concerns. Hence, therefore, it must be unwise in us to implicate ourselves by artificial ties in the ordinary vicissitudes of her politics or the ordinary combinations and collisions of her friendships or enmities.... Why, by interweaving our destiny with that of any part of Europe, entangle our peace and prosperity in the toils of European ambition, rivalship, interest, humor, or caprice? It is our true policy to steer clear of permanent alliances with any portion of the foreign world, so far, I mean, as we are now at liberty to do it.... Taking care always to keep ourselves by suitable establishments on a respectable defense posture, we may safely trust to temporary alliances for extraordinary emergencies.[6]

This early isolationist unilateralism was the product of an inward looking preoccupation with the vast tasks of exploration and development facing the new American nation. And the new nation, confident in the insularity provided by the great oceans and justifiably optimistic that the resources available here were sufficient to provide for the well-being of the population, had the luxury of an aloof moral superiority over the old world. As voiced by Thomas Jefferson in his first innaugural address,

> Kindly separated by nature and a wide ocean from the exterminating havoc of one quarter of the globe; too high-minded to endure the degradation of the others; possessing a chosen country, with room enough for our descendants to the thousandth and thousandth generation; . . . with all these blessings, what more is necessary to make us a happy and prosperous people?[7]

Contemporary unilateralism has widely divergent sources and manifestations. On one side are advocates of a highly constricted definition of U.S. interests that does not require the United States to help others protect their security and well-being. On the other side are those with a hegemonic, almost "imperial" view of the United States as a superpower that can largely "call the shots" in its military and economic relationships with the other industrial countries.

Inward looking pressures

Those with a constricted definition of United States interests are themselves a heterogeneous group. Some are domestic-welfare liberals who see foreign commitments and high defense budgets diverting scarce resources from government programs to help the needy in the United States. Some are fiscal conservatives who hope to reduce government spending and to balance the federal budget by cutting back on expensive military programs not strictly required for the defense of the United States itself. Others are trade protectionists attempting to insulate weak sectors of the U.S. economy from foreign competition. Still others are political nationalists worried over the loss of sovereignty that might be entailed in committing the United States to international decision processes and institutions.

Fortress America. Many of the divergent impulses for a more unilateralist foreign policy share the premise that the country's security requires only an ability to deter attacks on the United

States itself and that more extensive military commitments are either wasteful or dangerous or both.

A standard argument is that the revolution in military technology that has given the United States a capacity to strike a devastating blow at any country in the world from U.S. territory or the deep ocean has rendered obsolete U.S. forward bases in Europe and Japan. A softer version puts it that "they (the overseas allies of the United States) need us more than we need them." The Fortress America strategists reject the notion that the attainment of an intercontinental striking capability by the USSR, which neutralizes the U.S. strategic nuclear deterrent, revives the need for U.S. readiness to fight limited wars in order to contain Soviet expansion in Europe and Asia; on the contrary, they argue, it makes it all the more imperative for the United States to slough off overseas commitments that could draw this country into a confrontation and war with the Soviet Union over interests that are less than vital. The extension of the U.S. nuclear umbrella over allies who might be exposed to Soviet attack has lost most of its credibility; and efforts to shore up the declining credibility by maintaining U.S. troops in forward containment deployments as "hostages" to full U.S. involvement only underscores the basic obsolescence and irrationality of such commitments. (Presumably if the blood of Americans is being spilled in West Germany, the United States can be expected to regard an attack upon West Germany as tantamount to a direct attack on the United States.)

The logic of the Fortress America assumptions has been expressed in congressional pressures to unilaterally withdraw United States troops from West Germany (Most prominent have been the resolutions introduced year after year by Senator Mike Mansfield of Montana to cut the 300,000 U.S. troops in West Germany by half) and in George McGovern's 1972 presidential election campaign slogan, "Come Home America." It is also implied in the Mutual Assured Destruction (MAD)-only doctrine for U.S. strategic force planning because MAD equates U.S.-Soviet strategic war with mutual suicide and thus precludes the use of U.S. forces to retaliate against the Soviet Union for any Soviet moves short of a direct attack on the United States itself—even for an attack that is overwhelming Western Europe.

Isolationist impulses to pull back into a Fortress America are stimulated by perceptions that the NATO allies are not willing to assume a fair share of the military burdens of containing the Soviet Union. American resentments toward the Europeans (and the Japanese) for not pulling their weight in the common defense tasks of the coalition are intensified as the ability of these countries to compete with the United States (sometimes even to displace American industrial products) in the markets of the world grows. Why should we strain our economy to provide them with military security, it is asked, when they are gaining a competitive edge on us by avoiding defense budgets that would strain their economies? The existence of this resentment is played upon by high U.S. foreign policy and defense officials in their efforts to get the Europeans (and in recent years the Japanese as well) to contribute more to the pooled military resources of the alliance.

The popular notion that the NATO allies and Japan need U.S. protection for their security while the United States no longer needs them, leads, on occasion, to rather crude bargaining pressures on the Europeans and the Japanese. These pressures take the form of official U.S. suggestions that continued U.S. sacrifices in the mutual security field are "linked" to cooperation by the allies on economic matters. This type of linkage strategy was used by the Nixon administration against Japan at the time of the U.S.-Japanese negotiations on the return of Okinawa to Japanese control; and it was also threatened, at least by implication, in the tough negotiations between the United States and the European Community in the early 1970s on international trade and monetary issues. Secretary of the Treasury John Connally stated:

> To be perfectly frank, no longer will the American people permit their government to engage in international actions in which the true long-run interests of the U.S. are not just as clearly recognized as those of the nations with which we deal.[8]

Economic protectionism. There is always a politically powerful coalition in the United States for restricting the access of foreigners (usually sellers but sometimes also foreign investors) to the U.S. market. The arguments for keeping out the foreign goods, salesmen, and entrepreneurs are often presented in national interest terms: United States economic and social policies are likely to be distorted and possibly overwhelmed by fully opening the U.S. market to foreigners able to take sales, earnings, and jobs away from Americans. As often as not, however, such arguments are made by special interests draping themselves in a national interest flag, for there are always Americans who want to buy goods at world-market prices and many U.S. exporters who fear retaliatory barriers to their selling abroad by countries whose products are kept out of the U.S. market.*

In recent decades, economic protectionist sentiment has been stimulated by the activities of U.S.-owned multinational corporations that locate subsidiary plants in countries with lower "factor costs"—including cheap labor, special tax breaks, and the absence of environmental restrictions—and then reimport the products of these subsidiaries for sales in the United States market. But even when the foreign-produced goods are not reimported but only sold abroad, there is allegedly a loss of jobs and associated benefits to the American economy from the flight of corporations that otherwise would be producing their exportable goods on American soil. More than anything else, this phenomenon has turned American Labor into a protectionist lobby. In the words of some prominent spokesmen for organized labor,

> The age-old theory of comparative advantage... assumes that the factors of production remain fixed. This assumption no longer holds true.... U.S. multinational corporations have been investing overseas at phenomenal rates in recent years. The U.S. labor force, on the other hand, is not mobile. The result—products produced overseas that take advantage of cheap labor using the most modern of the U.S. or world's technology enter the world market and seriously disrupt job opportunities in the United States. Today, the comparative advantage is, in most cases, simply cheap labor.[9]

*The U.S. Civil War (1861–1865) was in large part a battle of the protectionist Northern industrial areas that wanted to keep European manufactured goods out of the U.S. market against the Southern agricultural areas that wanted to purchase the less expensive European goods and to earn foreign exchange by selling their products in Europe.

Such protectionist arguments tend to have widespread appeal during periods when the United States foreign trade balance is in deficit (when there is an excess of imports over exports) and when the country is experiencing high unemployment. At such times, it is comparatively easy to mobilize congressional majorities in favor of dollar devaluations (to make imports more expensive), tariff and nontariff import barriers, and export subsidies—in retaliation for the resort to such protectionist devices by members of the European Community and Japan who try to keep U.S. products out of their markets and to give their products a competitive price advantage over U.S. goods in world markets and even in the United States.[10]

The principal case against a retaliatory approach by the United States to the protectionist policies of other advanced industrial countries is that it can only reinforce the negative action-reaction cycle in ways that will reduce the overall volume of world trade to the detriment of all. No longer can the United States say with equanimity that "this will hurt you more than it hurts us." Relatively speaking, comparing the extent to which the various economies are dependent upon foreign trade, it is true that the United States will suffer less harm than other countries by a general international withdrawal into rigidly protected national and regional markets. The absolute harm, however, will be highly disruptive to the health of the American economy as well, given the fact that 40 percent of all U.S. farm acreage is devoted to producing crops for sale abroad, that over 20 percent of all U.S. industrial production is exported, and that one out of every six jobs in the manufacturing sector depends on the foreign sales of products made in the United States.

Alternatively, some economists argue for a third way—neither free trade nor protectionism—for the United States to respond to the growing competition from its industrial country competitors, which indeed emulates what some of these countries have been doing to enhance their own competitiveness: They argue for the strategy of *government-sponsored and guided structural adjustment.*

This strategy goes beyond recommendations by elements of United States Labor for reactive adjustment policies, such as temporary job creating projects and skill retraining programs to provide relief to local communities and particular industries adversely affected by foreign competition. Instead it involves a concerted effort by government, business, and labor to accelerate the transition of the U.S. economy into higher value-added and more competitive production. Uncompetitive firms would not be protected; they would be induced to close. Underutilized plant and equipment would be scrapped or put to more productive uses. Workers would be retrained and helped to move into industries on the frontiers of technological change—many of them would enter the "software" and knowledge industry fields as opposed to the "hardware" and commodity or finished goods fields.

One advocate of this policy, economist Robert B. Reich, proposes that the United States should "seek international agreements with other advanced industrial nations, establishing targets and timetables for capacity reductions, the scrapping and conversion of existing plants and equipment, and retraining of workers."[11]

The negotiated arrangements might include

> an international adjustment fund to help finance these transactions. Payments to the fund would be proportional to a nation's current employment in designated low-skilled, standardized businesses; drawing rights would be proportional to a nation's reduction in capacity and employment.[12]

Clearly, this strategy would involve ideological adjustments as well—against the prevailing bias that government interventions in domestic and international markets are bad in that they reinforce and reward inefficiencies. The task, say the strategy's champions, is to educate Americans to distinguish between undesirable government interventions and desirable ones. The latter are those that shift U.S. businesses into higher value-added production and more competitive outputs; such interventions can be eliminated once these shifts have been achieved. As put by Reich, we need to realize that "human capital formation" is becoming more important than "financial capital formation." It is investments in education, training, and group learning that now define a nation's comparative advantage and determines its capacity to develop products that will be competitive in the world market. He argues:

> The United States must understand that government expenditures in the form of subsidies, loan guarantees, and tax benefits designed to keep or lure high value-added emerging businesses within the United States, are no less legitimate investments in the education of America's labor force than are investments in the public schools.[13]

The "imperial" thrust

The breakdown of community building efforts and multilateral cooperation typically stimulates among some American policy makers an aggressive alternative to the inward looking Fortress America and simple economic protectionist responses. Instead of the withdrawal postures that say "since you won't play by our rules, we're picking up our marbles and going home," the alternative says, "since we still possess the greatest concentration of military power in the noncommunist world and are more powerful economically than any country on earth, you are asking for trouble if you refuse to cooperate with us."

There is, of course, no suggestion that the United States will use its power to directly coerce its coalition partners. But there is considerable hinting on the part of policy makers resentful of the lack of cooperation from the West Europeans and the Japanese (particularly when it comes to dealing with the Russians or the OPEC countries) that the United States may well be driven into charging its allies higher prices for the military protection it provides them.

One type of financial charge is the offset agreement whereby a country that hosts U.S. military deployments compensates the United States for the resulting draw on the U.S. balance of payments by purchasing equipment for its own armed forces from the United States. Another means of attempting to tighten the U.S. grip on its allies is to insist on alliance-wide standardization (not just compatibility) of military equipment and to try to ensure that it will be the U.S.-produced airplane or tank that is designated as NATO standard equipment. But attempts to induce conformity (and not incidentally to increase U.S. exports) by making allies dependent on U.S.-produced military equipment are increasingly resisted by allies whose domestic arms industries are capable of producing equally sophisticated military equipment. Consequently, this type of hegemonic assertiveness by the United States is likely only to worsen the nationalistic tendencies that it is attempting to counter.

The temptation is great, in a period of crosspressures and centrifugal pulls against the U.S. hegemonial system, for the United States to resort to heavy-handed unilateralism in both the military and the economic spheres—sometimes blatantly linking them—in order to present our uncooperative allies with the stark choice of either accepting U.S. leadership or being cast adrift in an anarchic world reminiscent of the unstable period between the two world wars.

Such a "take it or leave it" attitude was the hallmark of the Nixon administration's unilateral scuttling of the rules of the prevailing international monetary order (the Bretton Woods system) in August 1971 in an attempt to overcome an unprecedented U.S. deficit in international trade. Administration economists blamed the trade deficit on undervalued Japanese and West European currencies that made their goods artificially competitive in the United States market and on barriers that discriminated against U.S. goods in their markets. An unwillingness to compete freely with the United States was no longer tolerable, argued Secretary of the Treasury John Connally, given the ample financial reserves of the Common Market countries and Japan and their productive power. Taking Connally's advice, President Nixon suspended the conversion of the dollar into gold or other international reserve assets and imposed a tax of 10 percent on goods imported into the United States. These actions were taken, Nixon explained,

> to make certain that American products will not be at a disadvantage because of unfair [currency] exchange rates. When the unfair treatment is ended, the import tax will end as well. . . . The time has come for exchange rates to be set straight and for the major nations to compete as equals. There is no longer any need for the United States to compete with one hand tied behind her back.[14]

The United States partly got its way by resorting to these tough tactics. The other industrialized countries adjusted their currency rates to better reflect their real values. Additionally, they agreed with the United States to allow the currencies of the advanced industrial countries to "float" against one another so as to allow market forces rather than government intervention to establish exchange rates henceforth. The result was, in effect, to permanently dismantle the postwar Bretton Woods system of negotiated adjustments and intergovernmental accountability on currency values. No longer able to dominate the multilateral Bretton Woods system, the United States decided to take its chances with a largely unilateralist regime, one rationalized by the classical economic doctrines of the free market.

Concerting East-West Policies among the Industrial Nations

The desirability of a concerted approach toward the Soviet Union and its coalition has never been at issue in the United States government since the end of World War II. The questions rather have been over the content of the common Western (and Japanese) positions and over how to conduct relations with the East when a Western consensus cannot be maintained. These questions are found on issues ranging from grand strategy to the particulars of defense, arms control, and commercial policy and also on ways of responding to the suppression of human rights and political liberties in the Soviet sphere. With the rebuilding of Western European countries and Japan after the devastation of World War II, and the resulting inclination of these countries to assert their own national interests within the coalition, the problems of the extent to which coalition policies should be concerted and then precisely how to deal with divergencies have become, more than ever, central to the important debates over U.S. foreign policy.

On military matters

One school of thought, still dominant in U.S. policy circles, is that anything having to do with East-West military balance and how the military forces of any coalition partner of the United States might be used against the Soviet Union or a member of its coalition must be the business of the United States. Put in extreme terms, the United States, since it is the principal protector of the coalition because of its arsenal's ability to incinerate the USSR and since, therefore, it is also the prime target of the USSR's strategic arsenal, *must have a veto* on any actions that could provoke an East-West military confrontation or could determine its course and outcome. Put in terms more acceptable to the alliance partners of the United States, there *must be full consultation* on such matters.

The more extreme formulation was expressed most openly by the high officials of the Kennedy administration in the 1960s, as a reaction to General deGaulle's unilateral force decisions for France and to the other NATO allies' insistent demands for more of a role in decisions on the use of NATO's strategic nuclear arsenal. When it came to employing nuclear weapons, explained Secretary of Defense McNamara, there could not be conflicting targets on the part of the NATO allies nor could there be more than one list of targets. The nuclear campaign would have to be based on strictly centralized command and control.[15] President Kennedy, when asked if the United States would consider sharing command and control with the European allies, replied:

> It is a very difficult area because the weapons have to be fired in five minutes, and who is going to be delegated on behalf of Europe to make this judgment? If word comes to Europe or comes any place that we're about to experience an attack, you might have to make an instantaneous judgment.... Now, it is quite natural that Western Europe would want a greater voice.... But...in the final analysis, someone has to be delegated who will carry the responsibility for the alliance.[16]

Another school of thought is willing to contemplate, on grounds of political realism, the existence of more than one center of military decision making in the alliance. Indeed, it is asked, how could we avoid this once the French decided to deploy their own nuclear deterrent and to pull out of the integrated NATO military command structure? Rather than stubbornly insisting on a centralization of command and control that can no longer be sustained, the United States should explore ways of devolving greater political and military authority to a West European entity within the alliance that might merge French, British, and German capabilities. The contention is that this "dumbbell" arrangement for the alliance would be preferable to independent nuclear forces among the membership. Henry Kissinger, both before assuming his high posts with the Nixon administration afterwards, has suggested the importance of at least exploring the logic of such an arrangement.[17] In office, however, he appeared to be no less anxious to keep tight control over military strategic matters than were any of his predecessors.

In the 1980s some analysts see the deployment by the United States of intermediate-range nuclear missiles on the European continent (Pershing IIs and Ground-Launched Cruise Missiles) as paving the way toward a partial devolution of control over such weapons to a West European strategic nuclear entity. Others see exactly the opposite purpose being served: namely, that the United States, by putting such weapons on European soil, reestablishes the belief in its willingness to engage in a strategic nuclear war to deter a massive Soviet attack on Europe, and thus it reduces the incentives on the part of the West Europeans to have their own nuclear deterrent forces.

These intra-alliance debates (and debates within the United States) over the authority to order and direct the use of nuclear weapons in NATO are intimately related to the existence of conflicting opinions on the following issues concerning the military protection of Western Europe: how large and long a non-nuclear war NATO should be prepared to fight to deter Soviet attack on Western Europe and to defend Western Europe in case deterrence fails; when and under what circumstances to resort to nuclear weapons; and what the role is that will be played by nuclear weapons—battlefield, intermediate-range, and intercontinental.

The official United States position, since the Kennedy administration rejected the Eisenhower administration's primary emphasis on nuclear threats to deter Soviet attacks and provocations in Europe, has been one of flexible response: Prepare to defend as far forward and as long as possible with conventional weapons, but also be prepared to initiate nuclear warfare to prevent Western Europe from being overrun. The forward-deployed conventional forces of the alliance in Germany, in other words, would be more than "hostages" or a "trip wire" to assure that a nuclear response would be delivered to Soviet aggression. They would be an actual fighting force, with sufficient strength to defend Western Europe without having to initiate nuclear war.[18]

The doctrine of flexible response was accepted reluctantly by the West Germans and the French and also without enthusiasm by the British. The Europeans read more American fear than flexibility into the new U.S. policy—fear by the Americans of being compelled to place their own cities in jeopardy of nuclear attack by the Russians—and suspected the existence of secret U.S. contingency plans to confine the American military response (in the event of a Russian attack on Europe) to the European Theater itself. The Americans clearly were preparing, and trying to get the Europeans to prepare, for a protracted conventional conflict in the event that deterrence failed. And whereas the American architects of the flexible response strategy claimed that this would shore up NATO's deterrence of a Warsaw Pact attack because it was more credible than nuclear retaliation, most European strategists disagreed. They argued that, on the contrary, it would undermine deterrence by signalling to the Soviets they could engage in aggression below the threshold of the American promise to do all that would be necessary (including a direct strategic attack on the Soviet homeland) to repel a Soviet attack. Now it looked as if the Americans were ready to equivocate on the original NATO promise of all for one and one for all.

Indeed, the Europeans have been partly correct in their suspicions that the doctrine of flexible response is a cover for a United States policy of keeping our options open even in the face of a massive Soviet blitzkrieg-style invasion of Western Europe. Some influential segments of the U.S. policy community would go even further and attempt to foreclose the option of a U.S.-Soviet strategic war over the fate of Europe. But other equally influential segments of the American policy community have been in accord with the dominant European view that a major war confined to the European continent is not to be contemplated, and the Soviets should not be led to believe that there is the slightest chance of starting such a war without it escalating into an all-out nuclear holocaust.[19]

This fundamental debate over NATO strategy resurfaced in the spring of 1982 with the publication of a proposal for *no-first-use of nuclear weapons* by four prestigious former officials of previous administrations: McGeorge Bundy, George F. Kennan, Robert McNamara, and Gerard Smith. Writing in *Foreign Affairs*, the four strategists base their proposal on the following premise:

> There is no way for anyone to have any confidence that [even the most restrained battlefield] nuclear action will not lead to further and more devastating exchanges. Any use of nuclear weapons in Europe, by the Alliance or against it, carries with it a high and inescapable risk of escalation into the general war which would bring ruin to all and victory to none.[20]

Recognizing that the original American pledge, expressed in Article 5 of the North Atlantic Treaty, was understood to be a nuclear guarantee, Bundy, Kennan, McNamara, and Smith argue for a no-first-use policy on grounds that the fundamental condition that might have made the nuclear guarantee rational in 1949 and the early 1950s—namely, the fact that only a Soviet conventional threat then existed—has changed. Any use today of nuclear weapons by NATO will subject members of the alliance, including the United States, to nuclear devastation themselves. This fact not only severely erodes the feasibility of a nuclear response to anything short of a nuclear attack, but, to the extent that any response to Soviet aggression puts us on the nuclear escalator, it is all the more likely that the willingness of parties not under direct attack to participate in a collective military response will be found wanting.

A principal benefit of an explicit adoption of the policy prohibiting the first use of nuclears, say the authors, is that "it would draw new attention to the importance of maintaining and improving the specifically American conventional forces in Europe." Once the military leaders of the alliance have learned to operate on the assumption that if a war has to be fought in Europe, it should only be at the conventional level, then the NATO forces "will be better instruments for stability in crises and for general deterrence as well as for the maintenance of the nuclear firebreak [between conventional and nuclear war] so vital to us all.[21]

Not surprisingly, the no-first-use proposal did not sit very well with the West European governments—that is, Germany, France, and the United Kingdom—which, apart from the United States, make the weightiest contributions to the common defense. And the very next issue of *Foreign Affairs* carried a rebuttal by four West German experts on NATO strategy (Karl Kaiser, director of the highly regarded Research Institute of the German Society for Foreign Affairs; Georg Leber, member of the Social Democratic Party and vice-president of the German Bundestag; Alois Mertes, a Christian Democratic member of the Foreign Affairs Committee of the Bundestag and foreign policy spokesman of the Christian Democratic Party; and Franz-Josef Schulze, commander in chief of Allied Forces in Central Europe from 1977 to 1979). "What matters most," argued the German strategists, "is to concentrate not only on the prevention of nuclear war, but on how to prevent *any* war, conventional war as well." And the prevailing NATO doctrine and deployments, confronting the adversary with "a full spectrum of deterrence and hence with an uncalculable risk" is better able to prevent any war from starting than would the doctrine and deployments that would be associated with the no-first-use policy. "The tight and indissoluble coupling of conventional and nuclear weapons on the European continent with the strategic potential of the United States confronts the Soviet Union with the incalculable risk that any military conflict between the two Alliances could escalate to a nuclear war."[22] By contrast, contend the Germans:

> A renunciation of the first use of nuclear weapons... would... put [the Soviet Union] in a position where it could... calculate its risks and thus be able to wage war in Europe.... Such a policy would liberate the Soviet Union from the decisive nuclear risk—and thereby from the constraint that has kept the Soviet Union, up to now, from using military force, even for limited purposes, against Western Europe....
>
> ...The proposed no-first-use policy would destroy the confidence of Europeans and especially of Germans in the European-American Alliance as a community of risk, and would endanger the strategic unity of the Alliance and the security of Western Europe.[23]

Similar arguments against the renunciation of the first use of nuclear weapons have been part of the standard reaction by the

United States government to the Soviet Union's periodic proposal for a joint Soviet-American declaration against first use. Their arguments were reiterated forcefully in 1982 by Secretary of State Haig in reply to the proposal by the four former U.S. officials. "NATO has consistently rejected such Soviet proposals, which are tantamount to making Europe safe for conventional aggression," said Haig, himself a former Supreme Allied Commander for Europe (SACEUR). If the West were to agree to extract nuclear weapons from its deterrence posture against conventional aggression, observed Haig, the only way it could restore deterrence would be for NATO to maintain conventional forces at least at the level of those of the Soviet Union and its Warsaw Pact allies. And he went on to castigate those in the West who advocate a no-first-use policy without facing up to the implications—namely: "that the United States reintroduce the draft, triple the size of its armed forces, and put its economy on a wartime footing."[24] Neither do the Western proponents acknowledge the severe consequences to the alliance, asserted Haig:

> A "no first use" policy would be the end of flexible response and thus of the very credibility of the Western strategic deterrence. In adopting such a stance, the United States would be limiting its commitment to Europe. But the alliance cannot function as a limited liability corporation. It can only survive as a partnership to which all are equally and fully committed—shared benefits, shared burdens, shared risks.[25]

The four American advocates of a NATO no-first-use policy claimed, in reaction to these objections, that their reasoning had been either misunderstood or distorted. They did face up to the implications of a stronger " conventional option." As to whether it would take the drastic measures pointed to by Secretary Haig to achieve a conventional balance against the Warsaw Pact, many experts, including the present SACEUR, were not nearly as pessimistic. In any case, the matter needed further study, especially in light of new conventional technologies that were emerging, such as precision-guided munitions. The authors of the proposal expressed sympathy with the view of "friends in Europe, which . . . seems to us mistaken: that since all forms of war in Europe would be equally catastrophic, one might as well place reliance on the nuclear deterrent and hope for the best."[26] But we have to insist, said Bundy, Kennan, McNamara, and Smith, that

> thermonuclear hostilities would be so entirely different, so much more terrible than all past wars put together, that the two kinds of catastrophe are not really comparable. It is precisely the overwhelming difference between thermonuclear warfare and any past disasters that makes the threat to resort to it at once so dangerous, so hard to believe, and therefore so unreliable as a deterrent.[27]

Similarly, the debate over the installation of U.S. intermediate-range missiles in Europe is the product of waning credibility in the American threat to engage in an exchange of strategic blows with the Soviet Union for any purpose short of protecting the United States itself. At the same time that people in the NATO countries were beginning to understand that it would be tantamount to mutual suicide for the United States and the Soviet Union to fight a strategic nuclear war against each other, the Russians began modernizing their intermediate-range strategic missile forces (those based in the western USSR capable of hitting the West European countries and those based in Eastern Russia capable of hitting China and Japan). Particularly worrisome was the Soviet deployment of the mobile, highly accurate SS-20 missile, which carried three nuclear warheads. Apparently the Soviets were planning to install over 300 of the SS-20s west of the Urals by the mid-1980s. Although largely a redundant addition to the Soviet strategic arsenal (with approximately 10,000 nuclear warheads on their ICBMs, the Soviets could attack all the targets to be assigned to the new SS-20s by using only a fraction of their ICBM force), the new, specifically Euro-strategic deployments were an awesome portent of the possibility that in a future East-West conflict over Europe the Soviets would hope to intimidate the West Europeans while holding the United States at bay.

To reassure the worried West Europeans that the United States strategic umbrella was still extended over them, the Carter administration authorized the Pentagon to develop and deploy in Europe a countervailing arsenal of intermediate-range missiles capable of striking the Soviet Union. But there was a surprising popular reaction in West European countries against this decision. Opponents of the impending U.S. deployments argued that the American and NATO defense planners had jumped the gun; they had neglected to even explore the arms control alternative of inducing the Soviets to negotiate a mutual reduction of Warsaw Pact and NATO nuclear forces in Europe as a means of achieving parity in the European Theater—they had simply assumed that the only alternative for NATO was a compensatory buildup.

The result of the popular pressures in Western Europe was the "Two Track" decision made by NATO foreign and defense ministers on December 12, 1979 to pursue "two parallel and complementary approaches to TNF [theater nuclear force] modernization and arms control." They included the deployment in Europe of U.S. ground-launched intermediate-range systems (108 Pershing IIs and 464 Ground-Launched Cruise Missiles) capable of striking the Soviet Union and Soviet-American negotiations for mutual limitations of intermediate-range strategic forces on each side in the European Theater. If these negotiations showed no success by the end of 1983, the U.S. deployments were to commence. If there was success, however, NATO would reexamine its force requirements.

The Reagan administration inherited this NATO decision but was initially inclined to defer negotiations until it had completed its planned buildup of United States military power so as to be able to negotiate from strength. However, Reagan's rearmament posture and statements by the president and other high administration officials supporting capabilities for fighting various sizes and shapes of nuclear war—including nuclear war that could be confined to the continent of Europe—served to stimulate a groundswell of transatlantic popular opposition to nuclear war strategies and nuclear armaments. New pressures from West European governments combined with a revived peace movement in the United States moved Reagan in the fall of 1981 to embrace the "Two Track" approach that he would have preferred to defer until the completion of the U.S. arms buildup.

One of the results of these popular pressures was Reagan's "zero option" proposal of November 18, 1981 offering to forego entirely the planned deployment in Europe of U.S. Pershing IIs and Ground-Launched Cruise Missiles in return for the Soviets dismantling all of their long-range theater nuclear forces (the SS-20s,

SS-4s, and SS-5s). The Soviets, though rejecting the zero option, agreed to undertake formal negotiations with the United States to arrive at a mutually acceptable agreement to limit Euro-strategic forces.

At the end of 1983, with the failure of the Soviet-American negotiations to produce an agreement on the limitation of intermediate-range strategic forces, the United States commenced deploying its Pershing IIs and Ground-Launched Cruise Missiles in Europe as contemplated in the NATO 1979 decision. This led, however, to Soviet threats to retaliate by deploying new nuclear missiles into Czechoslovakia and East Germany and by increasing Russian seaborn nuclear missiles within range of the continental United States. Because of these threats and in response to the flareup of antinuclear and anti-U.S. demonstrations by peace groups throughout Europe, early in 1984 strategists in NATO circles and in the U.S. policy community gave serious consideration to ways of arresting the new arms race now underway.

One alternative would be to induce the USSR back to the negotiating table by offering to hold back on all but the first "token" phase of the planned U.S. deployments in Europe provided that the Soviets indicated a serious intention to resume negotiations in good faith. The Reagan administration hinted as much in early 1984 soundings and conciliatory statements by the President; but as of this writing, the Soviets, having suspended all major arms control negotiations with the United States in reaction to the start of the new deployments, were adamant in their insistence that the United States must remove all its Pershing IIs and Ground-Launched Cruise Missiles from Europe *prior* to the resumption of serious negotiations.

Another alternative—of growing popularity among arms policy experts in NATO countries—would be to merge the negotiations on intercontinental strategic nuclear forces with the negotiations on the intermediate-range forces in order to reflect the reality that these are all strategic weapons and that the Euro-strategic balance cannot be separated from the overall global balance. In one variant of this proposal, not simply U.S. and Soviet forces but also any nuclear delivery systems under the control of any members of the NATO or Warsaw Pact alliances should be counted in the total. Opponents to this alternative argue that it would provide the Soviets with tempting opportunities to exploit differences between the United States and its NATO allies. Proponents claim that the risk of interallied dissension at the negotiation forum could be avoided by prior consultation among the allies.[28]

On economic matters

Parallelling debates within NATO over military strategies for containing the Soviet Union, and often linked with the military issues, are disagreements among the advanced industrial countries over East-West commerce. As their recovery from the devastation of World War II has allowed the West European countries and Japan to expand the scope of international economic activities and to revive interdependencies that were dismantled during the war, the United States has encountered more and more resistance to the notion that virtually all East-West commerce should be heavily constrained by cold war considerations and tightly coordinated within the alliance. The West Europeans and the Japanese perceive that cold war considerations plus tight alliance coordination add up to a perpetuation of U.S. hegemony; moreover, they have become increasingly less inclined to accept U.S. ideas and leadership on grand strategy for dealing with the East, and thus even in fields where they can be convinced that cold war considerations are appropriate, the U.S. partners frequently pursue policies at cross-purpose with those of the United States.

The often divergent approaches have been reflected in differences between the countries over how to conduct the commercial side of the detente relationship with the USSR. The countries differ on the timing and subjects of commercial negotiations and on their connection to other aspects of East-West relations.

Managing detente. There has never been any firm alliance-wide coordination of the positive side of East-West relations. The West Germans unilaterally developed and practiced their policy of *Ostpolitik*, of gradually enlarging economic and political interaction with the USSR, Eastern Europe, and—very cautiously—with East Germany in the face of official U.S. coolness to these initiatives prior to 1972. France, too, stepped out in front of the United States to expand commercial and diplomatic intercourse with the Soviet

Union and its satellites under President deGaulle's vision of a reconstructed greater European system from the Atlantic to the Urals.

The Nixon-Kissinger strategy of detente—giving the Soviets a stake in equilibrium—was added on to the detente relationships already established by the West Europeans; but once it had been adopted as part of the U.S. grand strategy in the early 1970s, Nixon and Kissinger unsuccessfully insisted that the West Europeans (and Japan) follow the American lead. Kissinger wanted to use the prospect of enlarged East-West commerce as a carrot to supplement the stick of military containment and to combine this with the U.S.-Chinese rapprochement so as to obtain maximum leverage on the USSR.[29] Unilateral forays in East-West relations by our allies would undercut the controlled and "nuanced" diplomacy that Kissinger believed he alone was qualified to carry out. In the economic realm of East-West interaction, no less than in the military realm, Kissinger would remind the Europeans and the Japanese that the United States had global interests whereas our allies had merely regional interests.[30]

At issue in the U.S. policy community was whether the persistent assertion by the United States of such a hegemonical role in virtually all East-West matters was productive or counterproductive to the coordination and mutual accountability among the allies that Kissinger claimed was necessary. Foreign policy experts in the Democratic camp now blamed Kissinger for alienating the West Europeans and Japan by insisting on a degree of U.S. leadership no longer consistent with the real economic relations of the advanced industrial countries.[31]

Kissinger's right-wing critics faulted him for imitating the soft approach of the West Europeans—for subordinating containment of the Soviet Union to shallow commercial considerations and for adopting a naive doctrine of economic linkage and leverage as a rationalization for appeasing the Kremlin's international expansionism.[32]

Managing economic sanctions. With the election of Ronald Reagan, Kissinger's right-wing critics assumed control of United States foreign policy. In attempting to reverse the detente policies of the 1970s, they escalated the tensions among the advanced industrial countries and stimulated a new debate in this country on the appropriate kind and extent of intra-alliance coordination of East-West commerce.

These issues were brought to a head by the clash between the Reagan administration's aggressive strategy for dealing with the USSR and the natural gas deals various West European governments negotiated with the Soviets.

The Reagan strategy for bringing maximum pressure on the Soviet system, as explained by administration spokesmen, included "diplomatic, political, economic, and informational components built on a foundation of military strength."[33] Its objective was to "convince the Soviet leadership to turn their attention inward," to "force... the Soviet Union to bear the brunt of its economic shortcomings."[34] An essential part of the strategy was tightened restrictions on the sale of technologies to the USSR that could help it overcome its economic difficulties.

Consistent with this strategy, President Reagan, responding to Soviet repressive policies in Poland, added to economic sanctions the Carter administration had imposed on the Soviets after their invasion of Afghanistan. On December 29, 1981, the president announced that in addition to restrictions on U.S. exports of electronic equipment and other high technology materials to the USSR and on suspensions of Aeroflot services of various negotiations on commercial, scientific and technological, and cultural exchanges, export licenses were now to be denied to firms providing the USSR with gas pipeline equipment. Such equipment included air and gas compressors, gas turbine engines for compressors, sensors, meters and mixing equipment, and pipeline laying equipment.[35]

The problem in implementing the embargo on gas pipeline exports was that to be effective it required similar export controls by the West Europeans, since some of the components on which the Russians were crucially dependent were manufactured in Europe by subsidiaries of United States corporations or by European firms. Predictably, the European governments refused to go along. They had indicated as much to Reagan during the seven-nation industrial summit in Ottawa the previous summer. They cited the economic recessions in their countries and the recent cutback by the United States on steel imports from the European

Community as compelling reasons for fulfilling their contracts to sell the Russians the pipeline equipment. Moreover, the Europeans were resentful at being asked to make economic sacrifices for sanctioning the Soviets when the United States, under Reagan, had removed the embargo of U.S. grain sales to the USSR that had been imposed by the Carter administration. Why, they asked, should the West European workers, instead of the American farmers, bear the brunt of the sacrifices required by the new cold war orientation in Washington?

The president and Secretary of Defense Weinberger (Secretary of State Haig was a dissenter from this policy within the U.S. government) tried to persuade the Europeans that their assistance to the Soviets in building the gas pipeline would add to Soviet leverage over them since the Kremlin, with its hold on Western energy supplies, could blackmail the Western governments in a crisis. Furthermore, the $10 billion annually the USSR could expect to earn from selling the gas would free it from economic pressures that otherwise might restrict its capacity to pursue an aggressive foreign policy.

The West Europeans and U.S. opponents of the gas pipeline embargo argued that economic coercion of the Soviet Union had not worked in the past and would not work now. If the USSR were denied hard currency earnings in the West and if this produced a constriction of Soviet development plans, the Kremlin would—typically—not arrest its military buildup but simply take it out of the hides of the Soviet people and continue to defer satisfying their needs. Moreover, the Soviets would be confirmed in their paranoid suspicion that the West was determined to destroy the socialist experiment in Russia. The result would most likely be an even *more* aggressive Soviet foreign policy. Opponents of the embargo also challenged the allegation that the West Europeans were making themselves vulnerable to Soviet political pressures by becoming dependent on the USSR for energy. At the most, supplies from Russia would constitute 5 percent of the West Europeans' total energy consumption—a gap that could be filled from other sources in the event of a cutoff from the East.

Rebuffed by NATO allies, Reagan decided to move unilaterally. In the spring and summer of 1982 he prohibited United States companies from transferring equipment or technology to the Soviets for the gas pipeline project and extended this ban to foreign subsidiaries of U.S. corporations and even to foreign-owned companies producing pipeline items under U.S. license. The West Europeans cried foul, claiming that their companies were manufacturing equipment and using technology under American licenses obtained before President Reagan's December 1981 sanctions against the Russians. In addition, the allies charged that it was an infringement of the sovereign authority of their governments for the United States unilaterally to impose such controls on the West European companies.

What began as an attempt by the United States government to confront the Soviets over their aggressive behavior in Afghanistan and Poland turned into an embarrassing confrontation between the United States and its allies as the president, in order to compel acquiescence with the U.S. embargo, instructed the Commerce Department to prohibit the export of goods and data to foreign companies that continued to provide equipment and technology to the Soviet gas project. Even Prime Minister Margaret Thatcher, the one ideologically closest to Reagan among the allied leaders, was provoked to speak out angrily: "The question is whether one very powerful nation can prevent existing contracts from being fulfilled. I think it is wrong to do that."[36]

The State Department worked to convince the president that the larger purposes of the embargo might be served just as well, and without counterproductive altercation with the allies, if the United States allowed the Europeans to go forward with the gas deal as they saw fit but was able to forge a consensus on a more restrictive policy for extending financial credits to the USSR and on stricter controls on the export of strategic materials. The Europeans, in response to feelers from new Secretary of State George Shultz, countered with suggestions for a full-blown review with the United States of Western commercial intercourse with the East.

Just days after the death of Soviet President Leonid Brezhnev, Reagan announced a lifting of the most stringent sanctions directed against the Soviet gas pipeline project. He was willing to do this, he explained, because the allies had agreed to "a plan of action... to give consideration to strategic issues when making decisions on trade with the USSR."[37] The Western alliance was now "fundamentally united," claimed the President:

> We have agreed not to engage in trade arrangements which contribute to the military or strategic advantage of the USSR or serve to preferentially aid the heavily militarized Soviet economy. In putting these principles into practice, we will give priority attention to trade in high technology products, including those used in oil and gas production. We will also undertake an urgent study of Western energy alternatives as well as the question of dependence on energy imports from the Soviet Union....
>
> The understanding we and our partners have reached, and the actions we are taking, reflect our mutual determination to overcome differences and strengthen our cohesion.[38]

But Reagan's attempt to raise a victory banner over his lifting of the embargo on items for the Soviet pipeline and his retraction of penalties against United States and allied country firms that violated the embargo caused the French government to publicly contradict him: There was no linkage between the American retraction of the embargo and the allies' willingness to discuss a concerted trade policy with Secretary of State Shultz—at least not as far as the Europeans were concerned. Moreover, the discussions on overall East-West trade were still going on, and Mr. Reagan's announcement of an agreement was premature. The British confirmed the French view. Embarrassed, Reagan insisted that there had already been "substantial agreement" at the time he made his statement. But the French would not let the Americans evade the issue. The embargo was simply bad policy. Reagan had backed down. French President Francois Mitterrand said that the Europeans had made no concessions. Statements to the contrary coming out of the White House "did not correspond to reality, as far as France [was] concerned.[39]

Editorials in major American newspapers were highly critical of Reagan's performance on this issue—his startling assumption that the allies would simply subordinate their perceived national interests to a strategy unilaterally conceived in Washington; his futile effort to coerce the West Europeans into conforming with the U.S. approach; and finally his humiliating backdown, which he tried to obscure with the fiction of a new NATO consensus on geopolitically significant East–West commerce. The upshot, chided the *New York Times*, was that the sanctions policy did more harm to the West than to the Soviet Union.[40]

The issue of how much unilateralism versus unity among the advanced industrial countries is appropriate for their dealings with the rest of the world gets even more complex as we move from matters that are centrally a part of the East-West rivalry. The threat to common values is then less clear, and the reasons for individual industrial countries (some of which have a tradition of maintaining special relationships with former colonies) or regional groupings pursuing their own relationships with particular countries are more compelling. Consequently, when the United States government wants a free hand for dealing with particular Third World countries or when it wants automatic support from its industrial country allies for some diplomatic initiative in, say, the Middle East, there is an inclination in Washington to define the situation in East-West terms. Increasingly, this tendency to reduce the manifold and crosscutting relationships into bipolar, cold war simplicities has itself become an issue between the United States and most of the other industrial countries; and—as shown in the chapters on United States policy toward economically disadvantaged countries and toward the Middle East—it has also become a matter of intense controversy among United States policy makers.

Notes

1. John F. Kennedy, Address at Independence Hall, Philadelphia, July 4, 1962, *Public Papers of the Presidents of the United States, John F. Kennedy 1962* (Washington, D.C.: U.S. Government Printing Office), pp. 537–539.
2. *Ibid.*
3. Zbigniew Brzezinski, *Between Two Ages: America's Role in the Technetronic Era* (New York: Viking, 1970), 293–309; quotation from pp. 296–297.
4. *Ibid.*, p. 301.
5. Jimmy Carter, Commencement Address at Notre Dame, 1977, *Public Papers of the Presidents of the United States: Jimmy Carter, 1977*, Vol. I (Washington, D.C.: U.S. Government Printing Office, 1977), pp. 955–956.

6. George Washington, Farewell Address, September 17, 1976, in James D. Richardson, ed., *Messages and Papers of the Presidents* (Washington; 1896), I: pp. 221–223.
7. Thomas Jefferson, Inaugural Address, March 5, 1809, *Inaugural Addresses of the Presidents of the United States* (Washington, D.C.: U.S. Government Printing Office, 1952).
8. John B. Connally, Remarks at the International Conference of the American Bankers Association, Munich, May 28, 1971 (Department of Treasury News Release).
9. Rudolph Faupl (International Association of Machinists), Thomas Hannigan (International Brotherhood of Electrical Workers), and Howard Samuel (Amalgamated Clothing Workers of America), in National Planning Association, *U.S. Foreign Economic Policy for the 1970s: A New Approach to New Realities* (Washington: National Planning Association, 1971), pp. 44–45.
10. For reportage on contemporary U.S. protectionist sentiment, see the numerous articles in the *Wall Street Journal* and *New York Times* during the first week of June 1982 in connection with the president's participation in the seven-nation "summit" of the advanced industrial nations held in Versailles, France.
11. Robert B. Reich, "Beyond Free Trade," *Foreign Affairs* Vol. 61, No. 4 (Spring 1983), pp. 773–804.
12. *Ibid.*
13. *Ibid.*
14. Richard M. Nixon, Television and radio address on August 15, 1971, *Department of State Bulletin*, Vol. LXV, No. 1680 (September 6, 1971), pp. 253–256.
15. Remarks of Secretary of Defense Robert S. McNamara at the Commencement Exercises, University of Michigan, Ann Arbor, June 16, 1962 (Department of Defense Press Release), No. 980-62.
16. John F. Kennedy, News Conference of February 14, 1963, *Public Papers of the Presidents: John F. Kennedy, 1963*, pp. 174–175.
17. See Henry A. Kissinger, *The Troubled Partnership: A Reappraisal of the Atlantic Alliance* (New York: McGraw-Hill, 1965).
18. William Kaufmann, *The McNamara Strategy* (New York: Harper & Row, 1964).
19. See Bernard Brodie, *Escalation and the Nuclear Option* (Princeton: Princeton University Press, 1966).
20. McGeorge Bundy, George F. Kennan, Robert S. McNamara, and Gerard Smith, "Nuclear Weapons and the Atlantic Alliance," *Foreign Affairs*, Vol. 60, No. 4 (Spring 1982), pp. 753–768.
21. *Ibid.*
22. Karl Kaiser, Georg Leber, Alois Mertes, and Franz-Josef Schulze, "Nuclear Weapons and the Preservation of Peace," *Foreign Affairs*, Vol. 60, No. 5 (Summer 1982), pp. 1157–1170.
23. *Ibid.*
24. Alexander Haig, "Peace and Deterrence," An address before Georgetown

University's Center for Strategic and International Studies, Washington, D.C., April 6, 1982, U.S. Department of State, *Current Policy,* No. 383.

25. *Ibid.*

26. McGeorge Bundy, George F. Kennan, Robert S. McNamara and Gerard Smith, "The Authors Reply," *Foreign Affairs,* Vol. 60, No. 5 (Summer 1982), *ibid.*, pp. 1178–1180.

27. *Ibid.*

28. See Subcommittees on International Security and Scientific Affairs and on Europe and the Middle East of the House Commitee on Foreign Affairs, *Hearings: Overview of Nuclear Arms Control and Defense Strategy in NATO,* March 18, 1982.

29. See Seyom Brown, *The Crises of Power: An Interpretation of United States Foreign Policy During the Kissinger Years* (New York: Columbia University Press, 1979), pp. 19–48.

30. Brown, *ibid.*, pp. 117–118.

31. *Ibid.*

32. *Ibid.*, p. 15.

33. Richard Halloran, "Reagan Aide Tells of New Strategy on Soviet Threat," *New York Times,* May 22, 1982.

34. Saul Friedman, "Reagan Called for Pressure on USSR," *Boston Globe,* May 22, 1982.

35. Ronald Reagan, Statement on USSR and Poland of December 29, 1981, *Weekly Compilation of Presidential Documents,* Vol. 17, No. 53, pp. 1429–1430.

36. Margaret Thatcher, speaking in the British House of Commons on July 1, 1982, quoted by James Feror, "Mrs. Thatcher Faults U.S. on Siberia Pipeline," *New York Times,* July 2, 1982.

37. Transcript of Reagan's Speech on the Soviet Union, November 13, 1982, *Weekly Compilation of Presidential Documents,* Vol. 18, No. 46, pp. 1475–1476.

38. *Ibid.*

39. "'Substantial Agreement' Reached With Allies, White House Insists," *New York Times,* November 16, 1982.

40. Editorial, "The Pipeline Pipe Dream," *New York Times,* November 16, 1982.

Chapter 6
Policies toward the Third World

> To those people in the huts and villages of half the globe struggling to break the bonds of mass misery, we pledge our best efforts to help them help themselves, for whatever period is required—not because the communists may be doing it, not because we seek their votes, but because it is right.
>
> —John F. Kennedy (Inaugural Address, January 20, 1961)

United States policies toward the so-called Third World—the nonindustrialized countries outside of Europe, most of which are former colonies of one or another of the European powers—are ostensibly for the purpose of furthering the development of economically underdeveloped or politically fragile countries. Presumably, special United States help or intervention is required by many of these countries for them to tend adequately to their people's material needs and to maintain internal peace and independence from foreign domination.

But *why* should the condition of such Third World countries be of major concern to the United States? The answers encountered in the policy community range from narrow self-interest concerns to universal imperatives to alleviate the suffering of others wherever in the world they might reside. Each answer has its own rationale and generates its own objections.

National Self-Interest Rationale

United States government programs to help other countries develop economically rarely obtain congressional majorities to fund them unless a convincing case can be made that the United States itself will benefit from such a diversion of the taxpayers' money from domestic programs. This condition often is satisfied by Buy American provisos stipulated by Congress on financial credits extended to countries that need money to purchase equipment, technology, or experts for their economic development projects. Such strings, of course, are not possible to attach to U.S. contributions to international development agencies, such as the World Bank or regional development banks, nor are they appropriate to attach to U.S. loans to governments to help them balance their budgets and pay off existing foreign debts.

In cases where immediate or quick payback through purchase of U.S. goods and services is inappropriate, other—indirect—benefits to the United States usually have to be demonstrated to gain congressional approval of a foreign assistance program. These indirect benefits to the United States can be economic, political, or both.

Straight grants, concessionary loans, and associated economic assistance to particular developing countries or to multinational regional development banks often will be championed as important stimulants to the economic growth of the recipients; and purportedly, the resulting economic growth will provide new markets for U.S. products and new opportunities for U.S. investments, including the location of subsidiaries of multinational corporations. These types of benefits to the United States private economic sector were a large part of the rationale in President Reagan's 1982 Caribbean Basin Development Initiative.[1] Though philosophically opposed to heavy reliance on market distorting mechanisms such as government-to-government loans at concessionary interest rates, free enterprisers such as Ronald Reagan and his economic advisers are willing to resort to them temporarily because they provide seed money for generating an initial development cycle. Then, the loans can, presumably, be eliminated as the potential for growth in the aided countries begins to attract private investment.[2]

Often the economic self-interest rationale for foreign assistance is less direct, focusing on the effects of the economic aid on the political conditions within the recipient countries—conditions that are thought to be inhibiting what would otherwise be a profitable market for U.S. products and a stable source of inputs for U.S. industrial processes. The political disorder that disrupts normal commerce is attributed to the resentment of the poor alienated masses who have lost all hope of improving their lives within the system and thus can be mobilized into radical revolutionary movements willing to use violence to topple the existing order. Progress in economic development is a necessary precondition, so the argument goes, for the minimum public order, which in turn, is the precondition for a degree of economic development that will allow for mutually profitable commerce with the United States.

The political self-interest rationale for the United States helping economically disadvantaged countries has two facets: (1) To the extent such help does indeed relieve economic conditions that otherwise would lead to widespread despair, alienation, and susceptibility to radical revolutionary mobilization, the opportunities for the Soviet Union and its friends to make easy gains among the world's poor will be reduced; and (2) To the degree that U.S. economic aid is perceived by recipients as essential to their development efforts, the United States will gain gratitude that can be cashed in, so to speak, for at least informal commitments by the recipients not to become client states of the Soviet Union or for political support (perhaps in votes in international agencies) on issues of importance to the United States. From some recipient governments, particularly those that want financial or other help in building up their military establishments, the quid pro quo for United States aid can be base rights and servicing facilities for U.S. aircraft and naval vessels, permission for the U.S. to operate intelligence gathering stations, or a formal mutual security alliance.

World-Interest Rationale

A broader national-interest rationale, sometimes called enlightened self-interest, holds that the United States will fare best in a world community where countries not only respect one another but assume some responsibility for one another's well-being, especially in cases of dire need.

A minimum starting point toward such a world community, it is argued, would be for the United States to accede to the request of developing countries that each affluent country devote some specified fraction of its annual gross national product (GNP) to improving the lot of poor countries—without political or economic strings attached. (The standard figure asked by the coalition of developing countries is seven-tenths of one percent of an industrial country's GNP).

In a more elaborate and generous gesture, the United States could embrace the philosophy and something like the general program of action put forward by the Brandt Commission in 1980:* The Brandt Commission argued that a major effort by the more affluent countries to cooperate with the poorer nations in reducing the gap between the rich and the suffering poor was required in the interests of world survival:

> Continued rapid population growth in the next century could make the world unmanageable; but that growth can only be forestalled if action is taken to combat poverty in this century. Much the same is true for the biological environment, which is threatened with destruction in many countries as a direct result of poverty—though in others as a result of ill-considered technological decisions and

*Willy Brandt, the former chancellor of the Federal Republic of Germany, at the suggestion of World Bank President Robert McNamara, appointed a commission of distinguished persons in 1978 to study the international issues arising from the economic and social disparities of the world and to recommend remedies. In addition to Brandt, the members were Edward Heath (Conservative prime minister of the United Kingdom, 1970–1974), Olaf Palme (prime minister of Sweden, 1969–1976), Peter G. Peterson (United States secretary of commerce 1972–1973), Eduardo Frei Monyalva (president of Chile 1964–1970), Adam Malik (vice-president of Indonesia 1977–1978 and minister of foreign affairs 1966–1979), Layachi Yaker (minister of commerce of Algeria 1969–1977), Antoine Kipsa Dakoure (minister of commerce of Upper Volta 1970–1976), Rodrigo Botero Montoya (minister of finance of Colombia 1974–1976), Lakshmit Kant Jha (Indian ambassador to the United States 1970–1973), Haruki Mori (Japanese ambassador to the United Kingdom 1972–1975), Joe Morris (Canadian Labor leader and chairman of the International Labor Organization Governing Body 1977–1978), Abdlatif Y. Al-Hamad (prominent Kuwaiti economist), Khatijah Ahmad (prominent Malaysian banker and economist), and Katherine Graham (publisher of the *Washington Post*).

> patterns of industrial growth. These problems—nuclear weapons proliferation is another—can only be solved by North and South acting in cooperation, and their mutual interests in doing so are only too obvious. The conquest of poverty and the promotion of sustainable growth are matters not just of the survival of the poor, but of everyone.[3]

Specifically, the United States would endorse and contribute to raising at least $8 billion annually for a special fund to overcome food deficits in poor countries through a broad program of increased food production and agricultural development. The United States would resist pressures from special industry and labor groups for protection against Third World products. The United States would support the use of the reserve assets of the International Monetary Fund (IMF), principally the Special Drawing Rights, to help developing countries with their financial problems. The United States, in addition to meeting the 0.7 percent target for official development assistance, would support certain forms of automatic international taxation to raise funds from those with great wealth to be transferred to the world's poor. (The Brandt Commission, in some of its most controversial proposals, suggested taxes on international trade, especially on arms exports, and taxes on users of the international "commons" areas—the ocean beyond national jurisdiction, the atmosphere, and outer space.) And the United States would be more responsive than it has been to price-stabilization agreements with the producers of basic commodities subject to devastating fluctuations in the international market.

The United States would also attempt to promote a more cooperative relationship with developing countries by allowing them more decision making weight in international institutions affecting their welfare, such as the IMF and the World Bank and by moving more in the direction of one-nation-one-vote arrangements in new institutions, such as those being set up to regulate the exploitation of minerals on the deep seabed.[4]

The Brandt Commission's recommendation for global negotiations, including periodic summit meetings among world leaders, to move toward the more "equitable world order" envisioned in its report, would be responded to positively, not begrudgingly in the manner of the Reagan administration, if this basically generous and accommodating approach to Third World demands for a restructured global political economy were to become United States policy.

Some Americans agree with Willy Brandt that "What is now on the agenda (and should be supported) is a rearrangement of international relations, the building of a new order and a new kind of comprehensive approach to the problems of development."[5] But clearly, not all Americans agree.

The case against a policy of apolitical generosity

Three kinds of objections to generous foreign assistance programs are raised in public and internal government debates over the ways and extent to which the United States should attempt to help the world's poor. The first, which can be called *economic nationalism*, emphasizes the need to tend to problems at home before devoting resources to the welfare of others. The second, the *conservative realpolitik* stance, is fearful of disruptions to the global political and economic status quo that are resulting from the unrealistic expectations and demands stimulated by the notion that there should be a global social-welfare approach to the world's poor. The third kind of objection, arguing from the premises of *classical economics*, holds that the best path for increasing everyone's well-being lies in a free international market, the emergence of which is retarded by the market distorting effects of artificial affluent-to-poor resource transfers.

Economic nationalism. Nationalistic objections to substantial programs of special assistance to economically disadvantaged countries are of two sorts: (1) those stressing that charity begins at home; and (2) those concerned over the presumed loss of U.S. profits and jobs that could result from giving the disadvantaged countries special subsidies and privileges to compete in the market.

In a domestic United States political and economic environment dominated by demands to cut down government expenditures and reduce taxes on personal and corporate incomes, the popular saying that charity begins at home has greater consequences for foreign assistance programs than it normally does.

Even in the relatively good economic conditions of the 1950s and early 1960s, policy makers advocating increased resource transfers to the disadvantaged countries had great difficulty in convincing their fellow Americans that it was just as important to spend the United States taxpayers' money on helping the poor in India and Peru as on helping the poor in Harlem and Appalachia. Therefore, during this period, the cold war rationale of competing with the Soviets for influence in the Third World was invoked to justify foreign resource transfers. Economic development assistance was subordinated to or made an adjunct of "security assistance," and claimants in the United States government for such resources for foreign assistance programs competed with one another to demonstrate the country or region within their bureaucratic responsibility would "go communist" or align with the Sino-Soviet bloc if the United States failed to come to its aid.

In the early 1980s, the burden of proof carried by the advocates of foreign development assistance became heavier than ever. Public funds for this purpose were harder to come by than at any time since the end of World War II. This meant that political merit criteria would push aside most other considerations in the allocation of scarce resources, and the definitions of political merit would be narrowly drawn to virtually exclude that which did not add to U.S. power in its global rivalry with the Soviet Union.

Conservative realpolitik. International disorder, chaos, disruptions in the normal functioning of the global economy, and opportunities for the Soviet Union and other opponents of the United States to fish in troubled waters are the likely results, from the conservative perspective, of giving in to demands to share wealth and power with the Third World. The inequality of nations, it is argued, is not a superficial condition imposed on the world by a few selfish and venal leaders, but rather it is the product of a long and profound process of historical evolution of the nation-state system itself. The nation-state system is structured around the norm of autonomous national political economies, each sovereign over its own resources, and an orderly system of trade and bargaining between the nation-states, sustained by the great powers. To grant the argument being pushed by Third World leaders and their supporters in the more developed countries that the affluent and powerful nations have a duty to share their wealth and power in the name of global social justice is to undermine the legitimacy of the evolved international order before the groundwork for any viable alternative world order has been laid. Such action will stimulate unrealistic demands, which will have to go unmet and which in turn, therefore, will intensify the frustrations and anger of the have-nots and prevent the reasoned discourse and moderate policies necessary for international peace and security.

The conservatives are particularly adamant in opposing attempts by developing countries to democratize the structure of international institutions, such as the International Monetary Fund, the General Agreements on Tariffs and Trade, the International Maritime Consultative Organization, and the International Telecommunications Union, set up to ensure an orderly functioning of the international economy and commerce. Decision making weight in these bodies characteristically rests with those countries with the most real resource power in the economic sector to be regulated. Moves in the direction of a one-country–one-vote decision process in such institutions will, according to conservatives, make for irreponsible decisions and will simply drive away the holders of real resources whose participation in any case is voluntary. Similar objections are raised to proposals to give developing countries more power in the allocation and approval of loans by the World Bank, which gets most of its resources from affluent governments and private corporations. If the World Bank's Board of Governors no longer represents the contributors when it sets the terms on loans, then the sources of the Bank's assets will dry up because the contributors will either revert to bilateral negotiations with recipients or form new multilateral lending consortia under the control of the donor countries.

This basic conservative stance was reflected in the Reagan administration's efforts to alter the Law of the Sea treaty provisions subjecting deep seabed mining and mineral exploitation to regulation by a thirty-six nation council in which the United States, Japan, West Germany, Britain, and France could be outvoted by a combination of Third World and Warsaw Pact countries. The Reagan administration, in voting against the treaty in the spring of 1982, indicated it could not accept a seabed council weighted against those countries with the heaviest investments in seabed mining.[6]

Classical economics. A third kind of objection to generous international income redistribution policies normally finds expression in the Treasury Department and among a large portion—perhaps a majority— of academic economists at American universities. The classical economists want to remove most man-made barriers to the free exchange of goods in the international market. From their point of view, anything that prevents individuals from buying as cheaply as possible and selling to the highest bidder anywhere in the world is unjust. International free trade—or as close an approximation to it as possible—suppposedly will result in the greatest good for the greatest number of people. It will induce procurers to locate where the factors of production (natural resources, labor, capital, managerial capabilities) can be obtained most efficiently and therefore result in goods that can be sold more cheaply. Everyone benefits. According to the classical theory, this basic free market process will tend toward a global distribution of production, and thus income earning capabilities, on the basis of the comparative advantage of various societies in providing factors of production more efficiently for certain kinds of products. This dynamic, in turn, will produce a specialization of production by particular societies and presumably therefore provide each of them with secure sources of income.

Ronald Reagan has been a devotee of the classical economic notions and has stated that they are the official premises of his administration's economic policies toward developing countries: "The societies which have achieved the most spectacular broad-based economic progress in the shortest period time . . . believe in the magic of the marketplace," he told the Board of Governors of the International Monetary Fund and the World Bank. "My own government is committed to policies of free trade, unrestricted investment and open capital markets."[7]

Any program to correct the flow of trade and investments (and their rewards in the form of income) that naturally occurs in the free market is, by these lights, considered to be a harmful distortion of those processes that eventually will stimulate the most economic development. Large-scale official development assistance, concessionary loans and debt forgiveness, and any form of international taxation are prime examples of such distortive mechanisms and must be opposed.

Responding to specific economic demands[8]

The various philosophical stances toward social justice claims of developing countries can be seen in debates in the United States policy community over how to respond to many of the specific demands put forward by the Third World coalition at successive meetings of the United Nations Conference on Trade and Development (UNCTAD) and at Special Sessions of the United Nations General Assembly (especially the sixth and seventh Special Sessions of 1974 and 1975).

On commodity agreements. The case for assuring that developing country producers of basic commodities (mostly agricultural products and other raw materials) receive minimum or floor prices, or for indexing the prices of such commodities to the international market prices of industrial goods, rests on claims of fairness as well as United States self-interest. It is grossly inequitable, so the argument goes, that poor countries with economies highly dependent upon export earnings from one or a few basic commodities should be thrown into sudden and severe depressions because of a slackening of international demand for these commodities or a decline in real earnings in relation to goods they must import. The more diversified economies of the affluent countries are better able to absorb demand and price changes in particular sectors. (Indeed, most of them subsidize their own vulnerable sectors, like grain farmers, with price supports and government purchasing arrangements.) Simple fairness, therefore, requires international guarantees to poor countries against disastrous export-income losses that are no fault of their own. Some participants in the U.S. policy debates over providing special protection to the disadvantaged commodity producers also grant the argument of many Third World people that the industrial countries bear a special responsibility for redressing the existing disparities because it was they—

the former colonial imperialists—who allegedly forced a specialization of one or a small number of primary products on their colonies in previous centuries. The U.S. self-interest argument for commodity price-stabilization schemes merely emphasizes the connection between having reliable markets for U.S. exports in the Third World and providing the developing countries with assured means of earning what they need to pay for U.S. goods. Surely, it is argued, guarantees of an equitable relationship between industrial prices and prices for primary commodity imports couldn't *hurt* the United States economy.

Objections to commodity agreements center on both their desirability and their practicality. According to the orthodox free traders, everyone loses over the long run by making purchasers of any goods pay more than they would if prices were allowed to reflect supply and demand. Especially where price declines reflect the entry into the market of new producers, the development of more efficient means of production, or the use of better substitutes, efforts to prop up commodity prices are unfair to the consumers—many of whom may also be poor. Artificially pegging the price of raw rubber to the price of automobiles and other manufactured goods, for example, will only increase the costs to everyone, rich and poor alike, of getting from place to place; and, the marginal increases are likely to hurt the poor more than the rich. Moreover, it is argued, such artificial pricing arrangements will either feed on themselves, by attracting even more producers into a particular commodity line and thus requiring even heavier controls on prices (most likely in the form of production quotas), or else they will collapse when the number of new producers extends supply beyond the point where restraining competitive selling underneath fixed prices is feasible.

Another type of objection challenges the relevance of commodity agreements to the global rich-poor gap. Those who produce commodities for exports, it is pointed out, are not necessarily poor. Most of the large industrial countries are also raw material producers and exporters. Futhermore, within the poor countries themselves, the exporting sectors are the most affluent and resistant to income redistribution policies and other social reforms in their own societies. More often than not, their profits are reinvested in banks and corporations outside of their own countries; and sometimes, as in the so-called banana republics of Central America, they operate in cahoots with foreign-owned multinational corporations to keep control of the economies and political systems of their countries.

On tariff preferences. Discrimination in favor of the products of developing countries by allowing them duty-free or low tariff entry into the United States market is one of the ways that these countries and advocates of their cause within the U.S. see to help them earn foreign exchange and diversify their economies. Some preferences were granted by the European Community and Japan in 1971 and then by the United States in 1975. The European countries have extended trading privileges in the Common Market to their former colonies, while denying them to other countries. Similarly, the United States, in President Reagan's Caribbean Basin Development Plan, favors a subset of developing countries willing to cooperate with the United States in political as well as economic matters affecting the hemisphere.

Objections to the extension of tariff preferences come not only from particular industry and labor groups that fear their products will be undersold, but also from supporters of the Most Favored Nation (MFN) principle of the General Agreements on Tariffs and Trade. In the eyes of many, MFN is the heart of the GATT system of nondiscriminatory trade in that it states that all nations shall have access to a country's market equal to the most favored nation. Without such a rule, the world economy would evolve into rivalrous trading blocs antithetical to the goal of universal free trade. But advocates of tariff preferences for developing countries cite the long tolerance of the United States for European Economic Community (EEC) trading arrangements that discriminate against nonmembers—especially during the years of post World War II reconstruction of the European economy—as a precedent for compromising with GATT principles when an important world-order objective is served thereby.

On official development assistance. Support for the proposition that affluent industrial countries should appropriate 0.7 percent of their gross national product to development assistance for disadvantaged countries (as recommended in various UN resolutions and the Brandt report) is very thin in the United States policy community and probably even thinner on the part of the general public. The small minority that argues for such an obligatory donation takes its stand largely on the premise that the world has become an interdependent community and on the ethical postulate that in a community the affluent are duty bound to help the poor. Some geopolitically oriented public officials, while not wanting to be tied to any specific percentage of GNP, regard official development assistance as a useful tool of foreign policy because it provides the government with leverage that is lacking in resources transferred through the private sector or through multilateral institutions.

Those who advocate a generous response to the needs of disadvantaged countries worry that bilateral foreign assistance will be used primarily to pressure recipient countries to conform to United States foreign policy objectives. In order to gain congressional majorities, the sponsors of foreign aid legislation must often accept a variety of riders to their bills, ranging from Buy American provisions, to human rights stipulations, to guarantees against expropriation of U.S. corporations. Economic development functions of the resource transfers more often than not are subordinated to the particular hobby horses of congressmen whose votes are required. Rather modest levels of transfers are burdened beyond their carrying capacity with the result that few if any of the hoped-for effects—least of all economic development—are realized; and, neither the United States as donor nor the recipient countries are satisfied. Instead it is just as likely that both sides become increasingly disenchanted, if not bitter, with each other.

Because government-to-government development aid is tempting for the donor country to use as a lever on the recipients, many developing countries would prefer to receive help from international institutions; and the constituency in the United States policy community championing selfless assistance to developing countries tends to support such a funnelling of aid through multilateral rather than bilateral arrangements. Yet not all developing countries want to compete equally against each other for the limited funds of international and regional banks. Some countries, particularly those that are favored military and ideological allies of the United States (like Guatemala or Thailand), are anxious to preserve their position as the preferred beneficiaries of any U.S. generosity. And the congressional and administrative backers of particular allies are equally desirous of keeping direct control of the resource transfers so that they can be used as rewards to those foreign regimes presumed to be most supportive of U.S. policies.

Thus, even controversies over basic types of official development assistance—multilateral versus bilateral—are, at base, debates over the extent to which the United States should be pursuing a long-term, politically neutral strategy of helping developing countries, as opposed to a more politicized strategy of attempting to affect immediate international alignment and ideological character of Third World countries. Equally important decisions on if and how much a particular country should be helped are infused with these controversies over the basic purposes of foreign assistance as well as arguments over whether the countries are politically and economically worthy of aid.

On debt and balance-of-payments relief. There is controversy over how to respond to the fact that, even with the availability of low interest loans and other concessionary resource transfers, many a developing country is unable to increase its national income enough to pay its debts to foreign lenders at previously negotiated rates. (Put another way, if the debts were to be repaid at the agreed rates, the debtor nation would substantially wipe out its annual margin of economic growth or, in extreme cases, even suffer a decline in national income.) Developing countries have been pressing for payments moratoria on such accumulated external debts.

The main argument for such additional concessions to developing countries is that without them the purposes of the original loans—to allow the recipients to generate development investments that would be unavailable out of current earnings—would be negated, and they would be unable to sustain their economic growth; worse yet, they might fall into total bankruptcy. The main arguments against debt moratoria are (1) that they would constitute, in fact, an additional loan by those who had already extended help at concessionary rates of interest, and that these lenders (including many nongovernmental contributors to the resources of financial institutions) would be driven away from future lending to developing countries if this becomes the pattern; (2) that debt moratoria tend to reinforce weak economic performance; and (3) that better risk borrowers, therefore, will have less funds available to them.

Although there is no agreement among United States policy makers on debt moratoria as a general policy, there is a consensus that the issue should be approached on a country-by-country basis to determine both the legitimate need and the consequences of a moratorium in each particular case. This, of course, provides just one more entry point for injecting political considerations into development financing, especially when the question is about debts owed the United States government directly.

Closely related to the debt problem are the severe balance of international payments deficits frequently incurred by developing countries, which are caused largely by their export earnings dropping far below their expenditures on imports. There is general support among United States policy makers for helping developing countries overcome temporary balance-of-payments deficits so that they can continue to purchase needed imports during a period of declining exports; the normal source for obtaining such additional financial reserves is the International Monetary Fund or regional multigovernmental financial facilities. Controversy, however, surrounds proposals to allocate Special Drawing Rights (SDRs) against the IMF funds to developing countries with balance-of-payments difficulties—that is, to have the needy countries obtain a larger share of IMF credits than they would have under normal IMF criteria. Some policy makers favor this SDR-development link, while others are against mixing development issues with the main purpose of SDRs—namely, to provide sufficient liquidity to tide high levels of international trade over the reserve depletions suffered periodically by major trading countries.

Opponents of the SDR link argue that a diversion of SDRs to development purposes may reduce their availability for this primary role of avoiding severe international recessions that might accompany constrictions in trade when there are liquidity bottlenecks in the system. Advocates of the SDR link to development aid contend that the amounts of SDRs transferred to developing countries need not be of such magnitude to detract from the larger liquidity providing functions of the IMF and that the principle problems with the SDR link are technical and administrative and can be overcome if the moral commitment is there.

The Political Intervention Trilemma*

When it comes to the issue of whether, under what circumstances, and how the United States should intervene to affect the *political* conditions in Third World countries, the debates become most intense for they reach to the very essence of what the United States stands for in the world. Three alternative philosophies contend for basic acceptance as U.S. policy:

1. *Help friendly regimes secure themselves against U.S. adversaries.* This policy—reflected in the 1984 report by President Reagan's Commission on Central America, headed by Henry Kissinger—rests on the geopolitical premise that the most important determinants of United States support are a country's international alignments in the big power games of vital interest to the U.S.: the U.S.-Soviet rivalry and the efforts of the industrialized countries to maintain access to the world's energy resources and other critical raw materials. A regime's domestic characteristics are of little account when it is on our side in these international power games. Dictators and democrats, conservatives and reformers, fascists and communists—all are, in principle, equally acceptable as allies of the United States as long as their international interests converge with ours.[9]

In practice, this policy normally inclines the United States more toward rightist than leftist regimes. Leftist governments are suspected of having a basic animus against the United States as the leading capitalist power and of being supported by movements hostile to the United States. Rightist governments are presumed to be motivated more purely by practical considerations of power and thus will be more grateful for whatever tangible assistance the United States can provide them against their internal and external opponents. They are believed to be dependent for their political

*The material in this section is adapted from my essay, "The Trilemma of U.S. Foreign Policy," *AEI Foreign and Defense Review*, Vol. II., No. 5 (1980), pp. 2–4.

survival on domestic, commercial, and military classes, and deathly afraid of what would befall them if the leftists, especially those friendly to the Soviet Union, gained control. In the Reagan administration's lexicon, rightist regimes of an undemocractic character warranting U.S. support are called "authoritarian" while leftist regimes of an undemocratic character are called "totalitarian" and normally would not warrant U.S. support (China being a glaring exception).[10]

United States assistance to regimes warranting U.S. support on the above grounds takes several forms: generous financial credits, technology transfers, military and police training programs, and a permissive weapons sales policy—all of which constitute in fact, if not by explicit design, a rather significant intervention into the domestic affairs of the client country to help keep the existing regime in power. Occasionally this policy—appropriately called "conservative *realpolitik*"—can take the form of U.S. attempts to destabilize potentially shaky leftist governments. (These attempts might be overt through highly restrictive lending and commercial policies or covert through assistance to opposition groups.)[11]

The main problem with the conservative *realpolitik* policy is that a United States-supported regime, such as the autocracy of the Shah of Iran, may lose credibility with its own people and succumb to a sudden coup or a long germinating swell of popular discontent. In such cases, the United States may find its reputation sullied by its close association with the deposed government. Moreover, the elements engineering the coup or directing the revolution might have aligned themselves with our major international rivals to counterbalance U.S. support for the established government.

Defenders of the conservative *realpolitik* policy grant these risks but argue that the world political arena, particularly the volatile Third World, is by its very nature an uncertain field of competition. Either we accept the risks and participate vigorously on behalf of our friends, or we leave the field open to our major rivals who will intervene to tip local balances in favor of themselves and their friends—and cumulatively, the global balance of power as well.

2. *Identify the United States with "progressive" regimes and political movements.*[12] The basic premise of this policy is that the dominant forces in world politics are those working to equalize the distribution of wealth, broaden political participation, and expand

human rights. This is assumed to be the outgrowth of the universal spread of literacy and the accompanying exposure of the world's peoples to Lockean and Marxist ideas; namely, that all persons are to be regarded as equal in their basic rights to life, opportunity for economic betterment, and political activity; that governments are legitimate only to the extent that they rest on the consent of the governed; and (in some socialist variants) that disparities in wealth and socioeconomic class are to be eliminated.

From this point of view, United States success in the global rivalry with the Soviet Union, and U.S. international influence in general, will depend on the resourcefulness of this country in championing *two* movements—those for liberty and those for equality. The United States, because of the philosophical roots of its independence movement and constitutional system, the evolution of its humane domestic social welfare policies, and the main thrust of its best foreign policy traditions of anticolonialism and anti-autocracy, can credibly identify its basic liberal ethos with the reformist forces of the contemporary world.

Proponents of the policy like to emphasize that they are not motivated primarily by altruism or even idealism. The policy is designed, they contend, to drive a wedge between the communists and the democratic progressives by providing the latter with sufficient financial, organizational, and military resources to allow them to operate separately from communist-organized leftist coalitions. If the United States were to provide hope and concrete assistance to the noncommunist left, then this country—not the Soviet Union and Cuba—would be the reformers. In addition to reducing the USSR's prospects of gaining new clients and satellites, such a policy, if it were well executed, presumably would gain the United States long-term access to petroleum resources, other raw materials, and important geopolitical bases in the Third World.

There are problems, however, with this "progressive" interventionary policy also: To be successful it requires almost omniscient knowledge about who's who and what's what in the political life of complex and unfamiliar societies. Despite our best efforts, the regimes or movements supported might fail. Equally important, political leaders whom we may believe to be "progressive" might, once they assume power, turn out to be autocratic and brutal. The ideologies they express concerning human rights, economic egalitarianism, and democratic constitutionalism may be nothing more than instruments to garner popular support on the march to power, only to be discarded for instruments of oppression designed to eliminate their opponents once they are in control. Moreover, a posture of nationalist nonalignment vis-à-vis the U.S.-Soviet rivalry might also prove to be little more than a temporary expedient to gain international support, whereas the deeper commitments of Marxist elements in a "progressive" regime might incline it toward the Soviet Union.

The United States certainly has the option of withdrawing its support from those who have betrayed our faith in them. But unless such withdrawal of support is accompanied by an active policy of destabilizing the regime in power—with all the risks that entails—it will be viewed as a futile gesture, only increasing the opportunities for our major rivals to make the regime more completely dependent on them. Furthermore, if such second-thought reversals tend to become characteristic of U.S. policy, the global influence of the United States will be weakened by an embarrassing reputation for inconstancy and incompetence.

3. *Maintain a posture of scrupulous neutrality toward indigenous rivals for power in other countries.*[13] This policy does not prevent the United States from assisting those currently in power in worthwhile projects nor from vigorously objecting to policies that might injure U.S. interests or seriously offend basic American values. Nor does it deny the United States the option of counterinvention when our international rivals have intervened in regional or local conflicts. But it does attempt to preserve a clear-cut distinction between projects and policies on the one hand and other personalities and parties on the other. Official and unofficial contacts with various elements of the opposition would be regarded as a normal feature of U.S. relations with other countries. In the event that internal turmoil erupts in countries with which this country has diplomatic relations, the United States would insist on keeping communications open with persons and groups that do not necessarily have the government's official sanction.

Under such a noninterventionist policy, the United States government would not support political activity or cause antiregime groups to agitate. It would be official U.S. policy, however, to encourage foreign governments to allow transnational organizations, such as labor unions, churches, and human rights groups, that support their fellow members across nation-state lines. Furthermore, the United States could make it clear that it would be strongly biased against funding or promoting projects of regimes that systematically suppressed dissent or political opposition.

The United States need not dispense with a capacity to change a local political situation that is detrimental to important U.S. interests or to affect the outcome of an ongoing local conflict whose results, in the absence of such intervention, would substantially injure important U.S. interests. Nevertheless, the basic policy would be one of nonintervention in the affairs of other countries. The advocates of intervention would have to demonstrate that a situation requires U.S. intervention and that the costs and risks of such action are less than the costs and risks of no action at all.

The problem with such a noninterventionist stance is that it could well tempt major adversaries of the United States (the Soviet Union in particular) to intervene first in situations that are below the threshold of a U.S. interventionist response, to establish a *fait accompli*, and to thrust on to the United States the awesome responsibility of choosing between initiating or avoiding a large-scale confrontation.

Advocates of this policy, therefore, usually are also advocates of international conflict control mechanisms, international peace keeping forces, UN-supervised (or other international or regional agency) cease-fires and elections, international arbitration, and the like to prevent deteriorating local and regional situations from giving our adversaries the pretext for unilateral intervention. Even if the international presence does not succeed in settling a conflict or stabilizing a deteriorating situation, it can provide a buffer against competitive outside interventions of the type that could spark a larger conflagration.

Notes

1. Ronald Reagan, Address to the Organization of American States, February 24, 1982, U.S. Department of State, Current Policy, No. 370.
2. Ronald Reagan, Address to the Board of Governors of the International

Monetary Fund and the World Bank, September 29, 1981, *Weekly Compilation of Presidential Documents*, Vol. 17, No. 4, pp. 1052–1055.

3. *North-South: A Program for Survival* (Cambridge, Massachusetts: MIT Press, 1980), p. 75.
4. *Ibid.*, the whole report.
5. *Ibid.*, p. 18.
6. Department of State, "Law of the Sea: January-February 1982," *Current Policy*, No. 371.
7. Ronald Reagan, Address of September 29, 1981, *Weekly Compilation of Presidential Documents*, Vol. 17, No. 4, pp. 1052–1055.
8. On the responses in the U.S. policy community to specific demands of the Third World Countries, see Richard N. Cooper, "A New International Order for Economic Gain," *Foreign Policy*, No. 26 (Spring 1977), pp. 65–120; and Roger D. Hansen, "North-South Policy—What's the Problem?" *Foreign Affairs* Vol. 58, No. 5 (Summer 1980), pp. 1084–1103.
9. The archpractioner of the conservative *realpolitik* approach toward the Third World was Henry Kissinger during the period 1969-1975. See his retrospective defense of the U.S. support for the Shah of Iran in his *The White House Years* (Boston: Little, Brown, 1979), pp. 1258–1264. See also my book, *The Crises of Power* (New York: Columbia University Press, 1979, pp. 107–140.
10. Jeane Kirkpatrick's "Dictatorships and Double Standards," *Commentary*, Vol. 68, No. 5 (November 1979), pp. 34–35 developed the distinction between "authoritarian" and "totalitarian" regimes and so pleased President-elect Reagan that he appointed her ambassador to the United Nations.
11. Justifications for U.S. interventions to destabilize leftist governments are found in the following policy statements by the Reagan administration: Ronald Reagan, Address to the Organization of American States, February 24, 1982, Department of State, *Current Policy*, No. 370; Ronald Reagan, Address before the British Parliament, June 8, 1982, *Current Policy*, No. 399; Richard Halloran, "Reagan Aide Tells of New Strategy on Soviet Threat," *New York Times*, May 22, 1982.
12. The principal Third World development initiatives of the Kennedy administration were an expression of the "progressive" interventionist stance, although the public presentation of these policies tended to stress the purely economic objectives. The political interventionary premises are detailed in Arthur M. Schlesinger, Jr., *A Thousand Days: John F. Kennedy in the White House* (Boston: Houghton-Mifflin, 1965), pp. 195–196.
13. The aloof noninterventionist rationale is most clearly articulated by J. William Fulbright, *The Arrogance of Power* (New York: Vintage Books, 1967). It also finds articulation in George F. Kennan, *The Cloud of Danger: Current Realities of American Foreign Policy* (Boston: Little, Brown, 1977). A pragmatic version of this approach, fused somewhat with interventionist reformism, was advocated in the Carter administration by Cyrus Vance. See his *Hard Choices: Critical Years in America's Foreign Policy* (New York: Simon and Schuster, 1983).

Chapter 7
U.S. Interests in the Middle East

> Our involvement in the search for Middle East peace is not a matter of preference, it is a moral imperative. The strategic importance of the region is well known.
>
> But our policy is motivated by more than strategic interests. We also have an irreversible commitment to the survival and territorial integrity of friendly states. Nor can we ignore that fact that the well-being of much of the world's economy is tied to stability in the strife-torn Middle East. Finally, our traditional humanitarian concerns dictate a continuing effort to peacefully resolve conflicts.
>
> —Ronald Reagan (September 1, 1982)

Merely to list the important United States interests in the Middle East is to expose the deeply cutting dilemmas that make the formulation and conduct of U.S. policy for that area of the world so difficult. Our interests include preventing the Soviet Union from achieving predominant influence in this geopolitically crucial bridge connecting Europe, Africa, and Asia; ensuring access to Persian Gulf oil for ourselves and our West European and Japanese allies; helping Israel to secure its existence in the midst of hostile neighbors; and making sure that the conflicting objectives and commitments of the superpowers in the region do not spark World War III. Each of these interests often seems to require policies that contradict the policies called for by some of the other ones. Brilliant indeed would be the statesman who could find a way of satisfying all of these interests, but as yet no one has come forward with anything even approaching such a resolution of the principal dilemmas.

The arguments over policies toward the Middle East are, more often than not, arguments over the priorities to be accorded various United States interests in particular crises; debates over ways of handling the crisis at hand are arguments over which policies will involve the least overall sacrifice of interests.

The Reagan administration began its tenure with an effort to overcome these dilemmas by subordinating all United States interests in the Middle East to a new grand strategy for containing Soviet expansion and by obtaining a "consensus of strategic concerns" with the countries in the region built around that objective. But as the inevitable Middle Eastern crises erupted, this grand strategy proved incompatible with the complexities of the region and the multiple interests the United States had been attempting to sustain there.[1]

All the important interests of the United States in the Middle East continue to contend for attention and support; it is this contention between them that shapes the debates over particular policies and determines the choices that are, in fact, made.

Limiting Soviet Influence

There is very little debate over whether the United States should attempt to limit Soviet influence in the Middle East. The proposition is widely accepted in the policy community that were the USSR to obtain a dominant influence over the resources of the area, it would pose a substantial geopolitical threat to the economic well being and military security of the NATO countries and Japan. The issues, rather, are how much to emphasize the objective of limiting Soviet influence in official United States rhetoric and policies and what means are most effective for accomplishing the objective.

It is rare that a high United States official will state as baldly as did Henry Kissinger in June 1970 that the object of U.S. policies was "to *expel* the Soviet military presence [from the Middle East] . . . before they become . . . firmly established."[2] It is also rare for the United States government to go as far as it did in the fall of 1977 when it courted Soviet cooperation in a joint statement issued simultaneously in Washington and Moscow. In this joint statement the Soviet Union and the United States, as cochairmen of a reconvened Geneva Conference to obtain a Middle Eastern peace, called upon all parties to the Arab-Israeli conflict, including the Palestinians, to negotiate a comprehensive peace under the aegis of the Geneva Conference.[3]

"Expelling" the Soviets at one extreme and establishing a superpower condominium with them at the other extreme bracket the range of approaches for limiting Soviet influence in the Middle East that have been considered (and adopted) by recent United States administrations.

Confronting the Soviets

Confrontation has been one of the prominent means of attempting to oppose Soviet thrusts into the Middle East since World War II. President Truman bluntly informed Generalissimo Stalin in 1946 that the United States would not put up with Stalin's failure to honor his wartime agreement with Churchill for a withdrawal of British and Russian military forces from Iran at the end of the war. If the USSR did not honor its commitment, Truman warned, the United States would be compelled to bring this Soviet malfeasance before the newly formed United Nations, and prospects for Soviet-American political cooperation would be severely undermined. The president punctuated his verbal demands with redeployments of U.S. naval forces. Stalin reassessed the stakes and pulled his troops back behind the Soviet-Iranian border.

In the 1973 Yom Kippur War, reacting to indications that President Leonid Brezhnev was preparing to dispatch Soviet paratroops into the Sinai to rescue the Egyptian Third Army Corps from the Israelis, the Nixon administration put United States forces on a high alert status around the world, and Kissinger announced that any

Soviet military intervention would spell the end of the detente relationship. Brezhnev backed off and allowed Kissinger to work on the Israelies in his own way to obtain a cease-fire with the Egyptians.

In response to the Soviet Union's December 1979 invasion of Afghanistan, President Carter threatened to use "any means necessary, including military force," to repel an attempt by the Soviets to gain control of the Persian Gulf region.

Such direct coercion of the USSR has the virtue of not necessarily requiring the cooperation of countries in the region. If the United States itself can establish a credible posture of opposition to a particular Kremlin power play in the Middle East and convey a resolve to put U.S. forces on the line if need be, the Kremlin presumably is more likely to be deterred than if indigenous forces are expected to hold the front line of defense against the Soviets.

The problem with reliance generally on a confrontationist approach for dealing with Soviet expansion in the Middle East is that in most cases where the Russians are presented with opportunities to enlarge their influence, the stimuli for such moves are likely to be local conditions to which the Kremlin can claim to be legitimately responding. Nor are the Soviet moves, except in unusual cases, likely to be of the overtly aggressive type against which a confrontationist countermove would be appropriate.

When an Arab country signs a "Peace and Friendship" treaty with the USSR and obtains new Soviet military equipment to balance an increase in Israeli military strength, the United States, since it provides most of Israel's advanced military equipment, cannot very credibly charge the Russians of having destabilized the regional balance of power. Thus the transfer by the Soviets to the Syrians in the late 1970s and early 1980s of surface-to-air missiles to counter Israeli air superiority did not lend itself to Washington-to-Moscow ultimata; our main countermove was to provide Israel with electronic countermeasure equipment for its aircraft. One of the results of this arms-supply competition, however, was a deeper Soviet foothold in the region.

Nor is a confrontationist stance toward the USSR likely to be effective in preventing the Kremlin from expanding Soviet influence by exploiting civil strife within Middle Eastern countries. If

Russian help is sought by one of the factions in a civil conflict, say by the Shi'ite Muslims against the Sunni Muslims in Iraq, United States objections to Soviet meddling are likely to fall on deaf ears, and the balance of naval power in the Mediterranean and Indian Ocean will be almost totally irrelevant to Soviet decisions. Similarly, if the long-feared Soviet attempt to exploit the post-Shah turmoil in Iran ever materializes, it will most likely be in the form of benign material and organizational help to indigenous leftist opponents of the Muslim fundamentalist regime instead of in the form of Soviet troops crossing the Russo-Iranian frontier. The United States may one day wake up to the stark fact of a powerful Soviet satellite on the Persian Gulf without having had the opportunity to invoke the Carter Doctrine.

Alliance building

Widening the containment line in the Middle East by reinforcing existing alliances and constructing new ones has been the favorite policy of United States governments since the Truman Doctrine. This policy was called into serious question, however, with the overthrow of "our man in Iran," the Shah Mohammed Reza Pahlavi, and his replacement by a fanatically anti-Western, anti-American regime. Even so, the alliance building strategy was reinstituted with trumpets at the start of the Reagan administration under the banner of "strategic consensus."

The heyday for alliance building in the Middle East was the period of John Foster Dulles' tenure as secretary of state (1953–1959). The secretary's renowned "pactomania"—his compulsion to rapidly sign a string of military allies all around the Sino-Soviet periphery—was reflected in a set of mutual security alliances with Pakistan, Turkey, and Iran and in an arrangement to tie these into the British alliance with Iraq through the Baghdad Pact. This network of alliances in the northern tier of northwest Asia would constitute a barrier to Soviet penetration of the Persian Gulf-Middle East region.

The Dulles alliance building strategy for opposing Soviet influence in the Middle East quickly ran into pitfalls very similar to those encountered in the present period by the Reagan strategic consensus approach.

First there is the reluctance of most countries in the region to identify with either the East or the West. National independence and international nonalignment are the stances with greatest appeal for political leaders in the postcolonial world. And the insistence that they stand up and be counted as part of the coalition against Soviet communism goes against their practical sense that their bargaining with both superpowers can be more effective if they are in the pocket of neither. Equally important is the fact that an East-West polarization is inconsistent with many local partnerships and rivalries (Arabs versus Israelis; Sunnis versus Shi'ites) that often are more significant—practically and emotionally—to the people of the region than are the cold war issues.

The second pitfall is that those regimes most willing to become part of the U.S.-sponsored anticommunist coalition tend to be the least in tune with the popular movements in the Middle East for reform or deposition of traditional monarchies and undemocratic oligarchies. If the United States becomes identified with the status quo regimes, the reformers inevitably will define the United States as their enemy, which will only pave the way for the Soviet Union and other international enemies of the United States to pose as friends of the reformers and to convert these friendships into client relationships when the reformers take control. This indeed is exactly what happened in Syria and Iraq in the 1950s and Algeria and Libya in the 1960s. The virulent anti-Americanism of the Khomeinists in Iran is the legacy of the decades of our close association with the Shah. And this syndrome could yet appear in strategic countries like Saudi Arabia and Jordan.

The third pitfall is in part the product of the previous two. It is that the polarization of the region between pro-Soviet countries and pro-American countries could lead to a larger Soviet presence than would be the case if the United States refrained from making loyalty in the cold war the test of a government's worthiness. This polarization effect drew Egypt into the Soviet orbit for nearly two decades. Iraq's status as a Soviet client is in part the legacy of past U.S.-Iranian and U.S.-Jordanian alliances. And, Iran's future receptivity to an alliance with the Soviet Union is likely to be enhanced by a strengthening of military ties between the United States and Saudi Arabia.

Finally, since the Soviet Union is unlikely to stop supplying arms to its clients, there is the objection that the inevitably increasing arms flows to United States allies in the Middle East will create a never-ending spiral of new military demands on the part of the recipients (some of whom are adversaries) to balance one another; worse yet, this arms race might dangerously destabilize existing balances between such U.S. allies.

This stimulus to local arms races was precisely the problem critics saw in the Reagan administration's 1981 decision to sell Saudi Arabia $8.5 billion in new arms, including sophisticated Airborne Warning and Control System (AWACS) aircraft and long-range fuel tanks and missiles that would enhance the combat performance of the F-15 fighter planes already in the Saudi arsenal. Israel's government angrily denounced the sale because it undermined its military balance vis-à-vis the Arab countries. That balance depended on Israeli air superiority to counter the more numerous soldiers and greater amount of military maintained by Arab ground forces. The Reagan administration defended the sale, however, by defining it as an enlargement of the overall anti-Soviet military potential in the Middle East under the concept of strategic consensus. The Israelis and their American supporters contended that they could not rely on the restraining power of mere concepts, that it was the capabilities in Arab hands that counted, and that therefore they would have to purchase compensatory equipment from the United States even though this would badly strain Israel's inflation-wracked economy. To the Reagan administration's embarrassment, an authoritative Saudi government spokesman gave credibility to the Israeli fears by objecting to the U.S. definition of the new arms package as necessarily a part of the strategic consensus against the USSR. Sheik Ahmed Zaki Yamani said that the arms were for the Saudis themselves to use in defense of their national interests as they saw fit. Furthermore, between the threats faced by Saudi Arabia from international communism and Israel, the threat from Israel was "far more tangible and more in evidence" and "obviously worse."[4]

These various pitfalls of the alliance building strategy, even if not perceived by top foreign policy makers in Washington, have become rather widely appreciated by government leaders in the Middle East. With nonalignment the order of the day among Third

World countries, the United States, if it persists in this strategy, often will find itself in the position of suitor rebuffed.

Superpower cooperation

This is the means of containing Soviet influence that was initially adopted by the Carter administration, taking its guidance from the Brookings Institution study, *Toward Peace in the Middle East,* in which Zbigniew Brzezinski had a large hand.[5] It starts from the premise that, despite the larger role the Soviets usually get to play as patron of the Arabs when Arab-Israeli tensions are high, the Kremlin is as deeply afraid as we are of a war between the superpowers growing out of our respective commitments to opposite sides in a local conflict. Accordingly, the Kremlin can be induced to moderate its aims and behavior in the region provided that the United States accepts the Soviet Union as an equal partner in efforts to get the local parties to resolve their differences and also as a guarantor of the peace. As indicated above, this philosophy was reflected in the October 1, 1977 joint U.S.-Soviet call for a reconvened Geneva Conference.

The Soviets would have to cooperate at least to the extent of not trying to sabotage peace arrangements that were constructed with their participation. Moreover, this way of dealing with the Soviet problem was seen as a resolution to the contradictions between United States support for Israel and our attempts to contain Soviet influence—the assumption being that the Soviet-American cooperation would bring about a durable Arab-Israeli settlement.

Opposition to such a joint Soviet-American approach to Middle Eastern affairs comes from countries in the region that do not want to be treated either as objects of a superpower condominium or as parts of the superpowers' mutually agreed upon spheres of influence. Anwar Sadat's historic trip to Jerusalem in November 1977 to start the first direct negotiations on a peace settlement between an Arab state and Israel was prompted in part by his fears of precisely such results from the October 1977 joint Soviet-American statement. Having recently severed Egypt's client relationship with the USSR after the recent Yom Kippur war, Sadat did not take kindly to the prospect of returning to such a relationship. Israel's government and its supporters in the United States were equally anxious to keep the Russians out of the peace process because they were suspicious of the Soviets' real motives.

The triangular Camp David negotiations between Israel, Egypt, and the United States grew out of this determination by Egypt and Israel to keep the Soviet Union far removed from the peace process. The exclusion of the Soviet Union and the Kremlin's hostility to the resulting accords were an ironic consequence of the initiatives taken by the Carter administration in 1977 to draw the Soviets into a constructive superpower partnership in the Middle East.

This outcome has been mixed in relation to the objective of limiting Soviet influence in the area. The Soviet-Egyptian connection was severed; the unpopularity of the Camp David accords with most of the Arab states and the isolation of the Egyptians from their fellow Arabs, however, opened up new opportunities for the Soviet Union to pose as the champion of the pan-Arab causes of Palestinian self-determination and restoration of Arab control over lands captured by Israel in the 1967 war.

Political and economic development

A fourth approach attempts to limit the Soviet Union's influence in the Middle East by reducing the need of the societies in the region to become dependent on Soviet help for security or economic well-being and by reducing the susceptibility of the local regimes and movements to subversion by Moscow leaning revolutionaries. The Soviet Union's opportunities to enlarge its influence supposedly will be reduced as the countries in the area gain in national self-confidence and political stability. The resultant economic prosperity might also help build up a substantial middle class committed to political and economic liberalism. Under this approach, United States policies in the Middle East are explicitly oriented toward country and regional development objectives. The containment of Soviet influence is simply a by-product.

The principal advantage of the focus on political and economic development objectives is that it does not require recipients of United States assistance to compromise their Third World and domestic legitimacy by sacrificing cold war nonalignment for the role of a U.S. pawn. And at the same time it provides a rationale for U.S. decision makers to favor relatively progressive governments, like Egypt, that are committed to work toward liberal modernization, and to bring pressure on traditional governments, like Saudi Arabia, to institute domestic reforms before they fall victim to the revolutionary tides sweeping the region.

This is the theory. Skeptics point to the inevitable messy complications. One is that, if seriously and consistently applied as conditions for United States assistance, the development criteria could well signal the end of alliances with countries on which the United States depends for military bases, servicing facilities, intelligence, and other cooperation in the event of our having to confront the Soviet Union in the region. Saudi Arabia, Jordan, Pakistan, and Turkey, for example, may simply not be ready to measure up to the development criteria that would qualify them as fit partners, and attempts to pressure them to institute reforms might only alienate or discredit the leadership groups that have heretofore been the mainstays of political-military cooperation with the United States.

Alternatively, the controlling regimes in these countries may angrily resist such pressures and threaten to go elsewhere (even to the USSR) for the economic, technological, and military resources they have been obtaining from the United States. This, indeed, was the strategy of the Shah of Iran in response to the Kennedy administration's efforts to pressure him to institute domestic reforms; the Johnson administration caved in to the Shah's counterpressure and let up on the imposition of development criteria; and the Nixon administration, in effect, gave the Shah *carte blanche* to purchase whatever he wanted from the United States, which was mostly glamorous military hardware. The Shah pursued his own course of domestic modernization, featuring the top-heavy economic structure and police-state persecution of opponents that led ultimately to his overthrow in 1979 and to the disastrous alienation of the post-Shah regime from the United States.[6]

Proponents of a development emphasis to United States policy in the Middle East cite the case of Iran as evidence for the wisdom of their approach: If the Carter administration, in implementing the new human rights policy, had only pushed the Shah to liberalize his police-state and, for technical economic reasons, had strongly demanded a more diversified development strategy, there might have been a chance to avoid the revolutionary upheaval of 1978–1979. This is the lesson of Iran, they maintain, and it must be applied as soon as possible in other countries, particularly Saudi Arabia and Jordan, or these countries might fall victim to similar revolutionary upheavals, which will turn them from the United States and perhaps open the gates to a larger Soviet presence.

Some strategists, notably Henry Kissinger and Zbigniew Brzezinski, stress the risks of undermining known friends of the United States by seeming to side with their domestic critics in times of turmoil within these countries. The last thing we should do, argue these strategists, is publicly imply that the shahs and the monarchs of the region are illegitimate for this will only give legitimacy to revolutionary movements (either Marxist or Moslem) that will bring on the civil strife and chaos the enemies of the United States are anxious to exploit.[7]

Ensuring Access to Persian Gulf Oil

A denial of access to Persian Gulf oil would threaten the security and well-being of the United States. On this proposition there is nearly unanimous consensus among policy makers, and it is based on the following stark facts: oil and the energy products it is turned into (including fuel for military weapons and transport) have become the lifeblood of industrial society and essential ingredients of military power; and the prospect is that oil will continue to serve crucial roles well into the twenty-first century. The United States imports about 40 percent of the oil it consumes, and about 30 percent of this comes from the countries of the Persian Gulf. Western Europe imports more than 80 percent, of which approximately 60 percent comes from the Persian Gulf. Huge fields of potentially exploitable oil lie in other regions of the world, but these are much more difficult to tap. Even as prices for oil from the Persian Gulf quadrupled during the 1970s and as the Arab oil producers demonstrated that they could and would embargo oil exports to countries supporting Israel, the import-dependence pattern of the Western industrial countries and Japan was not substantially altered. In the 1980s, the Persian Gulf countries remain the principal sources of imported oil and are highly likely to retain this preferred status in the 1990s.

There is considerable sentiment in the United States policy community for reducing this overdependence on the Persian Gulf and, indeed, on imported oil generally. But the experience of the 1970s indicates that a truly significant dependency reduction cannot be the assumption of foreign policy officials dealing with immediate and near-term issues, nor even of policy planners working within five-year and ten-year time frames.

Therefore, *how* to ensure access to Persian Gulf oil and not *whether* to attempt to ensure access is the preoccupation of policy makers. But on this question no solid consensus has emerged, one of the principal reasons being that the most obvious ways of attempting to secure access can contradict some of the other important policy objectives of the United States in the Middle East. The two most obvious ways of attempting to ensure access to Persian Gulf oil are (1) to cultivate friendly relations with oil producing countries; and (2) to maintain military capabilities for intervention against hostile governments or movements and for direct seizure of the oil production facilities.

Friendly relations

The cultivation of friendly relations with oil producing countries of the Middle East has been a standard feature of United States policy since World War II. In the early postwar period, U.S. diplomacy for securing access to the region's oil was largely a backup to arrangements made by the large oil corporations with the local governments to extract, process, and transport the oil. More and more, however, with the nationalization by Middle Eastern governments of oil resources and production (at least at the well-head side of the process), the United States has become deeply involved in negotiations with the producer-country governments and with the Organization of Petroleum Exporting Countries (OPEC) on the terms of trade, including price-per-barrel arrangements.

While American privately owned multinational corporations are still the actual purchasers of oil, the United States government now has to provide other essential parts of the deals made between the oil companies and the producer governments to make sure that the producer governments do not artificially manipulate the supply and price of their oil in order to gain political concessions from the United States.

Furthermore, because the oil producing countries have accumulated huge holdings of dollars and are able to recycle these petrodollars by purchases or investments in the United States, friendly relations with these countries are deemed necessary to ensure against large disruptions of the U.S. and world economy that could be precipitated by irresponsible or deliberately hostile use of these enormous monetary assets.

Particular Middle Eastern countries frequently disagree with the United States over what their friendly relationship requires of each. And U.S. policy makers divide over the degree to which the United States should cater to the demands of the oil producing countries for arms transfers and other indicators of friendliness and over the degree to which the United States should insist on alignment of countries with us on global issues, especially in resisting the expansion of Soviet influence.

These difficulties are central to the relationship between the United States and Saudi Arabia, the first-ranking source of foreign oil for the United States and the largest consumer for U.S. arms. As indicated above, U.S. efforts to define the purposes to which the transferred arms should be put are resented by the Saudis. Indeed, the Saudis frequently act as if their role of principal oil supplier gives them the right to make demands on U.S. foreign policy, particularly U.S. policy towards Israel. Sheikh Yamani has expressed the preferred Saudi definition of the bargaining relationship:

> Saudi Arabia . . . alone is in a position to inflict very severe damage on the world economy as a whole or on selected groups of nations. . . . If the Saudis simply cut production to the level needed to meet their own development, there would be a depression in the United States in which the rate of unemployment would at least double, the price of oil would double again and the inflation rate would rise.[8]

But most U.S. energy economists doubt that the Saudis would attempt to exercise this claimed power over the United States and its allies. As put by the Congressional Budget Office analysts:

> The likelihood is low that the Saudis would set a production level that would be crippling to the Western economy. Saudi oil sales and much of their investment portfolio are tied to the dollar, so that economic injury to the United States would be felt directly by the Saudis. Furthermore, a weakened economy would compromise the West's ability or will to defend the Saudi government from either an internal or a Soviet threat.[9]

Military intervention

Whenever United States access to the oil of important supplier countries is threatened, a debate ensues in U.S. policy circles over whether the United States should intervene militarily to secure access. The issue takes on a different cast depending upon the sources of the threat, its apparent purposes, and the political targets of U.S. intervention. A request from a government friendly to the United States for U.S. military intervention to help put down a threat by a guerilla organization or other subversive group to take over or sabotage the oil fields obviously calls forth a different range of options than a threat by a hostile government to deny the United States access. The variable of outside instigation or participation in the threatening actions can be of decisive importance for the formulation of military countermeasures. Is the Soviet Union backing the group or government that is threatening to interrupt the normal flow of oil to the United States? Is a government's denial-of-access policy part of a concerted effort by the Arab members of OPEC to coerce the United States to change its policies toward Israel?

Obviously the nature of contemplated United States military interventions and assessments of their feasibility and desirability change as circumstances change. They were different in the period immediately following the Yom Kippur war when the threat was the oil embargo imposed by Saudi Arabia from what they were in 1979 when we had to consider how to regain access to Iranian oil in the face of the intense anti-American stance of the post-Shah regime. They changed again in 1980 when, after the Soviet invasion of Afghanistan, we needed to assess what kind of force was required to deter further thrusts by the Russians toward the oil resources of the Persian Gulf.

Military intervention to counter an attempted strangulation of the industrial world by the oil producers was publicly contemplated by Secretary of State Kissinger. Asked by *Business Week* magazine whether he had considered military action to secure oil at reasonable prices, Kissinger replied that this would be "a very dangerous course," but added: "I am not saying there is no circumstance where we would . . . use force. . . . It is one thing to use it in the case of a dispute over price, but it's another when there is some actual strangulation of the industrial world."[10]

The debate over military intervention to secure oil after the Yom Kippur war was further spurred by the publication of a set of articles by Johns Hopkins University political scientist Robert Tucker in *Commentary* magazine.[11] Tucker's arguments still stand as the classic case for military intervention. Based on the premises of further exorbitant price hikes by the OPEC countries and continuing threats by the Arab producers to embargo oil destined for Israel's friends, Tucker foresaw major damage to the economies and societies of the NATO countries and Japan. And doubting that peaceful diplomacy not backed by a credible threat of military intervention would be sufficient to dissuade the Arab oil producers from using their oil as a weapon of extortion, Tucker concluded, "Elementary prudence counsels that we at least raise the question of employing extraordinary means for resolving the crisis."[12]

Tucker advocated that the United States maintain capabilities for seizing the coastal strip from Kuwait down along the eastern littoral of Saudi Arabia to Quatar—the locus of 40 percent of current OPEC production and an estimated 40 percent of the world's known reserves. Seizing and holding this area would be militarily feasible, argued Tucker, since the population was very sparse and there were virtually no trees. His most frightening scenario anticipated the destruction of oil-production facilities in the target area prior to their being seized by U.S. forces; but this, he speculated, should put the oil fields out of operation for no more than four months, and if U.S. forces were properly trained to restore and operate the facilities, then perhaps no more than sixty to ninety days.

Writing in 1975, Tucker regarded Russian counterintervention as implausible even though, according to standard military assessments, the Soviets would win a conventional war on the ground for control of the area. The critical factors, according to Tucker, were the Russians' lack of adequate naval forces for interposition and the fact that access to the oil was vital to the West whereas denying the West such access was hardly vital for the USSR. In other words, the United States' willingness to fight a big war with the Russians over the Persian Gulf was more credible than the Soviet threat to engage in such a fight; we could, therefore, call the Kremlin's bluff.

In the 1980s, however, the balance of capabilities and resolve for military intervention in the Persian Gulf no longer so clearly favor the United States. Soviet naval capabilities for combat in the region have improved; Soviet land-based airpower has rendered U.S. naval deployments more vulnerable; the Soviet occupation of Afghanistan puts them some 800 miles closer to the Gulf itself; and their potential interest in the area's oil for themselves as they near their anticipated condition of being a net oil importer in the 1990s increases the Kremlin's stake in an enlarged Soviet presence.

The United States thus faces a limited set of alternatives for preserving military options of the kind advocated by Tucker:

- The United States could substantially augment its conventional fighting forces in the region. This is being done to some extent by the organization of a rapid deployment force. However, there is a consensus among military planners that an effort to match Soviet conventional capabilities in the region would be too costly in material resources and manpower. It would also require a magnitude of prepositioned equipment and personnel that assumes more loyal U.S. allies in the region (willing to provide bases and servicing facilities) than is politically realistic.
- The United States could extend its nuclear strategic umbrella over the Gulf and thereby threaten strategic reprisal for Soviet moves against U.S. vital interests. But few analysts or policy makers are willing to revive this strategy today in the face of a Soviet nuclear arsenal at least as powerful as ours.
- The United States could employ a more flexible conventional reprisal strategy that did not require matching Soviet conventional fighting capabilities in the Gulf area; rather, the Soviets

could be threatened with U.S. military countermoves in places where the Russians were militarily inferior. United States rapid deployments to the area or on-the-spot interventions to control the oil facilities would establish a presence against which the Soviets would have to contemplate using major military force, with all the risks entailed of a U.S. response that widened the conflict. This indeed was the strategy adopted by the Reagan administration, as revealed in statements by the secretary of defense and various military planning documents.[13]

The more basic and general criticism of the notion that the United States should secure access to the oil of the Middle East by strengthening its military intervention capabilities is that the real source of threat to U.S. and allied access is the instability of many of the ruling regimes and their vulnerability to coups and revolutions by groups hostile to the United States—the Khomeinists' ouster of the Shah of Iran being a major example. Military intervention to forestall such regime changes or to attempt to reverse those that have occurred, it is argued, would be like trying to use a sledgehammer to kill flies. The resulting mess would be far worse than the initial threat.

The arguments for and against resorting to military force to secure access to Middle East oil thus parallel the arguments over how best to limit Soviet influence. One school of thought holds that United States vital interests will be sustained best by deploying units to militarily counter and defeat enemy forces in the region (including those sent there by outside powers). Another school of thought emphasizes the social, economic, and political roots of such hostility toward the United States and advocates policies that deal directly with those conditions as the more effective and durable means of warding off threats to U.S. interests in the region.

Helping Israel to Secure Its Existence

Since the founding of the state of Israel in 1947–1948, support provided by the United States government to the Jewish nation in the Middle East has been motivated primarily by moral considerations. The support for Israel is not, like the attempt to limit Soviet influence in the region and efforts to secure access to oil, motivated fundamentally by considerations of U.S. national security and economic well-being, even though these geopolitical considerations do shape the ways in which U.S. support for Israel is manifested. Particular kinds of U.S. material aid and political backing for Israel may stimulate or discourage Israel's Arab opponents to become more dependent on Moscow or to use oil as a political weapon against the United States. Any calculation of the East-West balance of power in the region, to be sure, includes Israel's impressive military capabilities and the logistics and intelligence support the Israelies can provide U.S. forces. And obviously a large Middle Eastern war that pits Israel, supported by the United States, against clients of the Soviet Union poses the danger of drawing the two superpowers into direct confrontation. But these geopolitical considerations are more the *products* of the U.S. commitment to Israel's survival than its determinants. The deepest sources of that commitment are found in the consensus of concern among American Jews and their fellow Americans for the fate of the Jewish people in the Middle East—a concern that became a U.S. national interest in reaction to the slaughter of millions of Jews by Hitler in World War II.

The consensus supporting United States help to Israel so that its existence is secure breaks down, however, over the following questions: What are the necessary and appropriate means by which the United States ought to provide such help? What are Israel's legitimate security requirements? To what extent should the United States endorse and tangibly back those requirements?

Some loyal American supporters of Israel would have the United States defer to Israel's own judgment of her security needs. This is the dominant thrust of lobbying by organized groups of the American Jewish community, who contend that no one can know better than the Israelis the state of Israel's security situation at any time. These loyal supporters come close to advocating blanket U.S. endorsement of the Israeli government's foreign policies. The rationale for such blanket deference is that only the government of a nation living in the midst of the volatile and extremely complex

Middle East is in a position to authoritatively assess that nation's survival needs.

American policy makers, however, cannot ignore the fact that there is considerable debate within Israel itself over the substance of Israel's security requirements. Moreover, even when there is widespread consensus in Israel on particular policies, the United States government is unlikely to equate its own security and other interests in the Middle East with those of Israel.

United States policy makers characteristically insist on making their own determinations of Israel's needs (as distinct from her preferences) and—most importantly—of the appropriate ways for the United States to help Israel. This lack of complete congruence between U.S. and Israeli national interests sometimes results in a severe clash of policies. Such clashes occurred in the Suez crisis of 1956 when the Eisenhower administration compelled Israel, under threat of a cutoff of U.S. aid, to withdraw her invasion forces from Egypt; in the 1973 Yom Kippur war when Kissinger pressured Israel to free the surrounded Egyptian Third Army Corps; during the Reagan administration, over the Israeli bombing raid on the Iraqi nuclear reactor, and over the conduct of Israeli military operations in Lebanon; and, finally, with respect to arrangements for Palestinian autonomy and eventual self-determination in the West Bank and Gaza areas.

Controversy in the United States policy community over the degree to which the United States should support or distance itself from Israeli policies and actions usually revolves around four issues: the nature and location of the "secure and defensible borders" Israel claims to require; the political status of the Palestinians and the characteristics of a future Palestinian territorial entity; the governance of Jerusalem; and U.S. arms supply policies toward Israel and other countries in the region.

The issue of secure and defensible borders

Since the 1967 Arab-Israeli war in which the Israelis tripled the size of the territory under their control by driving the Egyptian armies out of the Gaza Strip and the Sinai, the Jordanian army out of the West Bank area, and the Syrian army off the Golan Heights, there has been tension between the governments of the United States and Israel over the conditions under which this conquered territory is to be relinquished by Israel. Opinions vary among U.S. policy makers on the extent to which the United States should endorse the official Israeli positions on this issue.

The standard Israeli position has been that the location of its perimeter for self-defense depends on the willingness of Israel's neighbors to live in peace with her. If neighbors consider Israel to be an illegitimate state and regard Arab-Israeli relations as essentially those of enemies, then Israel's security as defined by successive Israeli governments, must require a more extended defense perimeter than would otherwise be the case. Israel's occupation of the Sinai desert was for the purposes of preventing a massive Egyptian blitzkrieg-type invasion of Israel and of securing Israeli shipping through the port of Elat and the Gulf of Aqaba. The military rationale for continuing to occupy Jordanian territory west of the Jordan River is that in order to prevent Israel from being cut in half by her enemies in a future war, she must thicken the narrow nine-mile waist of Israeli territory between the Mediterranean Sea to the Palestinian area of the West Bank. And Israel has insisted upon holding onto the Golan Heights on the grounds that prior to 1967 the Syrians had used these strategic hills to bombard Israeli settlements in northeast Israel.

In the aftermath of the 1967 war, the Arabs insisted that Israel's return of all these newly conquered territories was the necessary precondition for peace negotiations between the two countries.

The position of all United States administrations since 1967 has been essentially one of evenhandedness with respect to these seemingly incompatible basic demands by the Arabs and Israelis and rests largely on UN Security Council Resolution 242—which states that peace in the Middle East requires:

> (i) Withdrawal of Israeli armed forces from territories occupied in the recent conflict; [and]
>
> (ii) Termination of all claims or states of belligerency and respect for and acknowledgement of the sovereignty, territorial integrity and political independence of every State in the area and their right

> to live in peace within secure and recognized boundaries free from threats or acts of force.[14]

It further affirms the necessity of "guaranteeing freedom of navigation through international waterways in the area" and for "achieving a just settlement of the refugee problem."[15]

But when it comes to the *sequencing* of Israeli withdrawal and Arab recognition of the legitimacy of the Jewish state and the *means* of attaining both of these goals, the consensus in the United States policy community fragments. The pro-Israeli faction, which until the 1980s could command support from a majority in the Congress and usually from the president, backs the standing Israeli position that Arab acceptance of Israel is the necessary precondition for the relinquishment of territories captured in war. The faction more sympathetic to the Arabs, which comprises many career foreign service officers who have served in Arab countries and members of Congress with constituencies including multinational corporations with a stake in good U.S.-Arab relations, tends to think otherwise. It grants the logic of the case that full mutual recognition and peaceful coexistence are incompatible with Israel's holding onto Arab territory; rather, these should be the rewards of Israel's withdrawal.

The possible resolution of these differences through *simultaneous* withdrawal and recognition arrangements is acceptable—in principle—to concerned American policy makers of various opinions, and United States diplomacy has been directed toward achieving such arrangements. In practice, it has been very difficult to get the Arab countries and Israel to agree on exactly what steps should take place simultaneously and in what sequence. The notable and historically momentous exception has been the set of agreements between Israel and Egypt, starting with the Sinai disengagement of 1974 and 1975 (the fruits of Henry Kissinger's "shuttle diplomacy") and culminating in the Israeli-Egyptian Peace Treaty of 1979 that called for full Israeli evacuation of the Sinai in return for full normalization of relations with Egypt (the result of President Jimmy Carter's Camp David diplomacy when he mediated between Prime Minister Menachem Begin and Egyptian President Anwar Sadat).

Arrangements similar to those negotiated between Israel and

Egypt have not been feasible as yet with Syria and Jordan. No Syrian government has indicated a willingness to work out the kind of compromise Sadat did with the Israelis; the Israelis, for their part, have hardened their opposition to withdrawing from the strategically significant Golan Heights, and in the fall of 1981, they conveyed an intention of hanging onto the Heights for the indefinite future when they extended Israeli civil law to this occupied area. The occupied territories formerly under the control of Jordan are predominantly Palestinian and, therefore, arrangements for their governance are dependent upon some mutually satisfactory resolution of the Palestinian issue between Israel and her neighbors. Meanwhile, Israel has encouraged her citizens to establish civilian settlements in the West Bank area, called Judea and Samaria by Prime Minister Began to emphasize Israel's biblical claim to this land.

The settlements in the West Bank have become a contentious issue between the United States and Israel. "The United States will not support the use of any additional land for the purpose of settlements during the transition period," said President Reagan in his September 1, 1982 policy statement on the Middle East.[16] He went on to say:

> Indeed, the immediate adoption of a settlement freeze by Israel, more than any other action could create the confidence needed for wider participation in these [autonomy] talks. Further settlement activity is in no way necessary for the security of Israel and only diminishes the confidence of the Arabs that a final outcome can be freely and fairly negotiated.[17]

Predictably, Prime Minister Begin took angry exception to the president's position on the settlements. The settlements were, by design, the tangible and symbolic thrust of the Begin government's assertion of Israel's sovereignty over the area. In succeeding weeks, U.S.-Israeli relations deteriorated as the Begin government announced a major expansion of West Bank settlements, which would continue over the coming months and years. The State Department publicly rebuked the announcement as "most unwelcome" and as raising "questions about Israel's willingness to abide by the promise of Resolution 242 that territory will be exchanged for true peace."[18]

Not all Israelis were adamantly opposed to considering an eventual restoration of Jordanian jurisdiction over at least portions of the West Bank or other ways of establishing greater autonomy for the inhabitants. Apparently, even in the face of the predictable Begin response, the Reagan administration decided to cater to these Israeli sentiments, which were well represented in the opposition Labor Party. This U.S. policy option—of reaching beyond the incumbent Israeli government to tap opposition sentiment—had been rejected by past U.S. administrations as likely to be counterproductive. The government in power would charge U.S. interference in Israeli domestic affairs, and this would only solidify popular backing for the government's positions in Israel and the United States. This was exactly the allegation that Begin did in fact make. Whether the results would, over time, serve to enlarge the Israeli constituency in favor of compromise on the settlements and larger West Bank issue or whether it would boomerang to provide a larger constituency for expansionary Israeli policies was being debated by U.S. Middle Eastern experts at this writing.

Israel's attempts to secure her population against terrorist attacks from Palestinian guerillas based in Lebanon have also caused tension between the Israeli and American governments. President Carter was angered in March 1978 when, in the midst of his mediation efforts with Begin and Sadat, Israel, in retaliation for a terrorist raid that killed thirty Israeli citizens, sent her troops into Lebanon to occupy a six-mile deep security belt north of the Israeli-Lebanese border. Israel withdrew her forces from southern Lebanon a month later as United Nations troops took up positions in the area to patrol the cease-fire. President Reagan temporarily suspended delivery of F-16 jet aircraft to Israel in reaction to the July 17, 1981 Israeli air attack on Palestinian concentrations in a downtown section of Beirut that killed 300 persons.

The massive Israeli invasion and air bombardment of Lebanon in the summer of 1982, which culminated in the evacuation of Palestinian guerillas from Beirut in exchange for the Israelis lifting their seige of that city, resulted in the most severe rift between the United States and Israeli governments since the Suez crisis of 1956. The Reagan administration appeared ready to tolerate the Israeli invasion as long as it stayed within the confines stated initially by the Begin government—namely, that it was temporary and limited to clear a twenty-five-mile-wide border area of the Palestinian guerillas who had been attacking Israelis settlements in the Galilee. But when the Israelis, heady with success for having achieved their initial objective, transformed the invasion into an effort to drive the Palestinians completely out of Lebanon and to totally destroy them in their Beirut strongholds if necessary, the U.S. government disassociated itself from the basic thrust of the Israeli operation. As the news media focused on the civilian casualties produced by Israeli bombs, the Reagan administration—despite Israel's insistence that it was making military sacrifices in order to minimize harm to civilians and despite the charge that the Palestinian guerillas deliberately were using civilians as a shield—felt compelled to further distance itself from Israeli plans to flush the guerillas out of West Beirut. The Reagan administration, through the mediational diplomacy of Philip Habib, concentrated its efforts on stopping the bloodshed by obtaining a simultaneous evacuation of Palestinian guerillas from Beirut and a pullback of Israeli forces. Both would be monitored by a multinational peace keeping force of French, Italian, and U.S. units. The president allowed himself to be photographed making an angry phone call to Prime Minister Begin during which he implied severe cutbacks in U.S. aid to Israel if the Begin government did not pull the reins on Israeli bombardment of West Beirut during these disengagement negotiations.

American-Israeli differences were aggravated further when, in response to the assassination in September 1982 of the president-elect of Lebanon, Christian Phalangist leader Bashir Gamayal, the Israeli army returned in force to West Beirut to maintain order. Relations descended to their lowest point yet when, within the area supposed to be under control again of the Israeli military, Christian militiamen inflicted a retaliatory massacre on Palestinian refugees—many of them women and children—in West Beirut camps. Begin's opponents in Israel were outraged at his government's mishandling of the Lebanon affair, as were members of the American policy community. President Reagan ordered a larger contingent of U.S. marines to join the French and Italian units of the reconstituted multinational force. They were to take over the order-enforcing job from the Israelis in and around Beirut, while demanding that the Israeli troops withdraw immediately. American-Israeli relations improved in the spring of 1983 as Israel, Lebanon, and the United States agreed to the terms of a withdrawal of Israeli and Syrian troops from Lebanon. (This time only the Syrians balked.) Then, in the fall and winter of 1983, the Americans and the Israelies were temporarily drawn into a virtual alliance as the American marines came under attack from Druse militiamen and Muslim fanatics. United States fighter planes began to strike at Syrian air defense batteries that had attacked and downed U.S. aircraft engaged in reconnaissance.

But the Lebanon crisis raised the issue of how the United States can effectively bring pressure on Israel to moderate its aggressive policies when these are regarded here as unwarranted by Israel's legitimate security and defense requirements. Some editorial writers, columnists, and congressmen advocated threatening a cutoff or reduction of military and economic aid to Israel, citing as a precedent President Eisenhower's successful threat to cut off aid to Israel in 1956 at the time of the Suez crisis unless it pulled its invasion forces out of the Sinai. Those who opposed using such leverage argued that threats would only galvanize support in Israel for the aggressive go-it-alone policies.[19]

The forced evacuation of thousands of Palestinians from Lebanon refocused world attention on the issue of their future homeland—an issue on which the dominant definitions of Israeli interests (as asserted by Israel's government and its staunchest supporters in the United States) tend to diverge significantly from the dominant definitions of U.S. interests in the Middle East.

The Palestinian issue

Successive Israeli governments have rejected the notion that the legitimate rights of the Palestinians extend to the creation of a new Palestinian state on the borders of Israel, particularly if such a state were to be established in the territories now under Israeli control west of the Jordan River and in the Gaza Strip. All Israeli governments also have regarded as illegitimate the organization which purports to be broadly representative of the Palestinians seeking statehood—the Palestine Liberation Organization (PLO)—pointing out that the PLO program calls for the dismemberment and destruction of the state of Israel.

Palestine Liberation Organization (PLO)—pointing out that the PLO program calls for the dismemberment and destruction of the state of Israel.

Until the late 1970s, United States administrations, backed by Congress, had deferred to Israeli insistences on both the question of a future Palestinian political entity and the question of relations with the PLO. But the Carter administration assumed office in 1977 with a comprehensive plan for peace in the Middle East that departed considerably from the rigid Israeli stance on the Palestinian issue; and although the original Carter plan was not implemented, U.S. positions during the Camp David negotiations of 1978–1979 and subsequently in the Reagan administration's reactions to Israel's 1982 invasion of Lebanon reflect an increasing erosion of the rather solid consensus in the U.S. policy community, which until now had essentially endorsed Israeli policies for dealing with the Palestinians.

Statehood, self-determination, limited autonomy. As the cause of the Palestinians has come into greater prominence in the United States—partly through acts of terrorism by Palestinians to publicize their cause and partly through increased media coverage of the problems of the Palestinians living in Israeli-controlled areas and most dramatically of their rout from Lebanon in 1982—that aspect of their cause that asserts the right to national statehood has generated increased sympathy among Americans. More consideration is accorded in U.S. policy circles to the argument that the existence in the Middle East of some 4 million Palestinians who consider themselves a distinct nation that ought to have its own state will be a persisting cause of political instabilty and war unless such a state is established.

As of this writing, the official United States position—for reasons of maintaining good relations with Israel and of not alienating the American Jewish community—remains that of rejecting the concept of an independent Palestinian state, even as a future objective. As reiterated by President Reagan in his September 1, 1982 address on the Middle East, "The United States will not support the establishment of an independent Palestinian state in the West Bank and Gaza."[20]

But the formal position is not necessarily fixed; the search for ways of moving toward a sovereign Palestinian entity is continually under way. The Brookings Middle East Study Group proposals, which provided the premises of the Carter administration's policy, urged Israel to accept the principal of Palestinian "self-determination" and did not rule out the possibility that the Palestinian entity would be an independent state.[21] And President Carter go into an altercation with the American Jewish community for his remarks at a March 16, 1977 town meeting in Clinton, Massachusetts where he endorsed a "homeland" for the Palestinians.[22] Movement toward United States endorsement of the concept of self-determination, which does not rule out statehood, was also reflected in the Joint Statement by the United States and the Soviet Union of October 1, 1977 that urged a resolution of the Arab-Israeli conflict that would include ensurance of the "legitimate rights of the Palestinian people."[23] Despite Israeli protests that these are code words for the Palestinians claim to statehood, the phrase "legitimate rights" of the Palestinians has continued to appear in the rhetoric of U.S. officials in formal documents of the U.S. government. The Reagan policy statement of September 1, 1982 also used the terms "full autonomy" and "self government."

An alternative to an independent Palestinian state has been suggested from time to time by the Israeli government—namely, that Jordan be accorded the status of *the* Palestinian state. But most Middle Eastern analysts regard this as a rhetorical ploy, since the Israelis do not indicate a willingness to allow Jordan to resume sovereignty over the West Bank and Gaza, nor is there any realistic prospect that the Hashemite monarchy of King Hussein would be willing to further enlarge Jordan's ethnically Palestinian poulation, which already constitutes 60 percent of the country.

A variation on the Jordanian solution, advocated by some politically prominent Israelis, including Shimon Peres of the Labor Party, would establish a new Palestinian state in Gaza and part of the West Bank in a "federation" with Jordan, the idea being that Jordan would retain substantial control over the national defense and foreign policies of the new Palestinian entity. The Reagan administration endorsed the essence of this concept on September 1, 1982 in the president's statement that "it is the firm view of the United States that self-government by the Palestinians of the West

Bank and Gaza in association with Jordan offers the best chance for a durable, just and lasting peace." Reagan also strongly urged a "freeze" on any further settlement activity by the Israelis in these areas.[24] The Begin government angrily rejected the Reagan proposals as being in conflict with Israeli sovereignty over these areas and contrary to the letter and spirit of the Camp David *Framework for Peace* agreed to by Carter, Begin, and Sadat in 1978. However, the Political Bureau of the Labor Party welcomed the Reagan policy statement on the Middle East as "a basis for serious dialog."[25]

The Reagan administration's position, publicly supported by former President Carter, is that the Reagan statement of September 1, 1982 is fully consistent with the Palestinian "autonomy" provisions of the Camp David accords. The Camp David agreements outlined a negotiating process that would establish a "self-governing authority" to administer the West Bank and Gaza areas for a "transitional period" of not more than five years while negotiations continue between Egypt, Israel, Jordan, and elected inhabitants of the West Bank and Gaza to agree on the final status of these areas. During this transitional period, the self-governing authority would be an "administrative council" that would be "freely elected by the inhabitants of these areas" to replace the existing Israeli military government. A local police force would be established that could include Jordanian citizens, and Israeli forces would be redeployed into specified "security locations." The degree of autonomy eventually granted the self-governing authority or its successor institutions was not spelled out. The Israelis set the goal as that of "limited self government" under continuing Israeli sovereignty. The Egyptians claimed the objective is "full sovereignty" for a Palestinian state.

There was an important change, however, between Carter's Camp David approach and the new Reagan initiative. By focusing primarily on the autonomy negotiating *process* rather than on having the United States take a position on the substance of the competing claims, the Carter administration attempted to maintain good relations with various parties and to preserve its role as mediator. Now the Reagan administration, in endorsing a particular resolution of the Palestinian issue, was trading some of its effectiveness as impartial mediator for the leverage it hoped to gain by putting the prestige of the president behind this outcome. President Reagan appeared to be fully aware that this was the choice he was making:

> The United States has thus far sought to play the role of mediator. We have avoided public comment on the key issues. We have always recognized, and continue to recognize, that only the voluntary agreement of those parties most directly involved in the conflict can provide an enduring solution. But it has become evident to me that some clearer sense of America's position on key issues is necessary to encourage wider support for the peace process.[26]

Opposition of the United States policy community to Israeli stubbornness on the Palestinian issue has been on the rise. Some members, like former Undersecretary of State George Ball, have suggested strong sanctions against Israel, perhaps a cutoff of economic and military aid unless the Israelis went along with at least American proposals for a freeze on Jewish settlements in the occupied areas. The objections to taking such a hard line against the Israeli intransigence on the Palestinian issue are of three kinds: (1) the acceptance of the Israeli government's definition of its security requirements as in fact accurate (the position of loyalists in the American Jewish community); (2) the unwillingness to alienate the one country in the Middle East on which the United States can confidently rely in case of a Soviet-American confrontation; and (3) the anticipation that any ultimatum to Israel will stimulate even more unilateral moves by the Israeli government, such as formal annexation and full-scale settlement of the West Bank and Gaza and perhaps even preventive war by Israel against some of her neighbors to further consolidate her gains while the military balance of power is still in her favor.

Dealing with the PLO. The standing United States policy on dealing with the Palestinian Liberation Organization—the organization that claims to be the official international representative of the Palestinian nation—was crystalized in 1975 in a special accord signed by Secretary of State Kissinger and Israel Foreign Minister Yigal Allon. In exchange for Israel's 1975 pullback in the Sinai, Kissinger promised that the "United States would not negotiate with the PLO so long as the PLO does not recognize Israel's right to exist and does not accept Security Council Resolutions 242 and 338."[27] This would require the PLO to renounce the Palestine National Covenant of 1964, which calls for the destruction of the State of Israel.

This official United States policy is one of three essentially different positions that contend for adoption. Another would abandon the above preconditions and allow for direct negotiations with the PLO in order to move it in the direction of coexistence with Israel. The third would simply reject the PLO as a legitimate organization, regardless of whether it formally acquiesced to the Kissinger terms.

The case for dropping the preconditions so as to be able to deal directly with the PLO is one of diplomatic expedience. In 1974, the UN General Assembly voted 105 to 4, with 20 abstentions, to recognize the PLO, and more than 100 countries, including most NATO allies of the United States, grant some form of legal political recognition. The United States does deal with the PLO anyway, despite our formal nonrecognition policy, through the good offices of other countries and through unofficial contacts.* The United States could avoid this cumbersome posture by adopting a *de facto* recognition policy—namely, an explicit definition of our dealings with the PLO as based only on the fact that it is one of the actors with whom we must deal in the Middle East and indicating that such dealings in no way confer any endorsement of the legitimacy of the PLO's purposes.

The case for refusing to treat the PLO as a legitimate international actor, regardless of any formal modification it might make in its anti-Israel statements or even its covenant, is based on the premise that the guerilla organization is deeply committed to the destruction of the Israeli state and that, therefore, even if it can be persuaded to say it will accept the terms of UN Security Council Resolution 242, it cannot be trusted to pursue genuine peaceful coexistence with Israel. An independent Palestine on the West Bank and Gaza, ruled by the PLO, armed by the Soviets, and encouraged by other Arab nations, might attempt to drive the Israelis into the sea.

* In 1979, when it became public knowledge that the United States Ambassador to the United Nations, Andrew Young, had held "unauthorized" conversations with a PLO official, Young was compelled to resign.

The case for adhering to Kissinger's minimal conditions for United States recognition of the PLO and interpreting these as a pledge to treat the PLO at least as a legitimate negotiating agent for the Palestinians is that this could yet provide an incentive for a real modification of Palestinian demands and aims. The PLO, it is pointed out, is an umbrella organization for about ten "liberation" groups, many of which are more violent and many of which are more closely tied to the Soviet Union than is Yasir Arafat's own group, the *Fatah*. Indeed, Arafat, the erstwhile leader of the PLO, was driven out of Lebanon in 1983 by the more militant Palestinians backed by Syria. If Arafat could show some real progress toward the goal of a Palestinian state by moderating PLO tactics and image, then Arafat, the majority of Palestinians, plus many of the Arab countries in which the displaced Palestinians are lodging would have a stake in reinforcing the shift toward moderation. It might be a gamble to accept an initial adherence by the PLO to Resolution 242 on face value; but, it can be argued, the risk may be worth taking, especially since the United States could revoke recognition of the PLO if it resumed terrorist tactics or in other ways attempted to make war against Israel.

The governance of Jerusalem

Because the question of how Jerusalem should be governed is a potentially highly contentious one in American politics, let alone a source of tension between the United States and Israel, it has, for the most part, been deferred by officials responsible for formulating United States policy toward the Middle East. The basic U.S. principle has been that any arrangements for the city—whether temporary or permanent—must safeguard the rights and holy places of the three principal religious groups who consider Jerusalem sacred: the Jews, the Christians, and the Muslims. In practice, the United States has acquiesced to the exercise of political and legal authority by the military occupiers in those parts of Jerusalem that they have physically controlled. Between 1949 and 1967 this meant U.S. deference to Jordanian control of East Jerusalem (which contains the Old City and the most sacred places of each of the three religions) and to Israeli control of West Jerusalem. Since the

1967 war, in which the Israelies occupied all of Jerusalem, the U.S. government has continued to follow this *de facto* policy, avoiding a denial or endorsement of Israeli claims of full sovereignty over the city.*

The closest the United States government has come to endorsing Israel's claim of full sovereignty over all of Jerusalem was President Reagan's statement in his September 1, 1982 policy speech that "we remain convinced that Jerusalem must remain undivided, but its final status should be decided through negotiations."[28]

The Reagan administration, like the Carter administration before it, has refrained from direct comment on Israel's moves in recent years to formalize its control over the city (such as the Knesset resolution of July 1980 officially establishing Jerusalem as the capital of Israel and Prime Minister Begin's decision shortly afterward to move his office from West Jerusalem to East Jerusalem); but a negative attitude toward such unilateral moves is implied in the Reagan statement that the final status of the city "should be decided through negotiations."

Prudently, the Carter administration backed off of its earlier position that Jerusalem's status should be negotiated simultaneously with the question of Israel's borders and troop withdrawals as part of a comprehensive peace. Carter soon realized that some of these issues (particularly the one over Jerusalem's control) would hold up resolution of others that were ripe for negotiation. Notably, the Camp David accords did not deal with Jerusalem.

For the time being, the United States position appears to be similar to that of Jerusalem's mayor, Teddy Kollek, that "Jerusalem will be among the last items on the agenda as the Middle East's

* The policy of official neutrality toward the competing claims of the Arabs and Jews on Jerusalem was temporarily abandoned in the Carter administration's instructions to its ambassador to the United Nations to vote in favor of a March 1980 UN Security Council Resolution (No. 465) stating that "all measures taken by Israel to change the physical character, demographic composition, institutional structure or status of the Palestinian and other territories occupied since 1967, including Jerusalem, or any part thereof, have no legal validity." In response to an uproar from U.S. supporters of Israel, the White House disavowed support for the resolution as it finally passed, claiming that there had been "a failure to communicate" by the State Department to Ambassador Donald McHenry that all references to Jerusalem should be deleted from the UN resolution.

problems are solved, and we [the Israelis] must strive in the meantime to make the quality of life for all people in the city as attractive as we possibly can."[29]

Eventually, however, the United States will have to take an official position on the final legal status of Jerusalem. It will have to decide from among a number of alternatives:

1. *A restoration of Arab sovereignty over East Jerusalem.* This would mean that the controlling authorities were either Palestinian, Palestinian and Jordanian, or Arab multinational, and is the consensus position among the Arabs. It is based on the claim that a settlement consistent with Resolution 242 requires Israel to relinquish control over all areas captured in 1967. The Israelies have made it clear that they would go to war again to prevent this.

2. *Internationalization of the city.* The Vatican has been a champion of internationalization as a means of ensuring that Jerusalem will be primarily a religious center for the world's Christians, Jews, and Muslims; this official Roman Catholic position has been echoed by numerous other Christian churches. But the Vatican has come to recognize that the United Nations, because of its pro-Arab–anti-Israel majority, would not be an appropriate supervisory body. Nor has the Church been able to come up with a design for an international administration of the city that would not be paralyzed by its need to await an international consensus before acting on day-to-day matters (which are bound to be controversial given the overlap between religious and civic life in the ethnic groups who inhabit the city). In recent years, the Vatican has contented itself with demands that each religious group should be guaranteed free access to its holy places and that the city as a whole should not be under the exclusive control of any one of them.

3. *A system of ethnic-religious boroughs and special-purpose districts coordinated by a metropolitan council.* Each ethnic-religious group would have considerable autonomy over its own affairs (possibly including police functions) within specially demarcated boroughs and would be represented in the metropolitan council. The controversial question of whether the council should make decisions on the basis of majority vote or unanimity would be left to the negotiations between the parties setting up the system. Such an arrangement might well work provided there was suffi-

cient commitment on the part of the Israelis and the Arabs to cooperate in maintaining maximum local autonomy along with the necessary coordination and a willingness to continually negotiate with one another. This type of solution attempts to push into the background the issue of ultimate or residual sovereignty in the event the system breaks down, but this is precisely the issue over which the negotiations to set up such a system are likely to break down in the first place.

4. *Israeli sovereignty over the whole city.* The Israelis claim that the only regime for the city that is historically and ethically justifiable—and currently workable—is one premised on the perpetuation of their sovereignty over all parts of Jerusalem. Although no United States government would want to put the proposition to the American electorate, the argument that the immediate practical imperatives of running the city require that one state have recognized responsibility and authority does score well in the U.S. policy community; and, for the time being at least, Israel, clearly, is the only state capable of taking on that responsibility. But there is growing sentiment among U.S. policy makers against a perpetuation of total Israeli sovereignty and, therefore, there is a search for means of ensuring that even current Israeli administration of Jerusalem is accountable to a wide international group, even though the question of the future governance of the city is postponed.

U.S. Arms Supply Policies

United States arms supply policies in the Middle East reflect the variety of important U.S. interests in the region but to some degree merely represent the attempts of the U.S. government and the arms export sector of the American economy to take advantage of lucrative foreign sales opportunities. Inevitably, therefore, some of the military resources the United States gives and sells to countries in the Middle East may undermine some of the interests supposed to be served by other U.S. military aid or sales in the region.

Managing military sales and aid so as to satisfy the various United States interests in the Middle East has become an increasingly difficult problem as the U.S. has enlarged its role as a regional arms supplier. By the early 1980s, the United States was supplying arms to its regional clients at the rate of $10 billion a year, a tenfold increase over the early 1970s. This figure was accounted for in part by the petrodollars the region's oil producers have to spend on armaments, in part as a reaction to the increased arming by the USSR of its clients, and in part to the multiplier effect of arms sent to stabilize local military balances that had been destabilized by an increase on one side (the destabilization often being a result of preceding U.S. arms transfers!).

Basic United States policy is still supposed to be governed by the 1950 Tripartite Declaration between the United States, Britain, and France to limit their transfer of arms to countries in the region in order to avoid an arms race between the Israelis and the Arabs. But the restraints called for in the Tripartite Declaration were overwhelmed by Middle Eastern complexities from the start. The agreement did not restrict the British and French from supplying arms to their various Arab clients who were engaged in arms races against one another; and, indeed, the Eisenhower administration encouraged Britain to arm Arab states that were willing to be allies of the NATO countries in containing Soviet efforts to penetrate the Middle East.

The United States-sponsored Baghdad Pact of 1955 between Britain, Turkey, Iran, Pakistan, and Egypt's rival Iraq, and the U.S. rebuff to Egypt's request for arms turned Egyptian President Nasser toward the Soviet Union. The Soviets responded by arranging for their arms producing satellite Czechoslovakia to be Egypt's principal arms supplier.

The Czechoslovakian-Egyptian arms deal threatened Israel's ability to balance Egypt's power and stimulated an intensified search by Israel for additional arms. The United States and Britain refused to supply them, but France, anxious to divert Nasser from helping the Algerian rebels and lead him toward the Israeli-Egyptian borders, responded favorably to Israel's request for additional arms.

The United States took over France's role as Israel's main arms supplier in the mid-1960s following France's sloughing off of this role once she had withdrawn from Algeria and no longer needed Israel as a counterweight to Egypt. After the 1967 war, in the face of a major Soviet effort to help the defeated Arabs build up their armed forces against Israel, the Republican and Democratic platforms and the leading candidates of both parties in the 1968 elections pledged to work to end the arms race in the Middle East, but meanwhile, in the short run, to counter the Soviet-sponsored Arab buildup by supplying Israel with the latest U.S. supersonic aircraft.

The Nixon administration continued the transfer of arms to Israel initiated by the Johnson administration but manipulated the flow during the Yom Kippur war as a carrot-and-stick to pressure the Israelis on various cease-fire arrangements. Following the 1973 war, Nixon and Kissinger requested that Congress authorize $2.2 billion in military aid to Israel to prevent a new imbalance from the large-scale Soviet military resupply of Egypt and Syria. However, consistent with its policy of using arms transfers as a major tool of diplomatic influence, and with the Nixon doctrine of transferring responsibility for forward defense against Soviet expansion to local powers, the Nixon administration also dramatically increased its military sales to Iran, Saudi Arabia, and Jordan. Thus, the Iranian arms purchases jumped from $236 million during 1969 to over $4 billion in 1974, and the Saudis, who were buying only $4 million of arms from the United States in 1969, bought nearly $6 billion in 1976. By the time of Jimmy Carter's inauguration, Israel, Iran, and Saudi Arabia were accounting for more than half of all U.S. arms exports.

Jimmy Carter had hoped to institute a restrictive arms supply policy and issued a directive in May 1977 imposing a ceiling on further military sales. But the administration's other interests in the Middle East, principally the ones of maintaining local balances against Russian-supplied countries and sustaining Israel's ability to defend herself, rapidly took priority over the arms control policy. Paradoxically, Carter found that arms transfers were the most potent lever he had on both the Israelis and the Egyptians for inducing their compromises during the Camp David peace negotiations. Carter's 1977 request for congressional approval of the sale of seven Airborne Warning and Control System (AWACS) planes to the Shah of Iran was an early indication that balance-of-power considerations had already begun to overwhelm world-order considerations in his foreign policy. And the administration's 1978 request for congressional authorization of $4.5 billion worth of military aircraft to Israel, Saudi Arabia, and Egypt reflected Carter's new attitude toward the utility of arms transfers as an instrument of United States diplomacy in the Middle East.

Members of the Reagan administration had no philosophical problems with the use of arms transfers as a prime diplomatic instrument in the Middle East or any other region. Not only did they willingly implement the arms deals their predecessors had negotiated, but they also actively explored opportunities to win friends, solidify alliances, and make as many Middle Eastern countries as possible dependent upon U.S. arms supplies for their security. An active arms transfer policy could provide important inducements as well as cement for the strategic consensus that was to be the foundation for opposing Soviet influence in the Middle East.

The 1981 arms package sold to Saudi Arabia (including the five AWACS planes) was fully consistent with this approach. But the Saudi deal also illustrated that unintended and uncontrollable repercussions of this kind of arms transfer policy can contradict and overwhelm many of the objectives it is supposed to serve.

The Israelies protested that the 1981 U.S.-Saudi arms deal would alter the Arab-Israeli balance of power. In response, the United States government tried to get guarantees from the Saudis that the arms would not be used against the Israelis and certainly not in offensive operations to which the Saudis retorted angrily, arguing that to place such political conditions on how they might use the equipment they bought was an infringement of their sovereignty. To mollify the Israelis, the Reagan administration responded to Israeli desires for a U.S.-Israeli strategic cooperation agreement that would solifidy the U.S.-Israel special relationship. The resulting Memorandum of Strategic Understanding signed in November 1981 by Secretary of Defense Weinberger and Israeli Defense Minister Sharon[30] further alienated the Saudis and proved to be a domestic embarrassment to the Begin government. The Saudis saw the Sharon-Weinberger accord as a move toward a full-blown U.S.-Israeli alliance and demanded reassurances from the Reagan administration. Prominent Israelis, including members of Begin's cabinet, branded the terms of the Memorandum a humiliation, since they bound Israel to consult with the United States more than they bound the United States to consult with Israel. Furthermore, the Memorandum dealt almost exclusively with the Soviet threat in the Middle East (the primary concern of the Americans) but not with the primary threats to Israel's security from her Arab neighbors. Moreover, the Reagan administration's reassurances to the Saudis that the United States was evenhanded and impartial on all major Arab-Israeli issues were read with alarm in Israel as a decided shift away from the U.S.-Israeli special relationship. As a consequence, the Israelis pressed even harder—and successfully—for compensatory arms to redress the impending imbalance.

This recent record has fueled criticism that the policy of influence-through-arms-supply is counterproductive and that, if anything, it stimulates local rivalries and instabilities over which the United States tends to *lose* control.

Notes

1. For the Reagan administration's revision of its original "strategic consensus" policy, see Seyom Brown, *The Faces of Power: Constancy and Change in United States Foreign Policy from Truman to Reagan* (New York: Columbia University Press, 1983), pp. 612–617.
2. Kissinger's remark on "expelling" the Soviets from the Middle East is quoted by Marvin and Bernard Kalb, *Kissinger* (New York: Dell, 1975), p. 222.
3. Soviet-American Joint Statement of October 1, 1977, *Department of State Bulletin*, Vol. LXXVII, No. 2002 (November 7, 1977), pp. 639–640.
4. Sheik Yamani, quoted by Congressional Quarterly, *The Middle East* (Washington, D.C.: Congressional Quarterly, 1981), pp. 74–75.
5. Brookings Institution Study Group on the Middle East, *Toward Peace in the Middle East* (Washington, D.C.: Brookings Institution, 1975).
6. See Barry Rubin, *Paved With Good Intentions: The American Failure in Iran* (New York: Knopf, 1981).
7. See Henry A. Kissinger, *White House Years* (Boston: Little, Brown, 1979), pp. 1258–1264.
8. Yamani as quoted by Walter Levy in "Oil: An Agenda for the 1980s," *Foreign Affairs*, Vol. 59, No. 5 (Summer 1981), pp. 1098–1099.
9. Congressional Budget Office, *The World Oil Market in the 1980s: Implications for the United States* (Washington, D.C.: United States Government Printing Office, 1980), p. 26.
10. Interview of Kissinger by *Business Week*, January 13, 1975.

11. Robert Tucker, "Oil: The Issue of American Intervention," *Commentary*, Vol. 59, No. 1 (January 1975), pp. 21–31; Robert Tucker, "Further Reflections on Oil and Force," *Commentary*, Vol. 59, No. 3 (March 1975), pp. 44–55. See also letters to the editor of *Commentary* in the April 1, issue, Vol. 59, No. 4.
12. Robert Tucker, *Commentary*, January 1975, p. 25.
13. Caspar W. Weinberger, *Department of Defense, Annual Report: Fiscal Year 1983* (Department of Defense, processed). See also Richard Halloran, "Pentagon Draws Up First Strategy for Fighting a Long Nuclear War," *New York Times*, May 30, 1982.
14. United Nations Security Council Resolution 242, November 22, 1967.
15. *Ibid.*
16. Ronald Reagan, Statement of September 1, 1982, U.S. Department of State, *Current Policy*, No. 417.
17. *Ibid.*
18. Alan Romberg's statement on Israeli settlement policy, quoted in *Jerusalem Post*, November 7–13 issue.
19. A reflection on the contemplation of aid cutoffs to Israel in situations like Lebanon 1982 is found in James Reston's column, "The Tragedy of Begin," *New York Times*, September 22, 1982.
20. Reagan Statement of September 1, 1982, *Current Policy*, No. 417.
21. Brookings Institution Study Group on the Middle East.
22. Jimmy Carter, Remarks at Clinton Town Meeting, March 16, 1977, *Public Papers of the Presidents, Jimmy Carter, 1977* (Washington, D.C.: U.S. Government Printing Office, 1978), Vol. I, p. 387.
23. Joint Statement of the United States and the Soviet Union, October 1, 1977, *Department of State Bulletin*, Vol. 77, No. 2002 (November 7, 1977), pp. 639–640.
24. Reagan Statement of September 1, 1982.
25. Shimon Peres, quoted in *Boston Globe*, September 4, 1982.
26. Reagan Statement of September 1, 1982.
27. Kissinger-Yalon 1975 agreement quoted by Bernard Gwertzman, "Brzezinski Urges Talks with PLO," *New York Times*, August 13, 1981.
28. Reagan Statement of September 1, 1982.
29. Teddy Kollek, "Jerusalem: Present and Future," *Foreign Affairs*, Vol. 59, No. 5 (Summer 1981), p. 1041.
30. Text of American-Israeli Agreement of November 30, 1981 in *New York Times*, December 1, 1981.

Chapter 8
Grand Designs for World Order

Foreign policy must begin with the understanding that it involves relationships between sovereign countries. Sovereignty has been defined as a will uncontrolled by others; that is what gives foreign policy its contingent and ever incomplete character....

...In this setting, our immediate aim has been to build a stable network of relationships that offers hope of sparing mankind the scourges of war....

...But peace must be more than the absence of conflict. We perceive stability as the bridge to the realization of human aspirations, not an end in itself....We may have improved the mastery of equilibrium, but we have not yet attained justice....

...The opportunities of mankind now transcend nationalism, and can only be dealt with by nations acting in concert.

—Henry A. Kissinger
(at *Pacem in Terris III* Convocation
October 8, 1973)

Each of the basic arguments over the foreign policy alternatives analyzed in the previous chapters implies a design for world order. The participants in these debates do not always reveal their preferences for a particular kind of world order. Indeed, they are sometimes unaware of the world-order implications of the policies they are advocating. But truly informed and serious assessment of foreign policy alternatives requires that these world-order implications be traced and analyzed.

The world-order preferences that are prominent in American foreign policy debates—either explicitly or implicitly—can be grouped under five so-called grand designs: the balance-of-power system; world peace through world law; a world of regions; polyarchy; and the global city. These are not necessarily mutually exclusive patterns of world order. Some can be seen as outgrowths of some of the others.

The Balance-of-Power System

From the earliest days of the Republic to the present, United States foreign policy, for the most part, has been premised on an international balance-of-power system. The world is seen to consist of sovereign nation-states, without an overarching, supranational system of law and order. Each nation-state must be prepared, therefore, to fight militarily—by itself or in combination with allies—to secure its independence and other values.

Policy makers explicitly invoke balance-of-power concepts when their country feels threatened by foreign adversaries. In such periods, the protection of the nation's vital interests appears to require capabilities and national will to confront adversaries with sufficient countervailing power to prevent them from implementing their hostile intentions. Balancing the power of adversaries, in the sense of ensuring that they do not achieve predominant power, is seen as a necessary requirement of statecraft; typically, this involves creating and strengthening military alliances as well as tending to one's own military strength.

Jimmy Carter, when campaigning for president, said that it was time for balance of power to give way to world-order politics, by which he meant a global system of cooperative interdependence in which countries resolved their disputes through peaceful bargaining rather than confrontation. But Carter modified this view during his term in the White House. Worried that the Soviet Union, either by itself or working through proxies, would take advantage of any opportunity to augment its power, Carter was led to embrace the view of his national security adviser, Zbigniew Brzezinski, that balancing Soviet power was still an essential precondition for progress toward a world congenial to American values.

But Carter was reluctant to make this concession. Like his precursor six decades ago, President Woodrow Wilson, Carter continued to believe that the balance-of-power system was only a temporary and discardable evil necessity. An imperative of statesmanship was to attempt to move the world toward a condition where the balance of power could be supplanted by a less brutal system for adjusting conflicts between peoples.

The main difference between statesmen like Wilson and Carter on the one hand and Theodore Roosevelt and Henry Kissinger on the other hand is that the former view the balance of power as an aberration to be done away with whereas the latter regard it as the essence of world politics and doubt that another system for regulating conflicts among nations is feasible or even desirable.

Those who regard the balance-of-power system as an inherent feature of world politics assume that the basic structure of world society now prevailing—self-governing nation-states without a supranational governing body over them—is the only world order compatible with the diversity of the human population. Some defenders of the balance-of-power system regard it as the only *desirable* system—the alternatives, presumably, requiring a suppression of cultural and political diversity.

The balance of power, its practitioners and advocates point out, should not be equated with anarchy, even though it is not inconsistent with anarchy. The states in the balance-of-power system, while relying mainly on their own power (and that of their allies) to defend their sovereignty and other interests, may well subscribe to international rules for diplomacy, economics, war, arms control, and other self-limiting arrangements and may be members of regional and global institutions designed to facilitate cooperation and conflict resolution.[1]

Variation I: The bipolar balance of power

The dominant image animating U.S. statecraft from the late 1940s to the late 1960s was that of a two-sided balance of power. Most of the nation-states were seen as gravitating around either of the two magnetic superpowers, the United States and the Soviet Union. The political coalescence of the lesser powers around one or other of the superpowers was generally thought to provide a useful antidote to the otherwise anarchic tendencies of the highly decentralized balance-of-power system that twice during the twentieth century plunged human society into world war. The capacity of the older balance-of-power system to deter wars was weak, given its shifting alliances of uncertain commitment and credibility. In the bipolar variant, however, the greater certainty about who was in whose camp was supposed to provide a stronger deterrent to aggression.

Truman's secretary of state, Dean Acheson, and Eisenhower's secretary of state, John Foster Dulles, welcomed and encouraged the two-way polarization of the balance of power for the greater predictability and stability it presumably brought to international relations. Such a bipolar system would make it less likely that the rival superpowers would miscalculate the degree of commitment each had to smaller allies.

Top United States foreign policy makers during the Kennedy-Johnson years saw bipolarity as a means of discouraging the spread of nuclear weapons. If each superpower was a credible protector of virtually all countries not in the rival superpower's camp, then there would be much less of an incentive for the lesser powers to acquire their own nuclear deterrents. Similarly, bipolarity provided a rationale for maintaining centralized command and control over the nuclear arsenals in each coalition.

By the late 1960s, however, the concept of a bipolar balance of power no longer matched the pattern of international alignments. China had broken from the Soviet coalition and regarded the USSR as even more of an enemy than the United States. The West European countries and Japan were pursuing their own interests independently of, and sometimes at cross-purposes with, the United States—not only on important international economic issues but also in political dealings with the Soviet Union and the Third World. A majority of the Third World countries professed to be nonaligned with either superpower. Henry Kissinger, in an influential essay written for the Brookings Institution before he was appointed Nixon's national security adviser, described the world as still bipolar militarily but "multipolar" politically.[2] In office, under Nixon and Ford, Kissinger attempted to fashion a U.S. foreign policy responsive to these emerging—post bipolar—international alignments and antagonisms.

The Carter administration initially attempted to carry forward the adaptation of United States policy to the growing complexity of international alignments; but the visible maturing of the massive Soviet military buildup that had been underway since the Cuban missile crisis in addition to what appeared to be an increasing Soviet tendency to assert power aggressively beyond the confines of the Warsaw Pact moved Carter back to policies emphasizing the central role of the U.S.-Soviet power competition in world politics.

The bipolar model of world politics once again provided the organizing concepts for United States foreign policy as the Reagan administration took office in 1981 on a platform pledging a strong response to Soviet expansionism. All around the globe, events and U.S. interests would be viewed in an East-West context. In the Middle East and the Persian Gulf, efforts were launched to realign countries with the United States under a so-called strategic consensus that the primary threat to their independence and security came not from their local adversaries but from the Soviet Union and that, therefore, local conflicts—Arabs versus Israelis, Sunni versus Shi'ite Muslims, radical versus moderates—should be subordinated to countering the common enemy. The military and economic assistance programs of the United States would again give priority to helping those foreign governments that would join the refurbished coalition to contain Soviet expansion and that were determined to counter Marxist-Leninist movements within their own countries.

For its adherents, the fact that many countries and many local conflicts do not fit neatly into the bipolar balance of power is no reason to discard it as a model. Rather, United States grand strategies and particular policies should be designed to reenergize the magnetic pull of the East-West polarity on countries and political movements because this will provide a more stable and predictable international order and a better ability on the part of the anti-communist side to husband and concentrate its strength to contain the Soviet, Marxist-Leninist side over the long haul ahead.

Variation II: A concert of great powers

This pattern of international relations has been championed most prominently by Henry Kissinger and resembles in many respects the kind of world order instituted by the European statesmen of the nineteenth century following the defeat of Napoleon Bonaparte—the period of diplomacy that Kissinger wrote about in his scholarly study, *A World Restored: The Politics of Conservatism in a Revolutionary Age.*[3] Rather than being based on a long-term polarization of the world into two rival coalitions, the "concert" system contemplates a continuing negotiating process among the powers to produce adjustments in their power and spheres of influence that will prevent any one or a combination of them from dominating the others. The concert system is itself a variant of the "Classical Balance of Power" prevailing in Europe during the eighteenth century, characterized by shifting alliances to preserve an equilibrium of power that would discourage imperialistic states from attempts to dominate the rest.

The concert differs from the eighteenth century Classical Balance of Power, however, in that the classical system was supposed to be largely self-balancing—that is, states would realign themselves automatically and augment their military forces against an expansionist power threatening to overturn the balance. The concert, by contrast, is supposed to keep the system in balance by *negotiations* on the distribution and redistribution of power among the states. The hallmark of the concert system is a shared concept of the system's rules and the existing distribution of power as legitimate. Its preferred mode of operation is *conference diplomacy*—frequent consultations between the great powers to positively exploit opportunities for cooperation and to avoid the miscalculations of vital interests that could draw them into war against one another.

Such a concept underlay Kissinger's efforts in the early 1970s to institute consultative relationships between the United States and the Soviet Union and the United States and China.

In the detente with the Soviet Union and the rapprochement with China, Kissinger was following initiatives already begun by West Germany (under the *Ostpolitik* policies of chancellors Ludwig Erhard and Willy Brandt) and France (under the "Third Force" policies of President Charles deGaulle). Thus the movement toward East-West accommodation was also a movement out of the bippolar division of the world into a multipolar system, including the West Europeans and Japan as principal powers along with the United States, the USSR, and China.

A major objection to managing the balance of power through a concert of great powers is that such an approach cannot avoid alienating those countries that are not deemed important enough to be part of the concert. When regular consultations about how to run the international system were initiated between Nixon and Brezhnev in the early period of detente, other countries alleged that the superpowers were attempting to set up a "condominium" or "duopoly" of power to run the world. If China were to be in the consultative group (a remote possibility because of the bitter Sino-Soviet split), on what grounds would she be included? Population?—but then India, with a population vastly exceeding the United States or the Soviet Union should also be admitted. The possession of nuclear weapons?—but then countries with a nuclear weapons potential would have a special incentive to produce and deploy them. GNP?—but then the consultative group becomes a rich country club, and the North-South polarization is worsened. Or if some combination of economic characteristics, making for a major impact on the global economy, becomes the criterion for great power status, so that important energy producers, for example, could be included, then the regional rivals of these countries may feel particularly resentful. (If Venezuela, why not Brazil or Argentina? If Nigeria, why not Zaire? If Indonesia, why not Vietnam and Australia? If Saudi Arabia, why not Egypt? and so on.)

Despite these difficulties, much of the necessary international coordination among countries does take place in such limited membership concerts, as it were, formed around specialized clusters of issues. And the United States, typically, is both an influential sponsor and participant in these groups.

There is, for example, the so-called London Suppliers Group of the main countries exporting nuclear materials and nuclear technology. The London Suppliers Group meets periodically to formulate guidelines for regulating the competition among them in the selling of nuclear wares for peaceful use. Agreed guidelines are important for restricting the transfer of nuclear materials and processing equipment that could be converted into weapons, lest some of the competing supplier countries attempt to win customers by being less stringent about the risks of nuclear weapons proliferation.

Another limited member concert is the annual seven-country economic summit that since 1975 has brought together the heads of government of the principal noncommunist industrial countries—the United States, Canada, Britain, France, West Germany, Italy, and Japan—in an attempt to harmonize their often conflicting approaches to economic matters affecting them all. These meetings are a recognition of the deep interdependence of their economies, of the fact that inflation, unemployment, major economic growth, and recession in one part of the advanced industrial world have major impacts on other parts. Accordingly, the typical agenda of these annual economic summits includes not only the international subjects of trade and monetary relations but also matters traditionally regarded as purely domestic, such as their respective interest-rate policies and their basic fiscal and budgetary strategies. The economic summits also are used to coordinate basic policy—political as well as economic—toward the communist countries and the Third World. The record of accomplishments at the summits, however, is very slight and is reflected in their communiqués, which are for the most part abstract and vague general statements designed to obscure their disagreements.

As shown in the more detailed discussion in Chapter 4 of United States policies toward industrialized countries, the vision of a harmonious concert of these countries providing the central ordering structure for the world is a delusion inconsistent with the facts of international life. Each of the seven, even the four that are co-members of the European Community, has its own special cooperative and adversary relationships with the Soviet Union, China, various oil producing countries, particular developing countries, and with one another. The seven-nation summits, not surprisingly, exhibit as much dissonance as harmony. Attempts to concert policies among the seven may be necessary to world order, but they are hardly sufficient. Despite the sometimes high blown rhetoric surrounding meetings at the industrial summit, the participating statesmen in their more candid remarks and their actual policies show themselves to be acting more in terms of the polyarchical vision characterized later in this chapter.

World Peace through World Law

Some of the rhetoric of American presidents, secretaries of state, and other high foreign policy officials implies a vision of a global system of law and order analogous to the constitutional system that prevails domestically in the United States. Conflicts of interest between countries, possibly even between individuals and groups who live in different countries, would be resolved through debate in decisions by representative international institutions and enforced by international courts. The official rhetoric usually goes no farther than to suggest that the structure for such a world rule of law is already present in the United Nations Charter and that if the nations of the world would truly adhere to the charter's provisions, humankind could realize its dreams of international peace and justice. But within the policy community and the fraternity of international lawyers visions of a more radical transformation of the world polity also can be encountered—visions of a full-blown world government more powerful than any of the separate nation-states, enforcing the decisions of a parliament of man on nations and individuals alike.

Variant I: Relying more on the United Nations

The United States can help advance the goal of a peaceful and just international order, it is argued, if it will only channel more of its international dealings through the United Nations.[4] It should attempt to enhance the authority of the collective security and dispute-resolution processes of the world organization by relying on them more than it has in recent years. Similarly, it should be willing to subject the overall management of the global economy to the general oversight and standards of the most broadly representative bodies of the UN. Some advocates of relying more on the

United Nations see this as a way station toward a more centralized world law and order structure, leading eventually to a world government. Others regard the UN system as consistent with an enduring society of sovereign nation-states, as an instrument for moderating the anarchic tendencies of that society and for facilitating cooperation among the states of a world system that it is best to keep decentralized.

A careful reading of the United Nations Charter reveals it to be very much a part of the existing international system of sovereign nation-states. The acts of the United Nations are resolutions, not laws, passed by bodies in which each national government has a vote. The member governments are obligated to implement the resolutions passed by the United Nations, but there is no mechanism in the system to compel them to do so unless the Security Council finds that a state's nonadherence to the terms of a particular resolution is a threat to international peace and security and mandates the formation of a multinational military force to compel compliance.

Any UN enforcement action, because it is supposed to be under the aegis of the Security Council, requires the concurrence of the council's five permanent members (the United States, the Soviet Union, China, the United Kingdom, and France)—a requirement which, because of the bitter rivalries between some of the Big Five, normally is impossible to satisfy.

Despite this inhibiting veto arrangement, the Security Council in 1950 did mandate a UN enforcement action to be directed by the United States against the North Korean invasion of South Korea. The enabling resolutions passed by virtue of the extraordinary circumstance of the Soviet Union being absent temporarily from its seat on the council. (China's seat was still occupied by the anticommunist government in exile on Taiwan.)*

The Security Council also authorized policing actions in 1961 in the newly independent and strife-torn Congo, through rather vaguely worded resolutions that the UN Secretary General inter-

*To bypass a veto on further UN actions of this sort, the United States persuaded the UN General Assembly to pass the so-called Uniting for Peace Resolution of 1950, giving the General Assembly the authority to mandate peace and security enforcement actions when the Security Council was unable to act.

preted permissively as allowing for military operations against the secessionist province of Katanga.

Both the Korean and the Congolese enforcement actions, however, are highly controversial for their legality under the charter and remain exceptions to the general norm that the United Nations can act within the territorial jurisdiction of any country only with the approval of that country's government.

Characteristically, the United Nations does respect the sovereignty of its member governments and refrains from actions within the territory of any country that are opposed by that country's government. Thus in 1967, the United Nations Emergency Force, which had been stationed on Egyptian soil to prevent hostile encounters between the Egyptians and the Israelis, was removed by UN Secretary General U Thant at the behest of Egyptian President Nasser (an act which precipitated the Six-Day Arab-Israeli War). And consistent with the norm of national sovereignty and the absence of supranational enforcement mechanisms, the United Nations, despite a long string of condemnatory resolutions against the Republic of South Africa for its racial apartheid (separation) policies and despite resolutions requesting UN members to boycott goods produced in South Africa, has not been able to bring any direct sanctions against the government in Pretoria to compel it to modify its racial policies.

Variant II: World government

A more drastic restructuring of the nation-state system than that provided for in the existing United Nations Charter is urged by some Americans, either explicitly or implicitly in proposals in particular fields such as disarmament or global economic development. The model for a more centralized and authoritative world organization most frequently resembles the domestic constitutional systems of developed industrial democracies. As argued by Grenville Clark and Louis B. Sohn, architects of one of the more detailed blueprints for a new world structure:

> It is futile to expect genuine peace until there is . . . adoption on a world-wide basis of the measures and institutions which the experience of countries has shown to be essential for the maintenance of

> law and order, namely, clearly stated law against violence, courts to interpret and apply that law and police to enforce it.[5]

The Clark and Sohn plan. Clark and Sohn would provide a revised United Nations with substantial law making and law enforcement powers, but these would be limited to the fields of war prevention, common resource management, and environmental protection. Legislation and law enforcement in other fields would be reserved to the nations and their peoples. But the new world law in the enumerated fields would apply

> to all individual persons in the world as well as to all the nations—to the end that in case violations by individuals without the support of their governments, the world law could be invoked directly against them without the necessity of indicting a whole nation or a group of nations.[6]

Clark and Sohn would lodge the basic laws of the strengthened world authority in its charter, so that members would know their primary rights and obligations before ratifying them and joining.

The principal institution for implementing the charter, through legislation and directives to other world agencies, would be the General Assembly, where member countries would be alloted seats according to population (subject to the proviso that each country would have at least one seat and no country would have more than thirty seats).

A seventeen-member Executive Council would be elected by the General Assembly and would be responsible to and removable by it, much as the British Cabinet is responsible to the House of Commons. The four largest members of the General Assembly (assumed to be China, India, the United States, and the Soviet Union) would be entitled at all times to a seat on the Executive Council, and five of the ten next largest countries would serve in rotation. The remaining eight seats would be chosen by the Assembly from all the other members. No one country would have a veto; rather, action on important matters would require the affirmative vote of a majority of the nine largest members of the council plus a majority of the eight other members of the council.

The International Court of Justice would have compulsory jurisdiction, including authority to decide cases even if parties should refuse to come before the court, over disputes referred to it by the General Assembly and over questions regarding the interpretation of the charter, treaties or other international agreements, and acts of the United Nations.

A world police force, with a standing component of up to 400,000 full-time professionals (plus a reserve of up to 600,000) would be directed by a five-member military staff committee immediately responsible to the Executive Council. (Clark and Sohn assume and provide for a six-year process to effect complete disarmament of all countries, down to small internal police forces. All modern weapons, including nuclear weapons, would be turned over to the United Nations.) The troops, the commanders, and the military staff committee would be drawn from the smaller members of the United Nations, but the world police force would be more powerful than any of the internal public safety forces allowed to the member countries.

Popular demands upon the existing national governments to institute the attempted transfer of authority and power to such a world government, Clark and Sohn forecast, will be generated mainly out of the spreading awareness that the anarchic nation-state system is bound to bring on a global nuclear holocaust.

The "preferred world" of the World Order Models Project. The publications of the World Order Models Project of the Institute for World Order, directed by international lawyer Saul H. Mendlovitz, are also in the world federalist tradition exemplified by the work of Clark and Sohn.[7] Although the project has solicited models of world order and justice from around the world, it is the design for a new world system developed by the American international lawyer and political activist Richard Falk that is most vigorously disseminated by the project and its parent organization.[8]

Falk's Preferred World Polity, as he calls it, is designed to serve four basic values: the minimization of large-scale collective violence; the maximization of social and economic well-being; the realization of fundamental human rights and conditions of political justice; and the maintenance and rehabilitation of ecological quality. A World Polity Association is to be built around "a central guidance system" having all the attributes of a world supranational state (though Falk, wanting to avoid knee-jerk reactions to his schemes, avoids using the terms world government or world state). Its central legislative body would be a three-chamber General Assembly with different bases of representation in each chamber and checks-and-balances voting arrangements between the chambers to ensure that the world laws are based as much as possible on the consent of the governed.[9]

The World Polity would have armed forces of its own to ensure that the legislative and judicial decisions of its institutions are adhered to and to enforce the disarmament agreement that Falk assumes will have preceded the establishment of the new system. Falk hopes that most of the enforcement will be through nonviolent techniques, but he does not rule out the use of violent weapons by the security forces of the World Polity and would even allow it to maintain a nuclear arsenal for countering groups that might have retained or built weapons of mass destruction in violation of the disarmament agreement.

Falk recognizes that because his design for a new world order presupposes a substantial modification of the state system, it will remain only an abstract idea on the bookshelf unless the "advocates of the new system are aligned with important social and political forces within the existing structures."[10] A political "transition process," therefore, must be an essential part of the design, the objective of this process being to create constituencies for the new order that, by virtue of their size and political influence, will compel those with formal authority in the prevailing state system to negotiate the required structural transformations. Falk envisages three stages in this development.

1. *An era of consciousness raising.* The general population and special interest groups are educated to realize that their security and other values cannot be adequately maintained in the existing world system and that a drastic change along the lines of Falk's Preferred World Polity is necessary.

2. *An era of political mobilization.* The new consciousness is converted into active interest-group lobbying and electoral politics to pressure established political elites and to put forward new leaders in countries throughout the world so that the national governments (which remain the mainstay of the existing system

until it is transformed) become committed to the required institution building at the global level.

3. *An era of transformation.* The disarmament of the nation-states and a simultaneous buildup of the prescribed world institutions is undertaken and completed.

Falk and his colleagues recognize that the contemplated effort at consciousness raising must contend against powerful incentives, sanctions, and doctrines reinforcing majority acceptance of the status quo. And in their pessimistic moments they grant that it may take a catastrophe—a worldwide economic collapse, a global ecological crisis, or World War III—to shake loose the prevailing attachments to the nation-state system. Even so, they continue their writing and speaking to persuade as many as they can that the existing system is irrational and will ultimately destroy itself and that a new system is necessary and ultimately feasible.

A World of Regions

The growing realization in the decades following World War II that human society is nowhere near being able to institute the world order designs of either the advocates of a world state or the champions of a substantially strengthened United Nations has been accompanied by the flowering of the idea of regional integration as an alternative to the universal designs.[11] For some, the regionalist alternative is a way station on the road to a universal system of governance.[12] For others it is a sufficient concept of world order, the idea being that wherever there is a voluntary intermeshing of societies across nation-state lines, it is likely that disputes between the involved nations will be inhibited from escalating to war and that when there is a intraregional conflict, the presence of conflict control mechanisms within a region will reduce incentives for superpower intervention and confrontation.[13]

Indeed, the regionalist idea has been the most popular idealistic concept animating the international activists in the United States policy establishment since the late 1940s when it became obvious that the cold war was probably here to stay for the indefinite future. It was not enough to be simply *against* the expansion of communism. Regional institution building thus became the *positive* rationale for some of the major cold war initiatives of the United States—the Marshall Plan, NATO, and various regional associations in Latin America, the Middle East, and Africa.

The high positive value placed on regional political integration was reflected in the strong support of official Washington for the consolidation of the European Economic Community (EEC), even though the regional common market would mean discrimination against imports from the United States as the EEC moved to achieve free trade among its members. (See the discussion in Chapter 4 of the community building approach toward dealing with the advanced industrial countries.)

Since the 1960s, however, the regionalist concept has suffered a decline in the United States policy community. Experience with the European Community and with other regional efforts has shown that substantial political unification is a long way off, even for the Europeans, and that negative attitudes toward outsiders often constitutes a large part of the incentive for regional cooperation, and this may work against concrete economic and security interests of the United States.

For Western Europe, the most optimistic forecasts for the remainder of the twentieth century envision a loose confederacy with minimal supranational functions, primarily for coordinating monetary and trade policies. The enlargement of the starting group of seven countries (France, the Federal Republic of Germany, Italy, Belgium, the Netherlands, Luxembourg, and Portugal) to include Britain, Denmark, Ireland, and Greece has diluted the political-cultural homogeneity of the original continental core and encouraged the intensification of crosspressures. There is as much dissonance today in the EEC as there is harmony; and when harmony is attained by EEC members on international issues, it frequently is engendered by disputes with the United States.

Elsewhere the prospects are even less favorable for regional integration because the preconditions of a common political orientation, a generally homogeneous level of economic development, and basic trust between the members of their cooperative intentions are inadequately developed.

The members of the Association of Southeast Asian Nations (ASEAN), for example, have little in common apart from the fact that they all border the strategically important waterways connecting western and southern Asia with the vast open Pacific and that most of their peoples have a racial physiognomy which is basically similar. The differences in national culture are large. Indonesia is primarily Muslim; Thailand is 95 percent Buddhist; and the Philippines are 75 percent Roman Catholic. The only language in which the leaders of the region can communicate with each other is English—but not because of a common colonial experience. Indonesia was part of the Dutch empire; Singapore and Malaysia were mostly under British control; the Philippines were under Spanish and then U.S. rule; and Thailand has been an independent country for two centuries. The former French colonies of Indochina (Vietnam, Laos, and Cambodia) do not belong to ASEAN, and their professedly communist regimes are alienated from the other governments in the region.

Another regional organization, sometimes pointed to as an embryo from which more elaborate and extensive international integration could develop, is the Organization of American States (OAS). Almost all the countries of the hemisphere belong to this twenty-six–member organization, except Canada, which has only observer status, and Cuba, which has been excluded from formal participation since 1962. In effect, the OAS is the institutional vehicle through which the United States can simultaneously interact with most of the Latin American countries. The hemispheric policies of the United States are often the focus of discussion in the OAS—United States policies of economic assistance and U.S. policies toward communist-oriented governments and movements. Motivated to maximize its influence in the hemisphere, to limit the growing economic competition from the European Community and Japan, and to limit the influence of Cuba and the Soviet Union, the United States usually attempts to gain OAS endorsement of its policies. The Latin members, motivated to restrain the United States from political (and military) intervention and from economically dominating them, are pleased to sustain the U.S. interest in OAS endorsements for this compels the United States to be more accountable to them than might otherwise be the case. Indeed, the main source of solidarity among the Latin Americans is their common resentment at U.S. tendencies to treat the hemisphere as a U.S. sphere of influence.

But even the common resentment of the "colossus to the North" is a flimsy basis for Latin American unity. The differences in domestic regime and ideology are so wide among the countries of Latin America (some are military dictatorships, some capitalist oligarchies, some representative democracies, some socialist autocracies) that their supposed solidarity rarely operates on matters of importance to any of them.

Within Latin America there are special groups of countries whose goals are to coordinate their commercial policies and to reduce barriers to trade among themselves—notably the four-member Central American Common Market (Costa Rica, El Salvador, Guatemala, and Nicaragua) and the five-member Andean Group in South America (Bolivia, Colombia, Ecuador, Peru, and Venezuela). But domestic turmoil and local rivalries are currently too pervasive in these regional subgroups to allow for any substantial progress even toward harmonizing their trading relationships.

In short, where a common regional front has been forged, as among the Third World oil producers or among the Arab antagonists of Israel, the regional coalition as often as not is held together by anti-American sentiments. United States officials in recent years have concluded that they usually can make more headway in obtaining cooperation with U.S. policies if they deal with individual countries rather than with any bloc of countries.

Polyarchy

An alternative to all of these grand designs is to dispense with efforts to remold the world to fit United States preferences and, instead, to pragmatically adapt U.S. policy to the existing realities of world politics. The realities present a more complex pattern than the pattern assumed to prevail in either the balance-of-power system or a highly centralized world order.

The term *polyarchy* is more descriptive than the more popular term anarchy, for the latter means literally *no* rule. Polyarchy means *many* sources and patterns of rule, authority, and power. It recognizes the hold on people of various kinds of associations and identities (nation-states, ethnic groupings, religion, transnational ideological movements, multinational corporations, economic class, and professions) and the considerable role in world society played by intergovernmental institutions (of military alliances like NATO and the Warsaw Pact, of economic blocs like the EEC, the Soviet-run COMECON, and OPEC) and functional organizations (like the International Monetary Fund and the World Bank, the General Agreements on Tariffs and Trade, the International Telecommunciations Union, the International Civil Aeronautics Association, and the International Maritime Consultative Organization).*

A foreign policy based upon this assumption of a complex polyarchy attempts to maximize United States world influence by positively exploiting the opportunities available to the U.S. in a wide range of these associations. The United States, the most global of the global powers, has tangible interests and assets in virtually every region and economic sector of the world. Some of its people have ancestral or current familial ties with nearly every nationality and religious group.

* Such a polyarchic structure of world politics is called a "New Mediaevalism" by Hendly Bull in his book *The Anarchical Society: A Study of Order in World Politics* (New York: Columbia University Press, 1977). Western Christendom in the Middle Ages is Bull's historical analog:

> If modern states were to come to share their authority over their citizens, and their ability to command their loyalties, on the one hand with regional and world authorities, and on the other hand with sub-state and sub-national authorities, to such an extent that the concept of sovereignty ceased to be applicable, then a neo-mediaeval form of universal political order might be said to have emerged. (pp. 254–255)

Bull is doubtful of the capacity of such a polyarchic society to provide adequately the basic amenities of social life for most peoples of the world. "If it were anything like the precedent of Western Christendom, it would contain more uniquitous and continuous violence and insecurity than does the modern states system." (pp. 264–277)

Building on these natural connections with other countries, the United States, operating under the assumption that polyarchy is a desirable state of affairs, would pursue an inclusionary rather than an exclusionary foreign policy. Instead of cultivating international alliances, which always are implicitly, if not explicitly, against some country or grouping of countries, the United States would pursue a basic international strategy of nonalignment. No long-term entangling alliances but flexibility to form and participate in a wide range of associations and temporary coalitions, reflecting the multiple and often crosscutting interests of the peoples of the United States—these would be the hallmarks of a realistic foreign policy pragmatically adaptive to the polyarchic patterns of world politics.

The virtues of this grand design are also its limitations. Diverse international interests and multiple foreign friendships make it more difficult to mobilize the country behind coercive diplomacy when this becomes necessary for there usually will be some segments of the American polity that will lobby against alienating their foreign partners, friends, or brothers and sisters. For example, the United States farm lobby has been an obstacle to embargoing grain shipments to the USSR, which was the most salient nonmilitary sanction against the Soviets in response to their military invasion of Afghanistan and their suppression of Polish nationalism. And the American Jewish community presents a weighty force against U.S. governmental opposition to the way the Israelis prosecute their conflicts with the Arab countires; at the same time, a fear of alienating the oil producing countries of the Middle East prevents the United States from overt opposition to Arab actions that otherwise we might strongly oppose. Flexibility, the presumed virtue of nonalignment, can lead to paralysis in crises, as positive ties to other countries are reflected in domestic lobbies capable of blocking decisive action.

In response to these criticisms of world polyarchy, it can be argued that the model is simply a picture of the frustratingly complex real world from which there apparently is no escape. Better to attempt to make the best of this imperfect world than to build illusory castles of a new (or romantically resurrected) world order and to bring on the inevitable bitterness and cynicism when the illusions crash.

The Global City

Optimists envision a transformation of the existing polyarchic pattern into a worldwide community in which the complex interdependencies are matched by political and legal processes and institutions, making people accountable to one another to the extent that they affect each other's lives. The model for such a world system is the ethnically diverse modern greater metropolitan area, such as the New York metropolitan area or greater Los Angeles. These megalopoli comprise numerous municipal and special-purpose jurisdictions, many of which overlap, but they lack a strong central government for the whole metropolitan area. The global city could exhibit an analogous structure: Public services—public safety, education, cultural activities, public utilities—would be largely provided and financed within locally demarcated political units (most of them, still, the nation-states of the traditional international system); but where there is a need for a high degree of coordination across national jurisdictions—such as in the transportation and communications fields, in the use of "commons" (the oceans, the atmosphere, and outer space), and in the regulation of transnational economic activity—multinational or transnational institutions, with memberships and spans of control congruent with the interdependent relationships, would be accorded the responsibility for coordination, rule making, and even rule enforcement.[14]

Insofar as the global city would develop worldwide networks of accountability and as these would involve coordination of activities and the enforcement of rules across fields—say, a global standardization of responsibilities of multinational corporations to local populations, including minimum wage and labor welfare benefits, safety and environmental standards, taxes, and responsibilities to their stockholders—the global institutions would tend to resemble those of the more full-blown world government models outlined above.

The resemblance to world government, however, works against the appeal of the global city and probably is the main reason why it has not been explicitly embraced by top United States officials as the vision animating U.S. foreign policy. Political leaders are reluctant to challenge the deeply ingrained resistance of their constituents to the transfer of control over their daily lives to evermore remote institutions. Those directing U.S. foreign policy also perceive that the global city concept, particularly as formulated by Brzezinski in *Between Two Ages*, strikes foreigners as a design for reasserting U.S. hegemony. This is because the most institutionalizing of the growing interdependence would come first in the high technology fields of communications and transportation where the United States is preeminent and presumably, therefore, could dominate the new legal and political institutions.

The anticipated negative domestic and foreign reactions to the global city idea has kept policy makers from overtly embracing it, but nonetheless the concept is strongly in evidence in much U.S. foreign policy directed toward managing the increasing international interdependence.

Notes

1. Hedley Bull, *The Anarchical Society: A Study of Order in World Politics* (New York: Columbia University Press, 1977).
2. Henry A. Kissinger, "Central Issues of American Foreign Policy," in Kermit Gordon, ed., *Agenda for the Nation* (Washington, D.C.: The Brookings Institution, 1968), pp. 585–614.
3. Henry A. Kissinger, *A World Restored: The Politics of Conservatism in a Revolutionary Age* (New York: Grosset and Dunlap, Universal Library, 1964).
4. Relevant publications of the United Nations Association are discussed in the note on sources, p. 208.
5. Grenville Clark and Louis B. Sohn, *Introduction to World Peace Through World Law* (Chicago: World Without War Publications, 1973), pp. 11–12.
6. *Ibid.*
7. Saul H. Mendlovitz, ed., *On the Creation of a Just World Order: Preferred Worlds for the 1990s* (New York: The Free Press, 1975).

8. Richard A. Falk, *A Study of Future Worlds* (New York: The Free Press, 1975), pp. 224–248.
9. *Ibid.*, pp. 242–248.
10. *Ibid.*
11. See Ernst B. Haas, *The Unity of Europe* (Stanford: Stanford University Press, 1958); Karl W. Deutsch, *Political Community in the North Atlantic Area* (Princeton: Princeton University Press, 1957).
12. Amatai Etzioni, *The Hard Way to Peace* (New York: Crowell Collier, 1962).
13. See especially William P. Bundy, "International Security Today," *Foreign Affairs*, Vol. 53, No. 1 (October 1974), pp. 24–44.
14. Relevant "global city" literature is discussed in the note on sources, pp. 208–209.

Notes for Further Reading

These notes are for the lay person or student who would like suggestions for additional readings available in most general libraries.

The issue-by-issue approach of this book can be complemented by chronologically organized accounts of recent U.S. foreign policy that sustain the presidential perspective. Modesty does not preclude my recommending the only overview of the period since World War II that analyzes the choices facing the country as the president and his top foreign policy advisers saw them—namely, Seyom Brown, *The Faces of Power: Constancy and Change in United States Foreign Policy from Truman to Reagan* (New York: Columbia University Press, 1983).

The best way to gain an appreciation of the presidential perspective on foreign policy issues administration-by-administration is from the memoirs of the presidents and other high officials.

Harry S. Truman wrote two lively and informative volumes: *Memoirs: Year of Decisions* (New York: Doubleday, 1955); and *Memoirs: Years of Trial and Hope* (New York: Doubleday, 1956). Truman's secretary of state, Dean Acheson, left a gracefully written account of his experiences in *Present at the Creation* (New York: Norton, 1969).

Dwight D. Eisenhower's remarkably candid public record of his presidency is in his *Mandate for Change: The White House Years 1953–1956* (New York: Doubleday, 1963); and *Waging Peace: The White House Years 1956–1961* (New York: Doubleday, 1965).

Unfortunately, the most eloquent president of the recent period, John F. Kennedy, did not live to give the world his own account. But his special counsel and chief speech writer, Theodore Sorensen, has provided the closest thing to what might have been the JFK memoirs in his *Kennedy* (New York: Harper, 1965). Another adviser's detailed reconstruction of Kennedy's view of the world and decision making is Arthur M. Schlesinger Jr., *A Thousand Days: John F. Kennedy in the White House* (Boston: Houghton Mifflin, 1965).

President Lyndon B. Johnson left us his version of the events of his administration in *The Vantage Point* (New York: Popular Library, 1971)—a not particularly candid reconstruction. LBJ's more candid recollections appear in a psychological biography by Doris Kearns, *Lyndon Johnson and the American Dream* (New York: Harper & Row, 1976), based on intensive interviews of Johnson after he retired to his Texas ranch. President Johnson's foreign policy was dominated by United States involvement in the Vietnam war. *The Pentagon Papers: The Department of Defense History of United States Decisionmaking on Vietnam,* Senator Mike Gravel, ed. (Boston: Beacon Press, 1971) contains most of the important (previously secret) memoranda and position papers of high officials responsible for U.S. policies in Vietnam.

Richard M. Nixon's strong suit as president was foreign policy, and this is in evidence in his memoir *RN* (New York: Grosset & Dunlop, 1978)—an unevenly selective and transparently self-serving account of his preoccupations in the Oval Office. Henry Kissinger's memoirs—*The White House Years* (Boston: Little, Brown, 1979); *Years of Upheaval* (Boston: Little, Brown, 1982); and a third volume forthcoming—are indispensable for insights into the thinking of the top decision makers during the Nixon and Ford presidencies; but because these books are, as it were, a massive force feeding of the author's briefs for the wisdom of his official actions, a useful antidote is the highly critical exposé of Kissinger by Seymour M. Hersch, *The Price of Power: Kissinger in the Nixon White House* (New York: Summit Books, 1983). Gerald R. Ford, *A Time to Heal* (New York: Harper & Row and Reader's Digest, 1979) accurately reflects the limitations of the presidential world view from 1974 through 1976.

The Carter administration has already produced three major memoirs: Jimmy Carter's *Keeping Faith: Memoirs of a President* (New York: Bantam Books, 1982); and two other often contradictory accounts—one by Zbigniew Brzezinski, *Power and Principle:*

Memoirs of the National Security Adviser 1977–1981 (New York: Farrar, Strauss, Giroux, 1983); and the other by Cyrus Vance, *Hard Choices: Critical Years in American Foreign Policy* (New York: Simon and Schuster, 1983).

The current official word on United States foreign policies is issued almost daily in the Department of State series *Current Policy* and monthly in the *Department of State Bulletin.* All of the president's public statements, including his news conferences, are published each week in the *Weekly Compilation of Presidential Documents* issued by the Office of the President.

Chapter 1: Contending Concepts of the National Interest

A cogent assertion of the geopolitical foundations of the national interest is Hans J. Morgenthau, *In Defense of the National Interest* (New York: Knopf, 1951). The *Annual Report of the Secretary of Defense* (presented to Congress early each year by the Pentagon) usually projects presumably vital interests from geopolitical concepts. Reactions by skeptical analysts and members of Congress are found in the yearly *Hearings* on Defense Department authorization requests before the Senate armed services and foreign relations committees and the House armed services and international relations committees. A highly circumscribed definition of vital national interests is presented by George Kennan in *The Cloud of Danger: Current Realities of American Foreign Policy* (Boston: Little, Brown, 1977).

The notion that the national interest is the sum of the particular interests of the American people is reflected every four years in the foreign policy planks of the national platforms of the Democratic and Republican parties (usually available directly from the national headquarters of each party if not in the libraries). It is implicit in the Washington lobbying activities of many ethnic and economic interest groups, analyzed in Thomas M. Frank and Edward Weisband, *Foreign Policy and Congress* (New York: Oxford University Press, 1979) and in James A. Nathan and James K. Oliver, *Foreign Policy Making and the American Political System* (Little, Brown, 1983), especially Chapter 8 on "Private Power and American Foreign Policy." The most explicit public endorsement of this populist idea by a high government official in recent years was by President Carter in his commencement address at Notre Dame University, May 22, 1977, *Public Papers of the Presidents of the United States, Jimmy Carter, 1977* (Washington, D.C.: Government Printing Office, 1977), Vol. I, pp. 955–962. A criticism of the extreme pluralist, or populist approach to foreign policy making is Samuel P. Huntington's chapter in Michael J. Crozier, Samuel P. Huntington, and Joji Watanuki, *The Crisis of Democracy: Report on the Governability of Democracies to the Trilateral Commission* (New York: New York University Press, 1975).

Precursors of the contemporary view that the national interest is part and parcel of the world interest are analyzed in Robert E. Osgood, *Ideals and Self-Interest in America's Foreign Relations: The Great Transformation of the Twentieth Century* (Chicago: University of Chicago Press, 1953). Most presidents ritualistically sound this theme when addressing the United Nations. See, for example, John F. Kennedy's address before the General Assembly, September 20, 1963, *Public Papers of the Presidents of the United States, John F. Kennedy, 1963* (Washington, D.C.: Government Printing Office, 1964), pp. 693–698. A systematically argued case for a world interest rationale for U.S. foreign policy is developed by Robert C. Johansen, *The National Interest and the Human Interest: An Analysis of U.S. Foreign Policy* (Princeton: Princeton University Press, 1980).

Chapter 2: Who Decides?

All of the official memoirs referred to above, in addition to being accounts of the assumptions in United States foreign policy, are rich with stories of how particular decisions were made—who was consulted and who was in the room at decision time. Kissinger's memoirs stand out from the rest, however, in reflections on who *should* be consulted and be in on the decisions, which is not surprising, for more than any other of the American statesmen of the past few decades he came under attack for being excessively elitist and evidently felt the need to defend himself.

A comprehensive, yet succinct, overview of most of the issues raised in this chapter is in James A. Nathan and James K. Oliver, *Foreign Policy Making and the American Political System* (Boston: Little, Brown, 1983). John Spanier and Eric M. Uslander also cover essentially the same ground in their clearly written *Foreign Policy and the Democratic Dilemmas* (New York: Holt, Rinehart and Winston, 1982). A somewhat more academically oriented discussion is provided by Charles W. Kegley, Jr. and Eugene R. Wittkoff in their *American Foreign Policy: Pattern and Process* (New York: St. Martin's, 1982).

The contest between the president and the Congress for control of foreign policy is well developed in the authoritative book by Cecil V. Crabb, Jr. and Pat M. Holt, *Invitation to Struggle: Congress, the President and Foreign Policy* (Washington: Congressional Quarterly Press, 1980). A solid collection of case studies of the legislative-executive rivalry on particular policy issues is provided by John Spanier and Joseph Nogee, eds., *Congress, the Presidency, and American Foreign Policy* (New York: Pergamon Press, 1981).

The role of the CIA is thoroughly examined in the *Final Report of the Select Committee to Study Governmental Operations with Respect to Intelligence Activities* (Washington, D.C.: Government Printing Office, 1976), 94th Congress, 2nd Session. The *Final Report* summarizes and quotes liberally from the voluminous hearings conducted by the Select Committee between 1974 and 1976.

For the problem of control of foreign policy decision making within the administration, see Morton H. Halperin, *Bureaucratic Politics and Foreign Policy* (Washington: Brookings Institution, 1974); and Alexander L. George, *Presidential Decisionmaking in Foreign Policy: The Effective Use of Information and Advice* (Boulder: Westview Press, 1980). Reflections on the management of foreign policy decisions within the Carter administration have been published by one of Carter's National Security Council officials, Robert E. Hunter, in his *Presidential Control of Foreign Policy: Management or Mishap?* (Washington: Center for Strategic and International Studies, Georgetown University, 1982), Vol. X, No. 91. A particularly lucid exposition of how the system works within the executive branch and of alternative proposals for reform, is provided by an academic with experience in the White House and the State Department: Lincoln Bloomfield, *The Foreign Policy Process: A Modern Primer* (Englewood Cliffs: Prentice-Hall, 1982).

Chapter 3: Dealing with the Soviet Union

An excellent compendium of papers covering the range of assumptions about Soviet intentions and capabilities analyzed in this chapter is provided by the Committee on Foreign Relations of the United States Senate in its publication *Perceptions: Relations Between the United States and the Soviet Union* (Washington, D.C.: Government Printing Office, 1981).

George Kennan's famous "X" (his pseudonym) article, "The Sources of Soviet Conduct," *Foreign Affairs,* Vol. XXV, No. 4 (July 1947), pp. 566–582, still provides a frame of reference for official U.S. policy and for most alternative views. The extent to which U.S. policies toward the Soviet Union from the late 1940s to the early 1980s have reflected or departed from the Kennan assumptions is analyzed by John Lewis Gaddis, *Strategies of Containment: A Critical Appraisal of Postwar American National Security Policy* (New York: Oxford University Press, 1982).

The most complete statement of the school of thought that attributes aggressive and malign intentions to the Soviet Union is the book by Robert Strausz-Hupé, William R. Kintner, James E. Dougherty, and Alvin J. Cottrell, *Protracted Conflict* (New York: Harper & Row, 1959). The views of this school have been reflected in the publications of the Committee on Present Danger (to which Ronald Reagan belonged and from which he drew most of his top foreign policy appointees), as, for example, *What Is the Soviet Union Up To?* (Washington: Committee on the Present Danger, 1977). See also Richard Pipes, *U.S.-Soviet Relations in the Era of Detente* (Boulder: Westview, 1981). The opposing point of view, that the Soviets are mainly interested in protecting the security of the USSR, is well represented by Richard J. Barnett, *The Giants: Russia and America* (New York: Simon & Schuster, 1978) and by Fred Warner Neal, ed., *Détente or Debacle: Common Sense in U.S.-Soviet Relations* (New York: W.W. Norton, 1979).

Henry Kissinger's rationale for pursuing a policy of détente toward the Soviet Union is scattered throughout his memoirs. However, his principal arguments are also found in his testimony to the Senate Foreign Relations Committee on September 19, 1974, which has been reprinted in Henry Kissinger, *American Foreign Policy*, third ed. (New York: W.W. Norton, 1977), pp. 141–176. The most cogent critique of Kissinger's views from the "hard line" school within the Republican party is G. Warren Nutter, *Kissinger's Grand Design* (Washington: American Enterprise Institute, 1975).

Within the Carter administration, Zbigniew Brzezinski and Cyrus Vance represented different approaches to dealing with the Soviet Union; Brzezinski's arguments now appear in *Power and Principle*, pp. 146–192; 316–353; and 426–469. Vance's are recounted in his *Hard Choices*, pp. 99–119; 349–367; and 384–397. Secretary Vance was giving voice to arguments developed by his principal adviser on Soviet affairs, Marshall D. Shulman, whose fundamental approach had been published a decade previously in his *Beyond the Cold War* (New Haven: Yale University Press, 1966).

Differing assessments of the utility of engaging the Soviet Union in arms control negotiations are typified by Richard Pipes, "Why the Soviet Union Thinks It Could Fight and Win a Nuclear War," *Commentary*, Vol. 64, No. 1 (July 1977), pp. 21–34; and Sidney D. Drell, "Arms Control: Is There Still Hope?" *Daedalus*, Vol. 109, No. 4 (Fall 1980), pp. 177–188.

Chapter 4: Managing the Relationship with China

The changing assumptions in United States policy toward China are traced in Peter P. Cheng, *China: U.S. Policy Since 1945* (Washington, D.C.: Congressional Quarterly Press, 1980). For the period leading up to the Nixon-Kissinger effort to normalize relations with the People's Republic of China, see A. Doak Barnett, *A New U.S. Policy Toward China* (Washington: Brookings Institution, 1971). For the persisting dilemmas, one can do no better than Banning Garrett, "China Policy and the Constraints of Triangular Logic," in

Kenneth A. Oye, Robert Lieber, Donald Rothchild, eds., *Eagle Defiant: United States Foreign Policy in the 1980s* (Boston: Little, Brown, 1983). The considerations prevailing in the Carter administration are recounted by the NSC official with primary responsibility for China policy under Brzezinski, Michel Oksenberg, who wrote "The Dynamics of the Sino-American Relationship," in Richard Solomon, ed., *The China Factor: Sino-American Relations and the Global Scene* (New York: Prentice-Hall, 1981).

China policy alternatives now facing the United States are explored in The Atlantic Council of the United States, *China Policy for the Next Decade* (Washington: The Atlantic Council, 1983), report of the Atlantic Council's Committee on China policy.

Chapter 5: Dealing with the Advanced Industrial World

The best account of United States policy premises and debates within the policy community about the common defense relationships among the countries of the North Atlantic area is found in Robert E. Osgood, *NATO: The Entangling Alliance* (Chicago: University of Chicago Press, 1963). There is no book that puts it all together, as Osgood did, for the period since the early 1960s. The next best thing is a collection of essays edited by Kenneth A. Meyers, *NATO: The Next Thirty Years* (Boulder: Westview Press, 1980).

In the early 1980s the flareup of a fresh debate about the role of nuclear weapons in NATO sparked a flurry of written briefs on the issues, most notably: McGeorge Bundy, George F. Kennan, Robert S. McNamara, and Gerard Smith, "Nuclear Weapons and the Atlantic Alliance," *Foreign Affairs*, Vol. 60, No. 4 (Spring 1982), pp. 1157–1170; the reply to this article by Karl Kaiser, Georg Leber, Alois Mertes, and Franz-Josef Schulze, "Nuclear Weapons and the Preservation of Peace," *Foreign Affairs*, Vol. 60, No. 5 (Summer 1982), pp. 1157–1170; and the rejoinder to this rebuttal, entitled "The Authors Reply," in *ibid.*, pp. 1178–1180. A balanced overview of this debate is Jonathan Dean, "Beyond First Use," *Foreign Policy*, No. 48 (Fall 1982), pp. 37–53. The practical military and political implications of moving toward a NATO defense based on a strategy of no-first-use of nuclear weapons are explored in John D. Steinbrunner and Leon V. Sigal, eds., *Alliance Security and the No-First-Use Question* (Washington: Brookings Institution, 1983).

The other big NATO issue of the 1980s—the deployment of intermediate range strategic missiles in Europe—is the subject of *Hearings: Overview of Nuclear Arms Control and Defense Strategy in NATO*, conducted by the Subcommittee on International Security and Scientific Affairs on Europe and the Middle East of the Committee on Foreign Affairs in March 1982. An excellent guide through the tangled and often esoteric argumentation is provided by Richard H. Ullman, "The Euromissile Mire," *Foreign Policy*, No. 50 (Spring 1983), pp. 39–52. These sources expose the serious strategic debate on the issue within the policy community as distinct from the popular polemics, demonstrations, and counter-demonstrations that the issue has provoked among lay publics in many countries.

The issues in economic policy for dealing with the advanced industrial countries are given special attention in I.M. Destler, *Making Foreign Economic Policy* (Washington: Brookings Institution, 1980); William Diebold, Jr., *The United States and the Industrial World: American Foreign Economic Policy in the 1970s* (New York: Praeger, 1972); and David P. Calleo and Benjamin M. Rowland, *America and the World Political Economy: Atlantic Dreams and National Realities* (Bloomington: Indiana University Press, 1973). The Reagan administration's attempts to grapple with this problem area are delineated in Benjamin J. Cohen, "An Explosion in the Kitchen? Economic Relations with Other Advanced Industrial States," in Oye *et al.*, *Eagle Defiant*, pp. 105–130.

Trade policy in particular is discussed by Raymond Vernon, "International Trade Policy in the 1980s: Prospects and Problems," *International Studies Quarterly*, Vol. 26, No. 4 (December 1982), pp. 483–510; and by Thomas R. Graham, "Global Trade: War and Peace," *Foreign Policy*, No. 50 (Spring 1983), pp. 124–137. A way out of the free trade versus protectionism dilemma is proposed by Robert B. Reich, "Beyond Free Trade," *Foreign Affairs*, Vol. 61, No. 4 (Spring 1983), pp. 773–804.

For international monetary affairs, see C. Fred Bergsten, *The Dilemma of the Dollar: The Economics and Politics of United*

States International Monetary Policy (New York: New York University Press, 1975); David H. Blake and Robert S. Walters, *The Politics of Global Economic Relations* (Englewood Cliffs: Prentice-Hall, 1983), especially Chapter 3; and Robert Triffin, "The International Role of the Dollar," *Foreign Affairs*, Vol. 57, No. 2 (Winter 1978–1979), pp. 269–286.

On coordinating East-West economic policies with U.S. allies, see Jonathan P. Stern, "Specters and Pipe Dreams," *Foreign Policy*, No. 48 (Fall 1982), pp. 21–36; David A. Andelman, "Struggle Over Western Europe," *Foreign Policy*, No. 49 (Winter 1982–1983), pp. 37–51; and Robert Paarlberg, "Lessons of the Grain Embargo," *Foreign Affairs*, Vol. 59, No. 1 (Fall 1980), pp. 144–162.

Chapter 6: Policies toward the Third World

Economic policies toward the developing countries are analyzed and prescribed in John P. Lewis and Valeriana Kalleb, eds., *U.S. Foreign Policy and the Third World: Agenda 1983* (Washington: Overseas Development Council, 1983). The case for letting free competition in the global market take care of the needs of the developing countries is argued vigorously by Melvyn B. Krauss, *Development Without Aid* (New York: McGraw-Hill New Press, 1982).

Proponents of active opposition to Third World Marxists and anti-American "neutralists" include Daniel Patrick Moynihan, *A Dangerous Place* (Boston: Atlantic Monthly Press, 1978); and Jeane Kirkpatrick, "Dictatorships and Double Standards," *Commentary*, Vol. 68, No. 5 (November 1979), pp. 34–45.

The case for active support of Third World reformers—even if they are socialists or neutralists in the cold war—was popular among Democrats in the policy community during the Kennedy administration. On this, see my *The Faces of Power* (1983 edition), Chapters 12 and 14.

A more aloof, essentially noninterventionist stance, is championed by Cyrus Vance in *Hard Choices* and receives systematic and cogently argued endorsement in Richard E. Feinberg, *The*

Intemperate Zone: The Third World Challenge to U.S. Foreign Policy (New York: Norton, 1983).

Chapter 7: U.S. Interests in the Middle East

A useful outline of past and current policy debates over United States policies toward the Middle East is Congressional Quarterly, *The Middle East* (Washington: Congressional Quarterly, 1981).

The contention among strategies for dealing with the Arab-Israeli conflict during the 1967–1976 period is analyzed thoroughly in William B. Quandt, *Decade of Decisions: American Policy Toward the Arab-Israeli Conflict 1967–1976* (Berkeley: University of California Press, 1977). The second volume of Kissinger's memoirs, *Years of Upheaval,* is a must reading for an understanding of American policies in and surrounding the 1973 Yom Kippur War. Jimmy Carter's otherwise rather dull memoirs come alive in his account of his peacemaking efforts between Anwar Sadat and Menachem Begin at Camp David.

The Middle Eastern policy choices facing the Reagan administration and how they have been dealt with are analyzed by Barry Rubin, "The Reagan Administration and the Middle East," in Oye et al., *Eagle Defiant,* pp. 367–389.

An argument that the United States has been insufficiently vigilant against the Soviet threat to U.S. interests in the Middle East is developed by James H. Noyes, *The Clouded Lens: Persian Gulf Security and U.S. Policy* (Stanford: Hoover Institution Press, 1979). The argument that the United States has been too preoccupied with the Soviet threat is made by former Secretary of State Vance in *Hard Choices,* Chapters 9–12, 17–18.

On available U.S. responses to the actions of the Organization of Petroleum Exporting Countries (OPEC), see Congressional Budget Office, *The World Oil Market in the 1980s: Implications for the United States* (Washington, D.C.: Government Printing Office, 1980).

A wide ranging overview of U.S. Middle Eastern policy choices is John C. Campbell, "The Middle East: A House of Containment

Built on Shifting Sands," *America and the World 1981*, special issue of *Foreign Affairs*, Vol. 60, No. 3 (1982), pp. 593–628.

Chapter 8: Grand Designs for World Order

World politics as a balance-of-power system is the theme of the most renowned American textbook in international relations, Hans J. Morgenthau, *Politics Among Nations* (New York: Knopf, 1978). Although many high public officials have never studied this book, it could well serve as a codification of the model of international relations implicit in most United States foreign policy decisions.

Policy initiatives that urge, or would require, strengthening the United Nations are found in the reports of the national policy panels of the United Nations Association of the United States of America, all published in New York by the UNA-USA. See especially the following panel reports: *Stopping the Spread of Nuclear Weapons* (1967), chaired by Burke Marshall; *Controlling Conflicts in the 1970s* (1969), chaired by Kingman Brewster, Jr.; *World Population: A Challenge to the United Nations and its Systems of Agencies* (1969), chaired by John D. Rockefeller, III; *Space Communications: Increasing UN Responsiveness to the Problems of Mankind* (1971), chaired by Robert R. Nathan; *The United Nations in the 1970s: A Strategy for a Unique Era in the Affairs of Nations* (1971), chaired by Nicholas deB. Katzenbach; *Science and Technology in an Era of Interdependence* (1975), chaired by Franklin A. Lindsay; *The Global Economic Challenge: Trade, Commodities, Capital Flows* (1978), chaired by Robert O. Anderson; *A United States Initiative Toward World Food Security* (1980), chaired by Orville L. Freeman; *U.S.-Soviet Relations: A Strategy for the '80s* (1981), chaired by William W. Scranton.

Proposals for a fundamental restructuring of the world system to establish a centralized system of law and order are explored by Grenville Clark and Louis B. Sohn, *Introduction to World Peace Through World Law* (Cambridge: Harvard University Press, 1960); Richard A. Falk, *A Study of Future Worlds* (New York: The Free Press, 1975); Johan Galtung, *The True Worlds: A Transnational Perspective* (New York: The Free Press, 1980); Saul H.

Mendlovitz, ed., *On the Creation of a Just World Order: Preferred World for the 1990s* (New York: The Free Press, 1975); Warren Wagar, *Building the City of Man: Outlines of a World Civilization* (New York: Grossman, 1971).

Designs for world order through uniting countries in various regions of the globe are analyzed and advocated in Ernst B. Haas, *Beyond the Nation State: Functionalism and International Organization* (Stanford: Stanford University Press, 1964); Warner J. Feld, *The European Community in World Affairs* (Port Washington, N.Y.: Alfred, 1976); Leon Lindberg and S. Scheingold, *Europe's Would-Be Polity* (Englewood Cliffs: Prentice-Hall, 1970); Richard A. Falk and Saul H. Mendlovitz, eds., *Regional Politics and World Order* (San Francisco: Freeman, 1973); Bruce M. Russett, *International Regions and the International System* (Chicago: Rand McNally, 1967).

Efforts to build world order through guided evolution of the existing "pluralistic" or "polyarchic" system toward what is often called "the global city" are suggested by Zbigniew Brzezinski, *Between Two Ages: America's Role in the Technetronic Era* (New York: Viking, 1970); Seyom Brown, *New Forces in World Politics* (Washington: Brookings Institution, 1974); Harlan Cleveland, *The Third Try at World Order: U.S. Policy for an Interdependent World* (New York: Aspen Institute for Humanistic Studies, 1976); Lester Brown, *World Without Borders* (New York: Random House, 1972); Seyom Brown, Nina Cornell, Larry Fabian, and Edith Brown Weiss, *Regimes for the Ocean, Outer Space, and Weather* (Washington: Brookings Institution, 1977).

Acknowledgments

Quotation on page 15 from an essay by Dean Rusk, Robert McNamara, George Ball, Roswell Gilpatrick, Theodore Sorensen, McGeorge Bundy, in *Time*, September 27, 1982. Copyright 1982 Time Inc. All rights reserved.

Quotation on page 39 from James Reston's "Who's Now in Charge," *New York Times*, June 30, 1982. Copyright © 1982 by The New York Times Company. Reprinted by permission.

Material on page 63 adapted from Seyom Brown's "An End to Grand Strategy," *Foreign Policy*, No. 32 (Fall 1978), pp. 22–46. Used by permission of the publisher.

Quotation on pages 109–110 from the editorial, "The Pipeline Dream," *New York Times*, November 16, 1982. Copyright © 1982 by The New York Times Company. Reprinted by permission.

Material on page 128 adapted from Seyom Brown's "The Trilemma of U.S. Foreign Policy," *AEI Foreign Policy and Defense Review*, Vol. 2, No. 5 (1980), pp. 2–4. Used by permission of the publisher.

Index